MORE FROM A
COUNTRY CATHEDRAL ORGANIST

MORE FROM A
COUNTRY CATHEDRAL
ORGANIST

DAVID GEDGE

First Impression – 2008

ISBN 978 0 95585 960 1

A CIP record for this title is available from the British Library.

Printed and bound in Wales at
Gomer Press, Llandysul, Ceredigion, SA44 4JL

Dedication

To Jane Brooks, who as Organist of Ledbury Parish Church was an inspiration; energetically maintaining the last all-male church choir in Herefordshire.

Acknowledgements

Thanks to Eileen Jones and Bethan Moses for typing and preparing this book, also to Major General the Reverend Morgan Llewelyn C.B. O.B.E, D.L., for writing the foreward, not forgetting the countless number of people who have made music with me and made it such fun, also to my wife, Hazel, who has been so very long-suffering and supportive.

Foreward

By Major General the Reverend R.M.Llewelyn C.B, O.B.E, D.L.

It is a great privilege to be invited to write the foreward to the second volume of David Gedge's memoirs. This book will not only be of great interest to those who know or have known David, or know of his immense dedication to church music and particularly that at Brecon Cathedral, but it also provides an intriguing insight into the life of a very special person in very unusual circumstances. Readers will marvel at David's encyclopaedic knowledge of church music and will immediately recognise his deep and loving commitment to it. They will also appreciate that here is a man of great wisdom and creativity who has given unstintingly of himself, often in very difficult circumstances. His capacity for hard work and the amount that he has managed to pack into each day is breathtaking. This makes the story that he has to tell both full and fascinating.

David has given more than forty years' service as Organist and Choirmaster of Brecon Cathedral, the longest in the British Isles. He and his wife Hazel have been a husband and wife team in the fullest sense and David's appreciation of Hazel and their mutual love shines from every page. They are well known and greatly respected throughout the world of Cathedral music, and it is in great measure due to them that Brecon Cathedral is also so well known beyond the limits of provincial Wales. This was recognised in 2006 in the award to each of them of the Cross of Saint Augustine. The citation for the award, signed by Dr Rowan Williams, Archbishop of Canterbury, records that *"over the past four decades, Hazel has been the partner that David needed: loving, caring, understanding, unselfish and forgiving. His achievements and contribution to the diocese and the wider community are very largely the result of her understanding and loyal support on a regular basis."*

This citation also affirms that *"David devoted his whole professional life to the worship of God through Sacred Music."* David's commitment to the life of Brecon Cathedral has indeed been one continuous act of worship; but this has extended beyond his beloved music. Having known David well and worked with him in the Cathedral for two years, he immediately conjures up for me the words of J.S.B.Monsell's wonderful hymn *"O worship the Lord in the beauty of holiness."*

David's awareness and appreciation of the whole spectrum of beauty which is available to be offered up in an act of worship extends beyond his beloved music to include the colour and form of art and architecture to be found in the Cathedral about which he cares so deeply. It is this aesthetic and spiritual sensitively that caused him to mind so much whenever he felt that this sacred beauty was at risk of being damaged or intruded upon.

The hallmark of a robust and active Christian life is unselfish concern and compassion for others. This is perhaps the most valuable and least recognised aspect of David's long ministry to the Brecon Community. He has helped innumerable young people from the least privileged areas of Brecon find purpose, comradeship and fulfilment as cathedral choristers. His support for them has extended beyond the choir room to social and educational help in a hundred different ways. He has helped these youngsters to grow in confidence and to discover and develop talents that they never knew they had. One particular young man owes his musical education and his organ scholarship at Cambridge to David and Hazel's patient nurturing and is himself now passing on these qualities to other young people. In some cases there were, inevitably, pitfalls along the way; but David was always there to help pick up the pieces and continue the good work.

It is perhaps because unselfishness, generosity, caring and compassion are so much part of his own nature, that it hurt terribly when he found himself being denied similar treatment. It was especially painful for him when he occasionally experienced this at the hands of the clergy who failed to recognise his intrinsic saintliness (not that he would have recognised it in those terms himself!) and seemed to forget that Christ was, above everything else, compassionate and gives us all a ministry of reconciliation.

David tells us that Dean Gwynno James, whom he much admired, on hearing of David's appointment and that Hazel was herself such an accomplished organist, remarked that they had *"two for the price of one."* In reality, for forty years Brecon Cathedral has almost had two for the price of none. David and Hazel have worked for a pittance. Although in order to survive financially David also became Head of Music at Builth Wells High School-where he also made an immensely valuable musical, educational and pastoral contribution-he has worked tirelessly to ensure that his beloved Brecon Cathedral had the sort of service from its Organist and Choirmaster that other cathedrals have-and did so without any of the ancillary resources available to other cathedrals. He has achieved miracles, and has done so cheerfully and without resentment, although often at great personal cost. While I am not convinced that this has always been understood in Brecon, it is widely recognised further afield. Again, a verse from the same hymn resonates:

> *"Fear not to enter his courts in the slenderness*
> *Of the poor wealth thou wouldst reckon as thine:*
> *Truth in its beauty, and love in its tenderness,*
> *These are the offerings to lay on his shrine."*

David Gedge has written this memoir with great clarity, much modesty and with considerable humour. His own boyish sense of mischief and his glee at relating the naughty or the ridiculous is most refreshing. He is always ready to tell a story against himself and to admit a mistake. Considering his own transparent honesty, humility and good nature, it is not surprising that he is angered by perceived injustice and is irritated by pomposity and arrogance. Where tension is evident in this book, these are invariably the causes.

It is by any standard a good read. Perhaps one day it will become an important primary source for social and ecclesiastical history. It is, of course, much more than this. It is not just the record of a musical career for which he was rightly awarded an MBE for services to music in Wales. Nor is it merely an account of life in a provincial cathedral. It is the story of a person who is fully in touch with both the spiritual and human side of his being. David Gedge is someone whose ministry-and it is a ministry in both the pastoral and the spiritual sense-has spanned the home, the Cathedral, the school, the choir room and the pub in a seamless and entirely effective way. The present Dean of Brecon, John Davies, wrote to David after his first Holy Week in Brecon to thank him for having *"shared in an enriching journey of faith."* He continued *"What, I believe, we actually experienced was Anglicanism at its best-worship composed of a rich mixture of teaching, ceremonial, music, prayer and scripture."* David's heart is in all these things. It is not an exaggeration to describe David's journey with Hazel as a pilgrimage of practical Christianity.

Morgan Llewelyn
Llangattock,
Epiphany 2007.

XXXVI

The second Bishop of Swansea and Brecon that I worked with (or was it 'worked for' as he could be somewhat autocratic) was endowed with almost as good and holy an assemblage of names as his predecessor Bishop John James Absalom Thomas. Answering to Benjamin Noel Young Vaughan, his second name 'Noel' reminded everyone that he had been born on Christmas Day.

So, in 1948, he left his homeland, Wales, to work in Barbados, returning four years later to lecture at St David's College, Lampeter. After three years at this idyllic seat of learning he went first to Trinidad and Tobago, then to Port of Spain where he was Dean, before becoming Suffragan Bishop of Mandeville in 1961 at the age of forty-four years. On his elevation to the Bishopric of the British Honduras he remained in Belize for four years before finally returning home to Wales in 1991 as Dean of Bangor and Assistant Bishop in the diocese.

It was at Bangor that I first met him when Hazel, my wife, was invited to give an organ recital as part of a Flower Festival at the Cathedral. Arriving at the Deanery on that occasion, our knock at the door was answered by Mrs Vaughan who, in reply to our request to see the Dean, said, rather pointedly, that the Bishop was out. Some days after the recital Hazel received a letter of thanks signed by the 'Bishop/Dean' which began: 'Dear Mrs Gegg', and therefore added one more variation to the spelling of our surname, 'Gedge'.

The Bishop had grandiose ideas which is understandable because as a Bishop in the West Indies he had probably been used to being held in much higher regard there than as a Bishop in Wales; after all it is generally agreed that since the Second World War, Britain has become rather a godless country. Indeed, it has even been suggested that instead of sending missionaries abroad to propagate the Christian gospel, the church would do well to send them to work in some of the major cities in Britain. As far as I was concerned the first casualty of the new regime in the diocese of Swansea and Brecon was the lovely, monastic, Saturday morning ordination service. When I told Bishop Vaughan that the Clergy Choir sang at this service after having rehearsed on the afternoon before in the Cathedral Choir Room, then having had tea at Ely Tower, he had not been the least bit interested. So the clergy choir rehearsed on the Friday as usual and indeed did repair to Ely Tower for tea but there the singing clergy had to be content with having their refreshments standing on the verandah outside; as for the service itself, the Bishop managed to reduce this to a rather joyless affair. Afterwards, he asked me why it was not possible to have the Cathedral Choir on a Saturday morning and made quite clear his desire to do away with the clergy choir. I duly explained to him that the Cathedral Choir had quite enough to do on a Sunday and as the singers were voluntary it was rather much to expect them to give up an entire Saturday morning, especially when some of the Lay Clerks had family commitments. I also expressed sorrow at the demise of the Clergy Choir but to no avail despite the explanation that with a fifth of the diocesan clergy involved, this service provided an ideal opportunity to give some sort of basic musical instruction which could be of benefit to the diocese in learning new hymns and simple settings of the Mass. To me this represented a teaching opportunity lost and I bitterly regretted it: furthermore, to my amazement, at the next Ordination Service there was no choir of any sort and it was a most dismal affair. Yet out of this disaster there arose a fascinating alternative. Recently, through a recording made by Worcester Cathedral Choir, I had come to know the Mass for two choirs and two organs which the French composer Charles Marie Widor of Toccata fame, had composed for an Ordination Service in the great church of St. Sulpice in Paris. So I persuaded Bishop Vaughan to purchase copies, enough for the Cathedral Choir and some of the Swansea choristers which was an expensive proposition as French music is notoriously costly, then I set about organising a performance of this music for the next Ordination Service. The soprano, alto, tenor and bass parts which form the second choir, I taught to the Cathedral Choir, while the extra tenor and bass parts which form the first choir and would have been sung by the ordinands at the first performance, I taught to the Swansea choristers. This was good because in recent years diocesan choral activities had expanded to the extent that no longer did these choristers sing only an annual Evensong in the Cathedral, but in the autumn months they met with me in Swansea to prepare a Christmas Carol Service. In this way and using the excellent 'Carols for Choirs Book 1', it had been possible to standardise harmonies and descants of many popular Christmas Carols which had made it easier for choirs to come together for joint Christmas services if they so wished. Later an Advent Carol Service was introduced to extend their horizons even further. Now it became possible to involve Swansea choristers in the Ordination Services at the Cathedral, and it became a great source of pride to them that they could make a musical contribution to this great diocesan event. So the Bishop did what he had long wanted to do: he moved the Ordination Services from Saturday morning to Sunday afternoon and so from a gentle monastic service it became a triumphant diocesan occasion. The Dean, Ungoed Jacob, found the first of these Ordination Services very moving and wrote in 'The Beacon', the Cathedral Magazine:

> 'Two by two. Two organs (Cathedral and Bevington), two choirs (Cathedral and diocesan), two languages (English and Welsh), two eucharistic settings (Merbecke and Widor), two sets of hymns, two candidates for the priesthood, two hours long, that was the order of the day for the Ordination Service on Sunday, June 25th and it was a magnificent occasion with a packed church, tremendous congregational singing, and very fine choral singing too. The Charles Marie Widor setting of the Kyrie, Sanctus, Benedictus and Agnus Dei was composed for two choirs and two organs and was intended to be used at an

ordination, so Mr Gedge reminded us in a musical note and we are grateful to him for introducing it to us and for his work'.

The Gloria and Creed were sung as usual to the timeless music of John Merbecke but eventually the choirs replaced Merbecke's Gloria with the stunning musical setting by C M Widor; not for long however, because clergy opposition, particularly from three of the Canons, soon put a stop to that on the grounds that the choir and its music were monopolising the service. Yet it has always gladdened my heart that the congregation at Ordination Services in Brecon Cathedral has been able to sing not only the main hymns but also more hymns during the administration of the Holy Communion, along with Merbecke's Gloria and Creed, not forgetting the ancient plainsong Litany.

Dean Jacob actually was coming to the end of his time at the Cathedral when he had written so enthusiastically about the Ordination Service, and before 1978 was out he had retired. In some ways his career had ended on a sad note when is considered the potential of the man. On arriving at Brecon Cathedral back in 1967, it seemed that his sights were set upon the Bishopric of St David's but that was not to be. In due course this Bishopric became vacant and he had set off to the election at St David's Cathedral bristling with confidence yet the Bishopric went to another and he returned home a chastened, different man. From that moment onwards he had resigned from many committees and had concentrated on being the good parish priest that he really was, visiting his flock conscientiously. So in his last years the real, caring Ungoed Jacob revealed himself, preaching exceedingly erudite sermons in the Cathedral and becoming a much loved pastor which made one realise what an excellent bishop he would have made. He had come to Brecon with a national reputation for his work towards church unity, indeed he had represented the Church in Wales at an international conference in Uppsala, Sweden; at the same time he had very little understanding of the place music held in Cathedral worship. Yet at the end he was big enough a person to admit that while Cathedral Music had meant little to him initially at Brecon Cathedral, nevertheless, over the years, he had grown not only to love it but also to appreciate how it could bring all heaven before the eyes of worshippers. Above all, he had admitted how through daily worship in the ancient Cathedral, he had grown aware of the aura of beauty and holiness that pervaded this unique monastic building. Indeed, he was no longer the bombastic priest who had arrived twelve years before; who, when I had allowed a musically cocksure chorister to accompany a hymn at Evensong in St Mary's Church and the boy had made a mess of it, had ordered me never to do this again without his permission; who, when the choirboys had been misbehaving during a recording session had shouted at them to 'wash their mouths out', making no effort to understand how their unsocial backgrounds were the root of the problem; who had sent home a head choirboy shortly before a Choral Evensong because he wouldn't stop kicking a football against the boiler-house wall, without considering how the boy's home life made him react like this and, furthermore, giving no thought to the fact that the anthem at Evensong was bound to suffer because this boy had such a big voice and was such an excellent leader that his absence was sure to have a detrimental effect on the quality of the singing. Indeed, over the years, Dean Jacob had changed and had come to appreciate, as I had done a few years before, that Brecon people were individuals who could not be changed overnight, who had to be gently led. So he had grown more tolerant and had become almost a saintly man and the transformation was considerable; but then the old Benedictine Priory Church had that effect on some people.

Dean Jacob retired in November whereupon there followed a long but eventful interregnum which lasted until the arrival of the new Dean in September 1979. However, during those nine months the life of the Cathedral had to carry on as normal although with Bishop Vaughan taking a keen interest, there was rarely a dull moment. January 1979, for example, marked the one hundredth anniversary of the famous Defence of Rorke's Drift which has been immortalised in the famous film 'Zulu'. This great military action is now part of the folk lore of the old 24th Regiment, when Queen Victoria awarded VCs to eleven of the hundred or so soldiers who had held off more than four-thousand Zulu warriors, and the House of Commons unusually voted thanks to the two officers who had masterminded the defence. It is all commemorated in the Regimental Chapel in the Cathedral where the wreath of Immortelles which the Queen had attached to the Regimental Colours, is now preserved in a silver case. So in the new year, on Sunday January 21st, 1979, there was a truly great and emotional service in the Cathedral, made all the more splendid and impressive by the playing of the Regimental Band and by the singing of the Cathedral Choir in the old favourites: C. Hubert Parry's impressive, 'I was glad', C.V. Stanford's ever popular, 'Te Deum in B flat', and Sidney Campbell's extrovert, 'Sing we merrily unto God our strength'. Some days later, Major Egerton, a regular member of the Cathedral congregation who looked after the excellent museum at the army barracks, and who had much to do with the organising of this service, passed on to me a copy of a letter which he had received from a member of the congregation, that began:

'Dear Major Egerton,

If my memory is right it is usually the high-ranking officers in a regiment who collect the praise for any regimental function which takes place but the person most worthy of the praise is that usually modest, self-effacing and generally over-worked person – the Adjutant! So let me offer you my warmest congratulations on the splendid and impeccably ordered Centenary Parade on Sunday and especially the Church service. It was beautifully ordered and profoundly moving. In a longish life I do not remember ever having heard such beautiful singing in church nor such equally beautifully performed music with the organ so skilfully integrated with the Regimental Band – no mean musical feat I should imagine. Please convey my deep appreciation of this to the organist and to whoever it was who chose, arranged and rehearsed the music.'

Another letter thanked Hazel and me for not only 'preparing the music but (also) in fixing up the tea for the band rehearsals'!

Later that year, the Easter weekend of services and concerts continued as usual but with the addition of a small string instrumental ensemble to the concert on Good Friday which allowed Hugh Thomas to play J.S. Bach's Harpsichord Concerto in F minor – a legacy of the previous year's Germany tour. Indeed, the Lay Clerks performance of The Lamentations by Thomas Tallis, moved one listener to write a letter thanking them for a 'wonderful and moving experience'. On the next evening, Holy Saturday, the Cathedral Singers' performance of 'Messiah' brought to the Cathedral for the first time the stunning counter-tenor voice of John York Skinner; his singing of 'He was despised' is still talked about to this day. In time Brecon worked its magic on this great singer, (he had even sung solo at La Scala Opera House, Milan), and after a few more visits he made a home for his family nearby, across Mynydd Eppynt, at Cefn Gorwydd.

A month later, whoever it was that organised a Diocesan Sunday School Festival on Cup Final Day, May 12th, at 2.00 pm, set in motion a spontaneous, unexpected reaction that had far-reaching consequences. The service inexplicably ended at 2.55 pm and by 3.00 pm when the Cup Final started, the Cathedral was empty except for Minor Canon John Walters and me, leaving us with all the clearing up. Until that moment, as far as I was concerned, Brecon Cathedral was the most cluttered and carpeted cathedral that I knew about, consequently the acoustic was dead, especially unrewarding for musical performances. With bad grace, John and I dutifully put back everything to clutter up the building again until we arrived at the last item: a carpet that lived on the floor outside the Sacristy, beneath the organ chamber. We looked at each other, then said: 'Shall we or shan't we?' and promptly rolled up the carpet and hid it away behind the altar in the Havard Chapel. Over the next two weeks no-one said anything so next we set about an unnecessary, unsightly curtain that hung across the final arch of the nave. One night we made it fall down but to our consternation, by the next evening, dear old Ossie, the groundsman, had put it back up. Waiting a few days, we repeated our deed only this time we made sure that the curtain could not be put back by breaking one of its two wooden end supports. This time we succeeded in our aim. Next, we turned our attention to the nave itself where so many of the lovely stone arches were cluttered by a mass of wooden chairs; from that moment onwards, any chair that had so much as a pin-prick was removed to prevent the possible spread of woodworm, with the result that gradually the full beauty of the nave revealed itself. Meanwhile, more bits of carpet had been disappearing, again usually rolled up and hidden behind the Havard (Regimental) Chapel altar, although one piece found its way up to the Ringing Chamber at the top of St Mary's Church tower in the town centre. The biggest project was emptying the South Transept of its heavy oak pews which were never used because they had been designed to face east when they would have been more useful facing north towards the choir stalls. So with a lot of effort these were rehoused behind the font at the far end of the nave where they replaced more 'worm-eaten' chairs. The empty South Transept looked magical, indeed the entire South Nave Aisle leading into the Transept was a transformation, and the space created left the building to speak for itself; it was, I suppose, beauty by exclusion. While accomplishing this we had also moved two ancient dilapidated, dusty wooden corner cupboards from a dark corner opposite the door leading into the Garth from the South Nave Aisle, and put them into the Dean's Vestry where not only could their antique beauty be seen and appreciated, but also they could be put to good use. We were pleased with what had been accomplished and the improvement in the Cathedral acoustic was considerable, but I must own up and confess that most of the deeds had been instigated by me, often accomplished under the cover of darkness when the building was locked up.

One day, late in July, the Archdeacon of Gower, Harry Williams, escorted me into the Cathedral and while surveying the building, said: 'David, a new Dean is arriving soon and you have to get on with him; put it all back'. I went home to Garth Cottage and immediately telephoned the Bishop who, I knew, approved of what had been done, to ask him what I should do. 'David, my boy', he said, 'It's July, go on holiday!'. I do not know whether or not the Bishop said anything to the Archdeacon, but no-one ever again mentioned anything to me about the changes made in the Cathedral. On Friday, September 7th, the new Dean was duly installed at Choral Evensong, 'accompanied by trumpets and some magnificent music in the presence of His Grace, the Lord Archbishop of Wales', so the Bishop reported in his quarterly magazine. After the service, the Lay Clerks went down to The George Hotel to celebrate, while the new Dean went to his new home in the Close also to celebrate. Later that night, I, along with Kelvin Redford, Hugh Thomas, John Cynan Jones the Cathedral Music loving Conductor of The Treorchy Male Choir, and some of the Lay Clerks, crept back into the Cathedral armed with a heavy hammer, a crowbar and a small ladder. By the light of a powerful torch we set about removing one last curtain which was hanging on a rail that was wedged into the top of the arch that led from the South Nave Aisle into the South Transept. When the deed was done we returned to The George Hotel to celebrate. So far so good!

XXXVII

The new Dean burst upon the scene like a draught of fresh air, his deep, penetrating voice ringing around the Cathedral Close, his bushy eyebrows flashing away continuously, all the more so when he was under pressure. Very North Walian in his Welshness, his erudite sermons were punctuated with 'hms' and 'ahs' which the Lay Clerks used to count, possibly, we thought, because he was thinking in Welsh while speaking through the medium of English. He was a wise man. Bishop Vaughan had commandeered the enormous Deanery and was busily converting it into a Deanery Centre for diocesan activities, therefore somewhere had to be found to house the Dean and his family. At first it seemed that the diocese would have to part with a lot of money purchasing a house for them somewhere near the Cathedral until, quite by chance, the Almonry at the entrance to the Cathedral Close, became available. Our good friends the Archdeacon of Brecon, Elwyn Griffiths, and his wife, Joan, had been living there for a few years until disaster had struck when their youngest son, Martin, was found to have Leukemia while Elwyn himself suffered the massive stroke that brought about his premature retirement. Yet surely, people thought, the house, tucked away as it was between the Cathedral boiler house and the main gateway, surrounded by a high hedge, was too small and not nearly grand enough for someone as important as a Dean. Not so, was the verdict of the Dean. He was only too happy to move in with Meriel, his ex-teacher wife who was the perfect partner to him, his young daughter Nia, who was such a character that she was soon dubbed 'The Blessed Nia' and with Moggy, the much loved cat.

So began a golden age at Brecon Cathedral which was all too short in years simply because of the Dean's rapid promotion, but during which so much was accomplished. The Dean was especially good at galvanising people into action, also in interesting young people in the activities of the Church, just as his daughter was good at baiting the Cathedral choirboys. Soon a happy family atmosphere pervaded not only in the Cathedral and its Close but also in St Mary's Church where the Dean encouraged the Parish Church Council to take on teenage members as observers so that they could gain experience at running their own Church. One of his most valuable creations at the Cathedral was 'Dad's Army', made up of male parishioners who met regularly to work on maintaining, even beautifying the Cathedral grounds, and he led them from the front, working with them. Similarly his wife, Meriel, persuaded some of the lady parishioners to meet every Thursday morning to clean the Cathedral and polish the woodwork; again she led them from the front and would be found in the vestry serving a welcome cup of tea or coffee to them. Alwyn Rice Jones was not afraid of work, indeed more often than not a light would be burning in the Almonry sitting room at midnight which indicated that he was still hard at work on administrative matters. Many is the time that I knocked on this window while returning home from the pub after the Lay Clerks' Thursday choir practice, and joined him in the Almonry for a nightcap glass of whisky. His workload was such that his wife, Meriel, would be reduced to hiding away in the kitchen to smoke a furtive cigarette; if my wife, Hazel, passed by at this time, she would be invited in, also to have a fag! Yet it wasn't all work as Alwyn had a wonderful sense of humour. Boys choir practices always began with two choristers going to Pendre Post Office, opposite the Cathedral Lych Gate, to buy 'pop and biscuits' which would then be shared out among all the youngsters. One day, one of the two boys returned not only with the pop and biscuits but also with a large juicy carrot that he had taken as he had left Mr Timothy's shop. I told Alwyn about this as the choir began to line up for Evensong that particular day and he promised to take action. When the choir were ready he prefaced his vestry prayer with these words: 'Boys, I have something serious to say to you. Mr Timothy has told me that before any of you went to collect the pop and biscuits this afternoon, he counted the number of carrots in the box outside his shop, then after you had returned to the Cathedral, he had counted them again and found one missing! I expect the culprit to own up'. However, there was no need for the boy to do this because his neck and face had turned bright red in colour and he looked exceedingly guilty. This was a young boy who lived in a hostelry, near to Brecon; he had already achieved notoriety by adding a touch of 'Squeezy' washing up liquid to each of thirty-six curries prepared by his father for the day's bar snacks, before setting off for school. His father was equally unpredictable. Apparently, he had gone for a cycle ride with his son, then much younger, on a small seat on the back of his bicycle. As he struggled to cycle up the long hill at Rhydspence, on the border of Herefordshire and Radnorshire, the boy said urgently: 'Dad', to which his dad has snapped back: 'Shut up, wait until I get to the top'. This scenario was repeated at regular intervals until his father finally reached the top whereupon he relaxed, turned around, looked at his son and said sharply: 'Where's your shoe?', to which his son answered, 'That's what I was trying to tell you!'.

During the summer of 1980, the Cathedral Choir had the good fortune to sing services at York Minster and this boy came with us along with his father. We stayed at Read Grammar School, Drax, where Hazel and I had taught when we had lived at Selby. While staying there the boy's father had telephoned home to make sure that all was well. His conversation with his wife was suddenly cut off when she shrieked down the telephone: 'There's water coming through the ceiling'. This was the work of the youngest son, who was being bathed and who, with his mother out of the way, had turned the tap back on and let the water flow over the side of the bath. For this trip the choir had taken its own bus so that every morning we were driven to York Minster to rehearse for Choral Evensong. Unfortunately, on arrival we always had to wait around until one of the three Minster policemen was found so that we could borrow a key which would give us access to the Choir Vestry.

After two days we decided to remedy this annoying situation. On the third day therefore, we borrowed the key as usual, opened the vestry door with it, then while the choir started its practice, lay clerk John Evans rushed to an ironmonger's shop in the city and quickly had a replica key cut. Never again did we have to bother the Minster Policemen and no-one appeared to be any the wiser. Working in the Minster was a thrill but singing services there was even more special yet as quickly as one of the Minor Canons befriended us, not one of the Residentiary Canons spoke to us until Evensong on Friday, by which time we had sung four services. That evening Alwyn, our Dean, joined us at Read Grammar School, Drax, staying with us for the weekend when he preached in the Minster on the Sunday morning while the choir sang a Mozart Mass followed by Morning Prayer. Strangely as there was a diocesan service in the evening we were reduced to singing the Magnificat and Nunc Dimittis to simple Anglican Chants, something we had never done before; we retaliated by singing as an anthem, all eighteen minutes of S S Wesley's 'Ascribe unto the Lord', yet it did seem strange that such an indignity should happen to us in York Minster of all places. Two statistics remain in my mind from that visit to York Minster in the summer of 1980: that the Dean and Chapter employed around one hundred and ten people to run the Minster, including those three policemen, also that during the hour of 2-3 pm on the Friday afternoon, more than 2,500 people entered the building. By comparison, the Dean and Chapter of Brecon employed five people to run their Cathedral while on a busy day, twenty or so visitors might cross its threshold in any hour on a Friday afternoon during August.

The year 1980 was made all the more memorable for me by the most appalling BBC television 'Songs of Praise' programme which had been broadcast earlier in the year on Sunday, April 27th. Strangely, while membership of The Church in Wales has remained reasonably constant over the years, membership of Non-Conformist churches has declined far more rapidly yet still non-conformists seemed to monopolise influential jobs, especially in BBC (Wales). Our dealings with this august institution had led us to coin the phrase 'Non-Conformist Ears' because while at Brecon we had been involved in a few broadcasts and TV programmes from the Cathedral and so often the BBC sound engineers had placed a microphone in front of the organ pipes which left them and not us able to decide just how much organ was to be heard. It was noticeable, for example, how in programmes from non-conformist chapels, very often the organ was relegated to a background noise while the voices were allowed to dominate. Particularly irritating were dress rehearsals for broadcasts from the Cathedral because Hazel and I were never allowed to hear for ourselves how the balance between voices and organ sounded, nor even how the balance and blend between voices was shaping. As for this particular Songs of Praise, in the past we had made the selection of hymns for the programmes, but now BBC (Wales) stipulated certain hymns that it wanted. These included one with Welsh words sung to a long, drawn-out but pleasant tune named 'Pantyfedwen', which was a ripe candidate for being laboured in performance, also another hymn, one that I detest for its sentimentality: 'The Rugged Cross', which was an even stronger candidate for such treatment. The programme still could have been a success had not the BBC, in its wisdom and without any consultation, invited along the Aberhonddu Male Choir, sat them half-way down the nave and placed a microphone above them. Having the Cathedral Choir in its choir stalls, the Cathedral Singers in the front of the nave, and the Male Choir a considerable distance away, was a recipe for musical chaos; then with the organ pipes up in the chancel, at least thirty-five yards away from the Male Choir, the programme was doomed to failure. In my efforts to keep the singing moving I over-reacted, particularly in 'The Rugged Cross', and as a result received some disparaging letters after the broadcast:

> 'Dear Sir or Madam,
>   Which bus or train was the conductor of the (wonderful) chosen hymns hoping to catch.
>   The whole service was a mistake at that speed.
>   Slow down please Mr Conductor and get the feeling out of the words in the hymns and fairness to the congregation.
>   Yours etc. '

That came from a listener living in Peel, in the Isle of Man. Worse came from a listener in Theydon Bois, Essex:

> 'Dear Sir,
>   I have just finished listening to the mess which was offered this evening from your Cathedral in the 'Songs of Praise' programme. It is easily the worst I have heard!
>   The first hymn 'Cwm Rhondda' with its cacophony of introductory Music, the organ apparently trying to compete with the band and the band retaliating with extra banging on the drum! The whole thing rushed through with indecent haste and the congregation having barely time for a snatch breath between verses.
>   Far too much swank and show-off when reverence should have been the keynote. The children's hymn 'Horsley' was about the best effort, but when we got to 'Hyfrydol' with the trumpet screaming out its descant and doing its level best to disrupt the singers – well! The practice of rushing through the hymns so you are able to squeeze just one more in is to be deplored, invariably they are all spoiled in this way.
>   For what it is worth I will tell you that I am a Church Organist of many years standing so I think I can reasonably say I have some qualification to criticise.
>   I don't think either that this programme is helped each week by being announced by loud Organ music which bears no relation to the organ we later hear in the church which is broadcasting, though of course this does not come under your jurisdiction.
>   Yours faithfully '

It was an embarrassing episode in my life!

Better was 'Celebration 80' to mark the Diamond Jubilee of the Church in Wales, which took place at the National Stadium in Cardiff on Saturday, May 31st, 1980, the day before the first Archbishop of Wales was enthroned, sixty years before, on June 1st, 1920. Through Alwyn our Dean, I had been put in charge of the music for this important occasion but only on my condition that there be adequate rehearsal. The idea was to have a choir of two-thousand voices drawn from churches throughout Wales singing the Holy Eucharist, using John Merbecke's music for the Gloria and Creed, and singing the Kyrie, Sanctus, Benedictus and Agnus Dei to Healey Willan's unison Missa de Sancta Maria Magdalena; in addition a psalm and some hymns were to be sung in harmony. The event was the brainchild of Captain Derek Jones of the Church Army and it was certainly an exciting prospect. However, I suppose, the event fell foul of the physical shape of Wales with the bulk of its population in Cardiff, Newport and Swansea, leaving the remainder living mostly in small towns and scattered villages, some in very remote areas. If I had been realistic I would have wondered why although rehearsals in the dioceses of Monmouth, Llandaff and Swansea & Brecon were well supported, the only rehearsal in North Wales, at a church in Rhyl, was attended by barely twenty-five singers. Similarly why were plans to charter trains from North Wales to the gathering in Cardiff cancelled leaving church people to use the normal rail services which were not that plentiful at convenient times? Indeed, on the great day itself, the last train back to North Wales left Cardiff at 5.10 pm, yet still the event had generated much enthusiasm amongst youngsters. They marched through Cardiff in a torch-light procession the night before, from the Church of St Mary the Virgin, near Cardiff Docks – where they had watched a Church Army musical about a teenager of those times, to Llandaff Cathedral – where they kept an all night vigil. On the day itself, there was a huge procession of the faithful, accompanied by four military bands, from Cathays Park to the Stadium. Many city centre roads had to be closed for much of the day with traffic diverted to alternative routes. Nevertheless, the expected invasion of fifty thousand people had dwindled to thirty thousand but by the time the faithful had gathered together in the stadium, the experienced eye of the Manager put the crowd at fifteen thousand while the Western Mail reporter gave a more generous estimate of twenty thousand. Certainly the choir numbered around one thousand choristers instead of the hoped-for two thousand; even so they gave a good account of themselves firstly in leading the community hymn singing before the service, then in leading the singing of the vast congregation in the service itself. Throughout the service Hazel played a not very sophisticated electronic organ which had to be hidden away undercover, presumably to prevent her from being electrocuted, as a persistent drizzle added its own accompaniment to the proceedings. Because Hazel and I were used to working together we could cope with being unsighted from each other; however, we were sad that the expected 'de luxe' electronic organ had not materialised, especially as the instrument provided, when amplified, did not make the best of sounds.

Despite the unfortunate weather and the smaller-than-expected congregation, it was an inspiring occasion with the sight of the six Welsh diocesan bishops clad in flame-coloured Whitsun Eucharistic Vestments adding a welcome blaze of colour. Afterwards, the Archbishop of Wales wrote to us:

> 'Dear Mr & Mrs Gedge
> Though I have already had the opportunity to thank you by word of mouth, I should like you to accept this brief message of gratitude for all you did for our 'Celebration 80'. I know how many hours of work all the preparation meant and that it must have been with a degree of apprehension that you looked forward to conducting the choirs in those unfamiliar surroundings. It was a magnificent success, thanks to your superb leadership and one we shall always remember with gratitude and pride.
> Yours very sincerely
> **Gwilym Cambrensis** '

A letter from Naunton Liles, the Organist of St Augustine's, Penarth, hinted at the problems that had been overcome:

> 'Dear David
> I thought I should drop you a line to congratulate you on the success of Celebration Eighty and its music. There is no doubt many people were very impressed with the music on that occasion and you achieved wonders against the odds of a difficult committee and a dreadful organ on the day.
> Many of us thought that your wife must have had considerable difficulties hearing what was going on .....'

Most unexpected, but very kind, was a short letter from the Rector of Merthyr Tydfil:

> 'Dear David
> Just a little note to thank you for the splendid contribution you made to Celebration 80. I know of no-one in the Church in Wales who could have done it better.
> None of us will ever forget the experience, but we ought to remember and thank those who made it possible.
> Yours sincerely
> **David** '

While Hazel and I had been working towards *Celebration 80*, life at Brecon had continued as near as possible to normal. One of my oddest weekly engagements took me to the Cathedral at 7.30 on a Saturday morning to give an organ lesson to the remarkable Wyndham Northcott. Before retirement Mr Northcott had driven the local co-op delivery van, now in retirement and being a non-conformist Lay Preacher, he helped out in chapels by taking services, and helped out in churches by playing the organ. He was a gentle soul who never took offence; indeed when I returned from a holiday in Devon and told him that I could never work in that part of the world because people seemed to be so slow, he said to me meekly: 'O! I come from Devon'. He then went on to tell me how, many years before, he had been in service in that idyllic county and how happy he had been working for a kind and considerate employer; also how he had cycled fifteen miles to Lyme Regis every Saturday for his weekly organ lesson. Now a widower and many years older, he still worked hard for his organ lessons and I remember his pleasure and sense of achievement when at the age of seventy-five years he added an ATCL to the ABSM that he had acquired many years before. Sadly he suffered badly at the hands of some local clergymen who took advantage of his gentle nature. He came to his lesson one Saturday morning clutching copies of the J S Bach 'Pastorale' and the difficult C M Widor 'Toccata', saying that he had to learn these for a wedding. After five lessons on this music I asked him if he was being paid properly for this service as not only had he purchased the music but also he had to pay for his lessons. When he told me that he was being paid £1 as usual, I suggested to him that he asked for £3 (money had lower values then!). Next time we met I asked him how he had got on whereupon he told me how the Vicar had remarked that if he was not happy with his fee, a lady down the road would play for £1! He then recounted the story of how for a long time he had played the organ voluntarily in the chapel at Cwrt-y-Gollen, a small army camp near to Crickhowell, until the authorities had made some money available for an Organist whereupon the Chaplain, a local Vicar, had told him that his services were no longer required and duly installed his own wife on the organ bench!

One Saturday as I walked around the Regimental Chapel in the Cathedral listening to Mr Northcott playing the organ, I noticed that the priceless immortelle (wreath of everlasting flowers presented by Queen Victoria to the South Wales Borderers Regiment after the Defence of Rorkes Drift) was missing. Next time I met Alwyn our Dean I asked him about its whereabouts only to discover that he had no idea it had gone and it was only after he had made a few enquiries that we realised it had been stolen. In the weeks that followed nothing was discovered which could shed any light on the disappearance with the result that some detectives and senior army officials became convinced that the wreath had been taken by, or on behalf of, a military collector as nothing else was missing. It was their belief that an unscrupulous collector would have been prepared to pay several thousand pounds to own such a historic rarity and priceless relic, which could never be sold legitimately because of its uniqueness. However, this was a far cry from the eventual outcome of the mystery. One afternoon a few weeks later, our German friend, Dieter Edel, left The George Hotel with tenor Lay Clerk Tonlas Evans, after a lunch-time drink, and made for his holiday abode at Llandefaelog. As he approached the cottage he was puzzled to see the front door open as he was sure that he had left it closed. Entering the building he walked up the stairs checking for an intruder whereupon someone pushed past him running back down the stairs and out through the front door. So Dieter turned around and set off in pursuit but soon fell over losing the hairpiece that I did not know he wore. However, picking himself up he quickly resumed the chase, looking to all intents and purposes like a second person as he was now bald! Unfortunately, he lost the intruder but not before he and Tonlas had seen enough to enable them to give a good description of him to the police. Within a few hours the police had arrested someone answering to their description and when they entered his lodgings in Llanfaes, they found not only the proceeds of some 'cat' burglaries which had been puzzling them for some time, but also the missing wreath now removed from its silver case which the thief had hoped to sell to make a little money. With the mystery solved the wreath was duly repaired then replaced in its case and returned to the Regimental Chapel in the Cathedral, but not before a burglar alarm had been added to prevent the repeat of such a misfortune.

XXXVIII

By now, our son Nicholas was nearing the end of his time in the choir of St John's College, Cambridge; it had been a wonderful experience both for him and for us. He had risen up through the ranks to become Head Chorister and had sung solos regularly, one in particular on his twelfth birthday during a BBC Radio 3 Choral Evensong, when as he was singing a particularly doleful passage in Michael Wise's 'The Ways of Zion do mourn', the sound of a passing ambulance or fire-engine, I know not which as I was a long way away in Brecon, added to the organ accompaniment. During his final year he had also become Head Boy at the school, having played rugby, cricket and squash in school teams during his few spare moments. After all it had been a gruelling schedule, with six services to sing and ten choir practices every week, not forgetting the regular practice to keep going on two musical instruments, in addition to normal school lessons. Small wonder the first four days of every holiday were devoted to sleep. As for Hazel, Harriet and me, we had made many good friends there, in particular my fellow Southwark Cathedral Chorister Richard Marlow, and his wife Annette, not forgetting the Organist of St John's College, George Guest, and his wife Nan. Indeed, just occasionally George would write to us, always using the Welsh language that he had learned at Cambridge and according to a Welsh-speaking friend in Brecon, his use of this language was impeccable, real text-book Welsh. Another good friend was wise Peter le Huray whose scholarly editions of Early Cathedral Music I had long admired; his outspoken wife, Bridget, and Hazel became good friends as did his daughter, Sarah, and our Harriet. To rub shoulders with such people whom I had admired from afar for so long was a great privilege. The Hendries too were good to us, offering us beds in their large house in Madingley Road on a Friday night, so that eventually we developed a routine of leaving Brecon after choir practice at around 7 pm, having supper in The Duke of Cumberland near Aynho at around 10 pm, arriving in Cambridge at around 11.30 pm, letting ourselves into the Hendrie house and so getting a good night's sleep. One famous night we arrived to find the front door locked by mistake and so had to spend the night in the car! When Gerald found us next morning in a steamed-up vehicle he begged us to bring our bags into the house to make it look as though we had spent the night there otherwise his wife, Dinah, would have been upset as she was a very sensitive soul. Dinah we had known for years; not only had she been a fellow student when Hazel and I had been at the Royal Academy of Music but before that she had been a Junior Exhibitioner along with me, attending lessons there on Saturday mornings. Gerald Hendrie was Professor of Music at the Open University and Dinah worked with him as a Senior Lecturer, publishing at this time a course dealing with the early classical period symphony for which they produced much fascinating material, even down to assembling a professional orchestra to record some of the relevant music by little-known (then) eighteenth-century composers; the resulting book and record proved valuable for my more musical 'A' level pupils at Builth Wells High School. Gerald and Dinah allowed us to house-sit for them in August while they went on holiday which gave us the chance to explore Cambridge and discover some of its more interesting and historic parts, travelling on borrowed bicycles. By now we had got to know the school well and admired it greatly for what it achieved for its pupils. The choristers were looked after by 'Matey', a wonderful old matron, and supervised by a very special Housemaster, Michael Peacock. He was a marvellous, lovable character who played Real Tennis as well as many a professional, and who loved horse racing so much that year by year his Christmas cards were purchased in support of 'The Distressed Jockeys Fund'. He treated the choristers like equals but woe betide any of them who tried to take advantage of this and overstepped the mark by betraying his trust; that boy would quickly find himself propelled into outer darkness and reduced to size. I remember Nick telling us with glee how Michael Peacock had taken the four most senior boys to a race meeting at Newmarket and had given each one a small sum of money to try his luck with the bookmakers! One Sports Day I called on him at his rooms in the morning in the school and, as usual, he welcomed me heartily and, again as usual, he thrust a glass of whisky into my hand. It was raining heavily so over the next hour or two we drank a large number of Glenfiddich Malt Whisky miniatures, each one prefaced by his saying: 'Don't worry, old boy, these are prizes for the fathers' races but there wont be any sports, look at the rain!' As the end of morning approached, the sun suddenly broke through the clouds, the rain vanished, whereupon we realised that we had drunk all the fathers' prizes. The longer Nick was at St John's the harder it became to leave Cambridge after our Saturday visits. We came to know more and more people who claimed more and more of our time, furthermore Choral Evensong so often was followed firstly by a chat with Nan Guest and some of the boys' parents, then by a drink with the choral and organ scholars and sometimes George Guest himself in the 'Barron of Beef'; opposite the Chapel. Afterwards, we would call at the school to say 'Goodnight' to Nick and this inevitably involved us in a visit to Michael Peacock so that by the time we set off it could be nearly 10 pm, with the result that when we reached the 'Duke of Cumberland' near Aynho, the door was firmly shut, it being well past Closing Time. Highlight of the year always was the last week of that strange short term for students who needed to re-take examinations, or so I was led to believe, at the end of July and the beginning of August. With Brecon Cathedral Choir usually on holiday by then, Hazel, Harriet and I were sometimes able to stay at Cambridge for a long weekend during which all sorts of fun events took place. There was the choir summer picnic on the banks of the River Cam, this being prefaced by our punting down the river and back again afterwards, always in the hope that someone would be propelled into the river because his pole had become stuck in the mud. Then there was the annual cricket match between the choristers and the choral scholars, the latter team usually being bolstered up by a few parents. Never to be forgotten was the evening barbecue in the school grounds with a bonfire, gorgeous food and oceans of wine; the smell of burning wood and sizzling hot dogs is still with me. Always there was the final round of services. No choir sang psalms as magically as St John's College Choir; no choir sang Stanford in A Magnificat and Nunc Dimittis like St John's and always I would wait with growing excitement as the words 'And to be the glory of thy people Israel' approached because out would come the great 'Trumpet Real' stop for an arpeggio of A major against almost the full organ and I would be reduced to tears; a similar effect in the Agnus Dei of Jean Langlais's Messe Solenelle on the Sunday morning inevitably produced a similar result. Truth to tell, to us no choir sang like St John's but we were biased, yet to watch George Guest direct his choir through any of the Herbert Howells settings of the Evening Canticles, particularly the 'Gloucester' and 'St Paul's' Services, not forgetting the final cadence of the St John's Service, and hearing the resulting sounds as one long phrase piled on top of another to create a magical, spellbinding tension, was an unforgettable experience. The final Sunday Evensong on that long weekend inevitably became an highly emotionally-charged experience because for at least four of the choral scholars this was the end; their last service; never again, perhaps, would they experience such camaraderie and be part of such magnificent music-making. Usually the final hymn was 'The day thou gavest, Lord, is ended', and if that was not enough of a tear-jerker, the final organ voluntary was often 'Nimrod' from Elgar's 'Enigma Variations'; small wonder the four choral scholars were not the only ones reduced to tears. One chorister on that Sunday, August 2nd, 1981, had no idea that he had sung his last service in St John's College Chapel otherwise he too might have wept. That was our Nick who when he returned at the start of the next term, found that his treble voice had left him.

Nick had belonged to the choir during a golden age. As a chorister, he had toured Europe extensively, been to Ireland, gone as far away as Japan and Australia as well as Canada and the USA, all before the age of fourteen years. What a lucky boy! It had been a time of special Organ Scholars too, including John Scott, a future Organist of St Paul's Cathedral, David Hill, a future Organist of Winchester Cathedral, and Adrian Lucas, a future Organist of Worcester Cathedral, all of whom have been to Brecon Cathedral at some time, to give organ recitals. Yet Nick had much to look forward to because he, and we, had decided to continue his education in the private sector but the question was, where? Earlier that year he had competed for scholarships at various schools. The Headmaster, Alan Mould, had wanted him to try for a lucrative scholarship at a public school in Oxford; we, however, were more interested in my father's old school, Charterhouse; dear old Michael Peacock, always a good friend to Nick, said: 'Why not Eton?', and Nick agreed. The trouble was, earlier that year, a friend, Llanelli-born Neil Cox, who was Organ Scholar at Downing College, Cambridge, had done some teaching practice at

Eton College and had been so bowled over by what he had seen that he had persuaded Nick to spend a day there. Nick did just that and was so mesmerised by the experience that he fell in love with Eton. Hazel and I were happy with Charterhouse where the Director of Music, Bill Llewellyn, couldn't have been kinder and more helpful; we also looked at Clifton College which scored many points for an exceedingly fine concert, and Radley College which did exactly the opposite. Hazel and I plotted a little cunning for the audition at Eton College and had Nick playing on his violin an 'Allegretto on the notes GEDGE', which Edward Elgar had composed for two pupils, the Misses Gedges, who had lived in Malvern: however, alarmingly we heard nothing. Meanwhile, at Charterhouse, Bill Llewellyn was poised, ready to offer Nick a scholarship but, knowing that we were still awaiting a reply from Eton College, he kindly telephoned the Precentor, by which title the Director of Music at Eton is known, and in that way we learned that Nick indeed had been successful in the school of his own choice. Indeed, Bill Llewellyn, impressively big hearted, was among the first to congratulate young Nick on his achievement. However, Nick's award was not as much in financial terms as we had hoped, after all, I numbered among the lowest paid Cathedral Organists in England and Wales and still was only a part-time school teacher, but to our amazement, joy and gratitude, the authorities at Eton asked how much we could afford and then offered to pay the remainder. So Nicholas enjoyed his final term at St John's College School as Head Boy and his not being able to sing in Chapel was compensated for by his dreams of going to Eton College. It was bliss both for him and for us.

If there was never a dull moment in Cambridge at this time there certainly wasn't one in Brecon. Indeed one morning, while walking across the Cathedral Close, Hazel met up with Meriel, Dean Alwyn's wife, who was chatting outside the Canonry with the wife of the Canon in Residence for that month, an elegantly dressed, well made-up lady who liked to move in higher society than our's. 'Isn't it wonderful', she cooed, 'Lady Brecon's grandson is going to Eton'. 'Oh!' replied Meriel, innocently, 'Nicky Gedge is going too'. While that didn't go down well with the Canon's wife, for us it made up for a lot. A few weeks later, Lay Clerk John Evans did what no other Lay Clerk had done before nor has done since: he with three friends sailed across the Atlantic Ocean from the USA to Great Britain, in a boat that was small enough to fit into the Cathedral Choir Room. A photograph of John and the boat now hangs on the Choir Room wall to commemorate the event. Needless to say, on the Sunday before John set out, the final hymn sung at Evensong was 'Eternal Father, strong to save' with its constant refrain: 'Oh hear us as we cry to Thee for those in peril on the sea'!

While John was busily employed on the ocean, the Cathedral Singers gave one of their most imaginative concerts. Beginning with Edward Elgar's grandiose setting of Psalm 29, 'Give unto the Lord, O ye mighty', the Gwent Chamber Orchestra continued with Alun Hoddinott's 'Welsh Dances', op.64. The central item was Constant Lambert's 'Rio Grande' which had so impressed me when I had been involved in performances at school and at the Royal Academy of Music. For once in my life I was truly apprehensive about the outcome of this rendition as I gave the down-beat for New Inn, Pontypool pianist Chris Knott to start the work. However, I need not have worried; he played with such aplomb that the music took off and the resulting performance was such a happy affair that I have never dared to perform it again. Not so the next work, Benjamin Britten's Serenade for tenor, horn and strings, op. 31, sung by Rogers Covey-Crump with the young Jonathan Williams supplying the demanding horn part. After the performance of that wonderful work I just wanted to do it again to get to know the music better. The concert ended on a 'high' with a performance of Hubert Parry's luxurious music to John Milton's poem 'Blest Pair of Sirens', a work that has long been dear to my heart. Later, at midnight, after the inevitable party in The George Hotel, as some of the musicians walked through the Cathedral Close on their way to Garth Cottage for a whisky nightcap, each of the four horn players rendered a solo fanfare in honour of Alwyn, our Dean, standing on the Almonry lawn beneath his bedroom window. Many years later he was to tell me how he had lain in his bed blocking his ears with his fingers, cursing my name.

The next day there were the normal two Sunday services in the Cathedral and the afternoon offering was a service to mark the Internations Year of the Disabled. Alwyn was good at organising services like this, usually organising an accompanying exhibition in one of the spaces that had been created during the interregnum before his arrival. On this occasion he had devised an interesting service around the three sections of Samuel Sebastian Wesley's little-known but imaginative, fine and lengthy anthem, 'Let us lift up our heart'. Imagine my surprise therefore when I read in a 'Musical Opinion' three years later, the following admission from Richard Turbet, a Librarian from Aberdeen University, long known for his championing of sixteenth century choral music:

> '*For many years the music of S S Wesley was anathema to me. Infatuated with Byrd, Tavener et al. (I still am) I was appalled by all those German sixths, the excruciating sentimentality, the complacent pomposity, the insensitive part-writing. So fascinated was I by the extent of my dislike that I borrowed records of Wesley's music from the library to try to rationalise my revulsion. But even membership of a choir whose conductor championed Wesley, a fact unknown to me when I joined, further repelled me. My road to Damascus was Brecon Cathedral where, at a Festival Evensong for the International Year for Disabled People, I heard the Cathedral Choir sing the whole of 'Let us lift up our heart': the first two sections replaced the Magnificat and Nunc Dimittis, the last section was the anthem. Here, at last, I saw Wesley's complete eminence in his sphere, aided by the fact that I had previously heard too many dreadful performances of Wesley's anthems by mixed choirs, and here was a fine and conscientious one by a male choir. Now Wesley's long-windedness became his*

ability to construct on a grand scale; his sentimentality became good melodies allied to a bold and judicious combination of his own originality and of the harmonic language of contemporary Romanticism: all these within a decorum in which the music was right for the circumstances for which it was composed. Most of all, I realised it was possible to admire Byrd, yet still to relish Wesley for being Wesley, inheritor of the English choral tradition through Byrd, who sought guidance from Tavener when composing his Masses; through Purcell who copied out Byrd's anthems and from whom Wesley picked up the sort of inconsiderate part-writing that Purcell perpetrates with his E below the stave for tenors in <u>My heart is inditing</u>: and through his own father Samuel, who transcribed motets by Byrd and endeavoured to have them published. What I had loathed in Wesley's music I had, in a distorted way, really enjoyed all the time, but in my commitment to the music of the Renaissance and flight from that of the nineteenth century, I had sought to reject it.'

Unexpected compliments like that made life all the more worth living!

Three weeks after that service I was sitting with Brecon Cathedral choristers on a bus bound for Truro Cathedral for another of our singing holidays. As we trundled from Devon into Cornwall we marvelled at how the countryside around us resembled Pembrokeshire and wondered if millions of years ago the two lands had been one before the arrival of the Bristol Channel. Not long after arriving at Truro we learned that we had brought sunshine with us because from that moment until the moment we left, not a drop of rain fell in Cornwall. We had a riotous week as almost opposite the Choir School where we lodged, was a lovely, hospitable pub, while close by the Cathedral was another; what more could we want. The Cathedral itself, a creation of that great Victorian architect, John Loughborough Pearson, was magical both inside and outside, indeed a pleasant faint aroma of incense permeated the interior although that puzzled me because never did I see any being used in services. Later I discovered that the kindly Head Verger used to arrive early every morning, light a thurible full of incense and waft its fumes into the Cathedral's central heating pipes so to convey the odours of Edom around the building. Such a quaint idea! Our stay in Truro was enlivened by the antics of a young choirboy answering to the name of Nathan. He stubbed out a lighted cigarette on a painted window sill in the dormitory; not content with that, he filled a poo-poo cushion with water and dropped it out of the dormitory window only for it to land on the roof of Kelvin Redford's car with disastrous results; finally, as the bus hurtled up the M5 on its way back to Brecon, he, feeling rather hot, pushed open the roof-light but with such force that it took off and bounced back down the motorway, much to the consternation of the following motorists.

That autumn the Cathedral Singers were awarded the W S Gwynne Williams Award which was presented at the Annual General Meeting of The Welsh Amateur Music Federation. With the cheque for £250 was a citation which commended the Singers for their pioneering work in Mid Wales, particularly on behalf of the music by J S Bach. Then, as winter descended, early in December Hazel found herself playing the organ for our friend John Cynan Jones's Treorchy Male Voice Choir in Croydon's Fairfield Hall and part of this concert was broadcast on BBC Radio 2. However, this was but the calm before the storm for suddenly, on Sunday December 13th, Brecon was attacked by a blizzard, the like of which had not been seen for a long time. At Choral Evensong in the Cathedral none of the soloists arrived and the performance of J S Bach's 'Christmas Oratorio' part one, was restricted to the opening chorus accompanied by the organ and a string quartet as the wind players also had failed to reach Brecon. That evening only six singers reached St Mary's church in the centre of the town where a congregation of six people had managed to gather for an Advent Carol Service. A week later an evening of readings and carols for the Mayor of Brecon's Christmas Fund, a much enjoyed annual event in St Mary's, was made more difficult by even more snow. The snow lifted a little for Christmas and Christmas Day itself was enlivened by what had become the annual summons to the Almonry to play cards with Alwyn our Dean and his family. The trouble was: he cheated so much that the Blessed Nia and our Harriet used to get rattled and the air became blue with their disgraceful comments. Four days later I was deposited in Neville Hall Hospital to have a perotid gland removed from beneath my left ear. After the successful operation I spent much of my time wandering around the wards with a bottle of fluid in one pocket and a small bottle of whisky, given me by Tony Wainwright, in the other, serving tea to patients. Then the snow returned with a vengeance and temperatures fell to 20°F. It took three days to dig a way out from the Tithe Barn where we parked our car as we had to get Nick to Eton College to start his first term; indeed that we got there at all was a considerable achievement as the road conditions were atrocious to the extent that the motorway road markings were hidden by packed snow. I had to take a month off from my Cathedral and School work so for January Hazel took charge of the Cathedral Choir and I used to hide behind a pillar in the nave to listen to the choir sing Evensongs. As this weather continued so it gave the Cathedral Choir the opportunity to sing for an anthem John Christmas Beckwith's, 'He maketh the snow to fall apace', which always caused much amusement. However, the end of an era was nigh. On the day when a new Bishop of St Asaph was elected it had never entered my head that this could be Alwyn our Dean, but it was. To say that this came as a shock is to put it mildly; as for the Blessed Nia who had built up such a delightful relationship with the choirboys, she was devastated and the Minor Canon, Stephen Brooks, had to work very hard to persuade her to accept the situation. So as the spring moved into the summer, first the Cathedral Choir, then the Cathedral Singers, and finally The Gwent Chamber Orchestra all made their farewells to Alwyn, Meriel and Nia, while making guesses as to who would come to Brecon as the new Dean.

XXXIX

Although it was now twenty years since we had left London, we had never lost touch with the Taylor family, three of whom had sung in the choir at the church of St Mary theVirgin, Primrose Hill. However, with Harry now retired and living only with his wife, Peggy, and his youngest daughter, Susie, my Goddaughter, the three older children having left home, they had moved out of their large house in Hampstead into a smaller house further north, near to Finchley. Hazel, Harriet, Nicholas and I sometimes looked after their new abode when they went away during the summer holidays and in this way got a holiday ourselves which we would not otherwise have been able to afford, now that some of our money was tied up in keeping Nick at Eton. Since we had moved away Peggy Anne had married, gone to live in Kent and started a family. Tony also had married and now lived in Southampton, indeed Hazel had played the organ at his wedding in the lovely old church in Dartmouth, an occasion which had brought back to me happy memories of Southwark Cathedral Scout Camps at Kingswear on the opposite side of the River Dart. Nicholas Taylor on the other hand, was still single, furthermore he had yet to show signs of calming down and behaving more normally. Passionately fond of flying aeroplanes, he had gained a pilot's licence at the age of seventeen years, a year before he had taken his driving test for the first time, and failed; to him it seemed ridiculous that he could fly an aeroplane but not drive a car. At the age of eighteen years he was accepted into the RAF College at Cranwell but his time there was short as he performed one trick too many in the sky and was asked to leave. Undaunted, he talked his way into the Royal Naval College at Dartmouth but, in view of his previous escapade, was restricted to flying helicopters. It was at this time that I had asked him if he could get me some aerial photographs of Brecon Cathedral. Lo and behold, a few days later a helicopter appeared over Brecon, flying low enough as to draw adverse comments from residents, then, shortly afterwards, in the post arrived two lovely black and white photographs. When we met up again soon afterwards at Tony's wedding, I thanked him profusely for the photographs but said that I really needed them in colour. Lo and behold, a few days later a helicopter circled over Brecon Cathedral, then shortly afterwards, in the post arrived twelve lovely colour photographs of the Cathedral taken from all angles. By now Nick was on his way to achieving his ambition of flying Sea Harriers as a member of the Royal Navy's Fleet Air Arm. Towards the end of 1980, he had been married at St Joseph's Roman Catholic Church in the North Wales seaside resort of Colwyn Bay, with Hazel playing the organ. Soon he and his wife Clare had settled into an eighty-year-old farm cottage on the outskirts of Closworth, a few miles from Yeovilton, Somerset, Naval air base, where both of them were stationed, he a Lieutenant, she a Second Officer in the WRNS. They had been married for just eighteen months when the

Argentinians took it upon themselves to invade the Falkland Islands and Nicholas Taylor found himself on an aircraft carrier heading towards the conflict. It was after a Cathedral Singers rehearsal, followed by a visit to The George Hotel on a Tuesday night, May 4th 1982, that Hazel and I had returned home and switched on the television in time to see a newsflash stating that a Harrier pilot had been killed in The Falklands. I don't know why but we sat up waiting until eventually the pilot was named: Nicholas Taylor. Immediately we tried telephoning Harry and Peggy in order to confirm what we did not want to believe, but to no avail as their telephone was permanently engaged, so it was not until the next day that we finally did reach them to express our sorrow. Their Nicholas had meant so much to us to the extent that we had named our son after him, as had their own daughter, Peggy Anne. Yet this had not been surprising as he had been such a striking person, tall, good looking, with a lovely nature and so full of fun, an obvious leader, indeed so good at his job that once the Falkland conflict had been resolved, he was due to become a shore-based Test Pilot. However, that had turned out not to be as Nicholas Taylor entered the history books as the first British Serviceman to be killed in the Falkland War. Harry and Peggy were wonderful; they said all the right words to the British Press but what is more they said them with conviction because they had meant them. After all, years before, they themselves had both fought in the British Army during the Second World War to keep Britain free, and had lived to tell the tale. Now they were furious that the Argentinians had dared to take possession of a British territory by force and were proud of the fact that their son 'had died doing the job he loved for the country he loved.' This statement was emblazoned over countless newspapers and inspired a certain Helen Forsyth to compose the following poem:

> 'Your noble words have echoed in our heart.
> We share your sorrow and we share your pride.
> And though at first you felt the harsh tears start,
> In time a kinder feeling will preside
> And loss will find a leveller in love
> With all its vivid memories of your boy,
> That youngster who had set his eyes above
> To gain the skies and know a flyer's joy.
> But sterner duties called him and he left
> Knowing the perils that now lay ahead.
> He gave his life and left your own bereft,
> And yet his shining courage is not dead,
> For you have found the words to give it life
> Above the carnage of this bitter strife.'

On Friday, May 14th, there was a Memorial Service for Nicholas Taylor at the Royal Naval Air Station at Yeovilton when Hazel played the (electronic) organ and the poignant final hymn, 'The day thou gavest, Lord, is ended', tugged at many heartstrings. A few days later Peggy wrote in a letter to us:

'Hello Sweeties

You really are darlings to come chasing all over the country for us – I just don't know what we should do without you all. I only wish I was a millionaire – I would buy you an aeroplane – though I'm not convinced that I should trust David to do the driving – he'd probably be thinking of a new descant instead of paying attention to the steering!

It's just about impossible to realise that Nick will not be dropping in on us – but we are trying to take comfort by Sue's remarks that he did more in 32 years than most of us do in a life time though the exception to that must be the Gedge family. But we shall always be grateful to you Hazel and David for putting up with him – it was such an important part of his life.

I'm so sorry that we could not come up this weekend – the trouble with Harry is that he always takes on more than he can chew and I have to keep on thumping him! Also we must be about, our poor darling Clare is being such a good girl but is finding that its quite impossible to eat – so we shall have to thump her too.

We had a super 'phone call from Little Nick yesterday – Peggy-Anne is bringing the boys home for the summer!! Roger will come and join us for the last week in Aug. and they will all go back in Sept. and if those b—Argentines have shut-up and gone home we shall be going out at the end of Oct. for about 3 months – that should cheer Harry up – he wont have to watch the electric meter whirling around.

Our love to you all and a special hug for Nick –

See you soon
Love
Peggy '

The war did not last for much longer and soon the Argentinians were returning home with their tails between their legs leaving Harry and Peggy free to retrace the final journey of their son Nicholas. Soon they discovered that it was not all as it had seemed. Earlier The Times newspaper had published a moving account of Nicholas' burial:

'IF I SHOULD DIE THINK ONLY THIS OF ME: THAT THERE'S SOME CORNER OF A FOREIGN FIELD THAT IS FOREVER ENGLAND.' – Rupert Brooke.

The bleak and savage lands of the Falklands may not be foreign, but there is an unknown corner where Lieutenant Nicholas Taylor, the Sea Harrier pilot short down last Tuesday, today lies.

Last night the Argentines who killed him showed on television how they honoured him in death and buried him with their own war dead.

There was nothing British about the ceremony. Forty Argentine soldiers stood rigidly to attention with rifles gripped diagonally across their chests, in the howling wind, as a priest muttered softly in Latin and shivered inside his anorak. The blue and white Argentine flag cracked in the wind.

For 80 minutes Argentine television showed scenes of the Falklands. At one point two jets flashed by, their exhausts emitting a pall of red and white smoke, and they looked like Harriers. Suddenly there was an explosion.

The film, taken by a state television crew, switched to a crumpled, mangled and barely recognizable Harrier with an identification mark that looked like X243.

The burial was at Goose Green, where the Harrier was shot down. The Argentine announcer said it was brought down on Saturday, May 1, whereas Britain announced that the aircraft was lost three days later, on May 4. That was the Saturday the Argentines claimed to have destroyed two Harriers.

There was a line of small white wooden crosses and right at the end was the fresh grave of Lieutenant Taylor, covered with newly-dug turf. The Argentine major in charge of the party saluted, but his troops did not. No islanders were present and not a word of English was spoken. The Argentines gave him a strictly Argentine Roman Catholic burial, with not the slightest acknowledgement to the country of his birth.'

The report had gone on to outline the damage done to the airstrip at Goose Green by the three Harriers:

'The camera panned across the airfield in a two-second blur just to prove that it was still there and operable, but it was an absurd scene. For all the viewers could tell it was nothing more than a heap of rubble and a mass of holes.'

In a later passage, huge craters were seen in the earth around the airstrip. A military spokesman said they were 30 yards away and conceded that the airport entrance was badly damaged.

Now Harry and Peggy discovered that the three harrier pilots had been given a specific task: to destroy some stockpiles of napalm on the airstrip at Goose Green. This came as a shock because it added a chemical dimension to the Falkland War. As to the action itself, it seems that Nicholas Taylor was piloting the third of the planes to attack by which time the Argentinian soldiers had lined up their guns and his plane was hit. Nicholas Taylor's Harrier jet crashed onto the edge of a field close to the airstrip and here comes the strange twist to the sad tale. According to the farmer who owned that field, the Argentinians, far from giving Nicholas a military funeral, merely dug a grave at the side of the wreckage and placed his body there. Only later was Nicholas given a military funeral and buried alongside other British military dead at Port Stanley, the small capital of the Falkland Islands. In due course, Susie, who had accompanied her mother and father on this poignant trip, became Secretary of the association that was formed to hold together relatives of the British Falkland War Dead. However, there is one further strange twist to the Falkland War episode. Many years before, one of the Gedge family had gone to live in Buenos Aires, settled there and married an Argentinian girl with the result that there were Gedges living in Argentina; so when Argentina invaded the Falkland Islands, a Gedge was piloting one of their jet planes. However, the story does not end there because on the British side was a Squadron Leader Tim Gedge who may have known Nicholas Taylor because he, too, was based at Yeovilton. Had Nicholas Taylor had a premonition of what was to happen? On the night before the fatal mission, while in the Aircraft Carrier, he had written a lovely letter to his mother and father, apologising for all the trouble that he had caused them in his youth, and thanking them for being such wonderful parents. In Brecon Cathedral Choir Room, Nicholas Taylor's name lives on, commemorated by the first of those black and white aerial photographs which he had taken while flying a helicopter that he had commandeered from his base at Yeovilton, whether officially or unofficially I had never asked! This is now framed and hangs on the wall close to the door.

While Harry and Peggy had been courageously enduring this crisis, our lives meanwhile had continued on their relentless course. Around the time that Nicholas Taylor had begun his long journey to the Falkland Islands, Hazel, Harriet, Nicholas and I had attended our Shelagh's wedding in Sheffield. Since that Royal School of Church Music Course at Darley Dale, back in 1976, when Shelagh had entered our lives, she had become a different person largely through the efforts of Hazel who had persuaded her to attend evening classes to accumulate some 'O' Levels, also to take an interest in accountancy. Still Shelagh spent most of her holidays with us either at Brecon or at Kidwelly, in addition she had become a keen member of the Sheffield Ladies Cricket Team. Devoted to her church choir at St Augustine's Endcliffe in Sheffield, she had met a perfect soulmate in Nigel Carter, a young dentist from Croydon, who, like her, loved church music. Their wedding was a happy occasion, the only hiccup being the odd behaviour of her brother who had not been able to come to terms with the new life that she had made for herself; furthermore, the delightful reception was held close to another of her passion's, Sheffield Wednesday Football Club's ground. Fortunately, through this wedding we did not lose an adopted daughter but rather we gained not only a good friend in Nigel but also another good friend in his Best Man, Colin Nash, who soon began to join in Cathedral musical activities at Brecon and beyond.

A month on found Hazel, Harriet and me in the Rhondda Valley helping The Treorchy and District Choral Society with a performance of Handel's 'Messiah' at St Peter's Church, Pentre. Afterwards we went to a party at the home of our friend John Cynan Jones, conductor of The Treorchy Male Choir, and his wife Mary, who lived close by in Hermon Street; their daughter, Eldrydd, and our Harriet also were good friends. With Rhondda hospitality being what it is, we had such a good time that we did not set off for home until after midnight, with Hazel driving the car. So we wound our way along the empty, narrow road through the Rhondda Valley and up onto the Rhigos mountain where suddenly the car slid off the road and into a ditch! Hazel and I got out to survey the damage and quickly realised that there was no way we ourselves could get the car back onto the road, so we stood hoping for the Almighty to intervene. We did not have long to wait! Suddenly, in the far distance, we became aware of the lights of a coach threading its way along the windy mountain road towards us; when it reached us it stopped. By chance the bus turned out to be carrying a local Male Voice Choir which had been competing in an Eisteddfod at Hereford. Two of the singers alighted from the bus and came over to discover what had happened, eyeing Hazel and me in such a way as to make obvious that they thought we'd been up to no good in the back of the car. Hazel was silently fuming just as she had been when I had first set eyes on her fifteen years before, but then their eyes alighted upon young Harriet and their attitude changed as they listened to our explanation. When Hazel uttered the magic word 'Messiah', in telling of how earlier that evening she had been playing the organ in a performance of this masterpiece by George Frederick Handel, the two singers rushed back to the bus uttering loudly in awe the words: 'Messiah, boys, Messiah', and within a few seconds more of these Male Choir choristers were disgorged from the bus to lift bodily from the ditch our car, then cheerfully to wave us on our way back to Brecon.

Another month on found the Mayor and Corporation of Brecknock attending Morning Service at Brecon Cathedral one Sunday, but on this occasion, there was a fatal break with tradition as the reception was not held in the Guildhall but on the lawn between the Canonry and Clergy House, alongside the Cathedral. The sun shone down and the occasion sparkled but unfortunately, just as I was about to stagger home for lunch having imbibed a fair amount of wine at the expense of the taxpayer, I spied the figure of the Canon-in-Residence standing at the door of the Canonry beckoning me inside. As I went through the door he trust a tumbler of whisky into my hand and thereafter, no matter how much I drank, Canon Wynford Rees always saw to it that my tumbler was full to the brim. I have only hazy recollections of Choral Evensong that day on which the choir were due to sing an awkward anthem by Henry Purcell – 'I will give thanks unto the Lord', but I do remember that Alwyn who at that time was still our Dean, spent most of the time sitting down so I can only assume that he too was in a similar condition. I recovered consciousness in time to play the organ for the 6.15 pm Evensong at St Mary's Parish Church after which I retired to bed only to spend most of the next day worrying about that Choral Evensong. That evening I was going to Swansea for a church choirs rehearsal and 'Orrie', now singing alto in the Cathedral Choir, was coming with me. When he arrived I asked innocently: 'How did the anthem go at Evensong yesterday?' to which he replied: 'I don't know, I can't remember anything about it'. Apparently he, too, had enjoyed the reception.

These trips to Swansea continued to be a source of fun and usually I was accompanied by some of the younger Lay Clerks. One Monday evening we had all enjoyed our customary 'after the rehearsal drink' in a Swansea pub with some of the local choristers, whereupon we set off for home with Hazel driving. Orrie and Dai Tim – as David Timothy was called, were with us and, as was customary, we stopped just beyond Ystradgynlais Churchyard to allow the two lads to relieve themselves in the churchyard. Suddenly Hazel and I heard sounds of a commotion coming from behind us and looked back to see 'Orrie and Dai running up the road towards the car as best they could, doing up their trousers, pursued by an irate elderly Vicar who was shouting: 'You dirty buggers, you dirty buggers'. Knowing the Vicar as we did we thought quickly: if we waited for 'Orrie and Dai he would catch up with them and discover us, so we drove off and parked again, half a mile nearer Brecon, leaving them to catch us up, safe in the knowledge that the Vicar would never run that far! Another Monday evening, as Hazel was busy and couldn't come with us, there was room for a third lad, young Ian Robson. Our destination on that occasion was Cockett, a suburb of Swansea, where the local Vicar at that time was Fred Secombe, brother of the famous (Sir) Harry Secombe. On the way to St Peter's Church, Ian took great delight in embarrassing me while we were waiting at some traffic lights, by innocently asking a passer-by how he could get to Cockett! One other of these trips found me 'taken short' on the way home, just after leaving Abercraf. As we approached Crai Mountain I saw a gate leading into a field which contained a barn, so I persuaded Hazel to stop the car. Climbing over the gate under the cover of darkness, I ran over to the barn where I proceeded to relieve myself only to find a security light unexpectedly come on to illuminate the proceedings!

One longer journey that summer took Hazel and me northwards to St Asaph. We had been unable to go to the service at Bangor Cathedral when Alwyn our Dean had been consecrated Bishop of St Asaph but we were able to go to the service when he was enthroned as the seventy-seventh Bishop of St Asaph. It was a splendid and dignified occasion in St Asaph Cathedral yet for us, one that was tinged with sadness as afterwards we had to make our farewells to Alwyn and Meriel who we had come to love and admire so much at Brecon; however, for Alwyn, this was the beginning of a new and important stage in his life which culminated in his eventually becoming a very wise Archbishop of Wales.

The journey to St Asaph and back on Saturday, July 17th, had been long and tiring but there was one even longer journey that summer on Monday, July 26th, when Russ the Bus drove the Cathedral Singers all the way to Scotland to Trinity College, Glenalmond in lovely Perthshire, where Jim Wainwright, brother of our bass doctor friend Tony Wainwright, was a Housemaster. For the next twelve days Jim's school house became our home and what a congenial one it turned out to be. We started by turning the library into a bar that remained open until whichever Wainwright was on duty as Bar Tender, became too tired to stand up any longer. Interestingly, because 'Last Orders' was never called, there was no drunkenness; furthermore, despite lower club prices being charged for drinks there was still a healthy profit of £300+, which was donated to the 'Gerontius Fund' as the Singers were hoping to perform Edward Elgar's 'Dream of Gerontius' next summer and that was an expensive project. Initially, the Wainwright Bar-Tenders had underestimated the alcoholic capacity of the Cathedral Singers as the stock purchased for the first few days was demolished on the first night alone. At the Wainwright House in Trinity College, every day started with the same ritual: unfortunately, Russ had found a trumpet and had taught young David Jermyn, son of contralto Myra Jermyn, to play the first three notes of the song 'Day by Day', which he would then sing in a very loud voice followed by an explosion of infectious laughter as a third member crashed around on some cymbals. This unlikely and unwelcome trio would wend its way around the house daily at an early hour, performing at every vantage point, until everyone was well and truly awake. Every day was fun as the Singers enjoyed the most beautiful countryside and the most lovely weather. As the school grounds included a magnificent cricket field and as there were enough Wainwrights to field a cricket team, so the Wainwright families took on The Cathedral Singers. It was a game to remember because at one priceless moment, umpire John Cynan Jones, our Treorchy Male Choir Conductor friend, substituted a haggis for the ball which bass Geraint Jones promptly bowled to Chris, son of Tony and Beth Wainwright; he struck it good and hard to send guts flying in all directions.

During their time in Scotland, the Cathedral Singers gave concerts in Dunblane Cathedral, a wonderful mediaeval building which to my sorrow was no longer an Anglican place of worship and therefore only a cathedral in name; in St Paul's Cathedral, Dundee, designed by Sir Giles Gilbert Scott in 1853, where the charismatic and friendly resident Organist, Robert Lightband, soon became known as 'Robert Lightbulb'; in St Andrew's Church in the university town of St Andrew's, where the performance was given a pleasing review in the local paper; also in St Ninian's Cathedral, Perth, a building designed in 1850, by William Butterfield and very dear to my heart because of the part it played in the early history of the Anglo-Catholic movement – those Singers who belonged to the Cathedral Choir also sang an Evensong here and discovered afterwards that no-one had remembered to unlock the main Cathedral door, so unaccustomed were people there to having weekday choral services. Most fantastic was Glasgow's St Mungo's Cathedral, a giant mediaeval edifice again, sadly, no longer Anglican, where in the crypt, deep down in the bowels of the building, is a shrine to St Kentingern who numbered among his disciples none other than St Asaph. In this magnificent building an organ screen separated the nave from the chancel and here, from the roof, hung the hugest curtain I had ever seen. Here also the console of the Fr Willis organ was so far away from me conducting the choir on the floor of the nave that Kelvin Redford lay on the floor of the screen and relayed my beat to John Cynan Jones who duly tapped it out on Hazel's shoulder. When we had arrived at the Cathedral we had been advised by the police not to stray far away in a certain direction because as likely as not we would be mugged; when we left the Cathedral we persuaded Russ to stop his bus outside a Fish and Chip Shop so that we could sample Haggis and Chips! Our one Sunday in Scotland was spent in Sir Giles Gilbert Scott's masterpiece, St Mary's Cathedral, Edinburgh, singing the Vaughan Williams Mass in the morning and an Evensong later; in between we had time to meet up with dear Dennis Townhill, the Cathedral Organist, and his charming wife, Mabel, who were such delightful company. By taking a few instrumentalists with us to Scotland we had been able to vary our programme by including a G F Handel organ concerto or a J S Bach violin concerto in addition to providing instrumental accompaniments to Pelham Humfrey and Henry Purcell verse anthems. Russ the Bus again fell in love with the broad tune that opens Mendelssohn's 'There shall a star from Jacob come forth', at the start of that composer's unfinished oratorio 'Christus'; once more it became known as 'Russ's Anthem' with the result that wherever Russ drove us on tour, this had to be sung!

So another happy singing tour staggered to its inevitable conclusion but not before one final act of madness. This involved two very dear, elderly characters in our party. One was Haydn Bond, a chirpy violinist from Pontypool, who could remember the days of the silent films and who, around 1947, had the distinction of being the first peripatetic violin teacher appointed in Wales. Some of the violinists in the Gwent Chamber Orchestra had at some time numbered among his pupils and he himself played in the band, sometimes unconsciously decorating the violin parts with portamentos reminiscent of the 1930s. For years he had cared for a sick wife but recently she had died leaving him free to roam around with Brecon Cathedral Choir and The Cathedral Singers. The other was Mrs Muggeridge, a very dear lady from Brecon's Coryton Close, whose son, Wyndham, had been a Cathedral Choirboy, whose daughter, Maggie, had looked after Harriet and Nicholas in their younger days, who herself had helped Hazel a lot in Garth Cottage – strangely, by chance, some of her distant relatives who lived in Towyn, Merionethshire, had worked alongside me on the Talyllyn Railway when I had spent my summer holidays there in my youth. Mrs Muggeridge had gone on many choir trips to help cook and bottle wash, in addition to helping with the youngsters, and always her help had been particularly valuable because she was so good-hearted. Anyway, everyone agreed that a mock-wedding of Haydn Bond and Mrs Muggeridge would be great fun and a fitting conclusion to the trip, even Haydn and Mrs Muggeridge themselves. So John Cynan Jones became the Minister and Kelvin Redford was nominated the Preacher, while my wife, Hazel, dressed up as a village organist, with Beth Wainwright and Dotty Phillips suitably attired as Bridesmaids; finally, violinist David Walker undertook to be Haydn's Best Man. A real live piper was engaged to lead the wedding procession around the school grounds and a real fresh salmon was purchased for the marriage feast. Best of all was the stag party attended by everyone in a remote Perthshire pub to which we were driven in the bus by Russ dressed in drag as a Char Woman. When after careering through narrow leafy lanes the bus drew up outside the chosen hostelry and disgorged its cargo of strangely attired passengers, the locals looked on in utter amazement; when the tall stocky figure of Russ emerged from the driver's cab, heavily made up, clad in a dress, with high-heeled shoes on his feet, and a scarf tied tightly around his head, constantly emitting loud bursts of deep, raucous, noisy laughter, their eyes almost popped out. It was hilarious!

XL

Bishop Noel Young Vaughan had now been at Brecon for around six years and, having the initials BNY, was generally referred to as 'Binny'. A man of vision, he had arrived full of ideas and good intentions, also he was fortunate in having an excellent and loving wife, Nesta, to help him travel along the right path. He enjoyed a good show but sometimes, in his efforts to create such an occasion, unknowingly brought about mayhem, as had happened at the farewell Choral Evensong for Dean Jacob a few years earlier. On this occasion he created such genuine confusion at the end of the service that the Dean was unsure as to whether he was to bless the Bishop or the Bishop was to bless him and as usual, it was not the Bishop who ended up red-faced with embarrassment. Sadly, along came tragedy: Nesta was found to be suffering with cancer from which she died a few months later, leaving him like a rudderless ship, without her guidance. Nesta's funeral was turned into a great public display of grief, the like of which had never been experienced before at the Cathedral and certainly not since. Afterwards Bishop Vaughan settled down as best he could and battled on courageously, but alone. When a long journey had to be undertaken – and there were plenty of those in the vast diocese of Swansea and Brecon, he would enlist the additional driving skills of Bill Rees, a Lay Reader from nearby Llanfrynach who was also the local Health Inspector. The irony of this arrangement was not lost on many people for while two famous comic characters on TV at this time were 'Bill and Ben the Flowerpot Men', here also at this time were 'Bill and Ben the Episcopal Men'. Although Bishop Vaughan and I did not always see 'eye to eye' he was nevertheless very supportive of musical matters, ideed for the Diocesan Choral Festival in 1983, the sixtieth birthday of the Diocese, he provided me with £300 to commission a setting of the Mass for congregation and/or choir from Dr Arthur Wills, the Organist of Ely Cathedral, who was also a composer of some note. So was born 'The Brecon Mass'. This was based on Joseph Parry's famous hymn tune 'Aberystwyth' which is sung to Charles Wesley's hymn 'Jesus, lover of my soul'; the Kyrie is particularly fine as is the Agnus Dei, but the remainder is difficult to perform well.

One of Bishop Vaughan's most interesting ideas had been to send Alwyn our Dean, Canon Arthur Howells, the Diocesan Youth Chaplain, and me to Taizé, to experience worship in that remarkable religious community. My two abiding memories of this excursion were firstly, Alwyn our Dean – the future Archbishop of Wales, hogging all the driving in France which was not always good for the nervous systems of his three passengers, and, secondly, the music at the services. I had always been led to believe that this was spontaneous but it was not so because some of the pilgrims were invited to the daily music workshops where they were instructed into how to sing the chants that have now become famous. Afterwards, at the services, they infiltrated the hordes of worshippers and led them in the 'spontaneous' singing of what, I suppose, would now be called 'Worship Songs'. Strangely but, I suppose, typically, after our return to Brecon, no use was made of my new found skills as Bishop Vaughan turned his mind to other matters. However, he was for ever scheming and among his most visionary schemes was the creation of a Deanery Centre out of the rambling old Deanery which originally had been attached to the Cathedral when it was a Priory, and used as the Prior's House. Initially, the Bishop had a vision of the Old Deanery becoming a centre for church music but unfortunately for him my reaction was lukewarm; being the lowest paid Cathedral Organist in England and Wales, I had to continue teaching at Builth Wells High School where recently my job had become full-time, also I still had my Cathedral Singers and Gwent Chamber Orchestra to rehearse and conduct, in addition to my work with the Swansea choristers. What did cross my mind was the idea that perhaps the Royal School of Church Music could be persuaded to use the place for day courses catering for choristers from South and Mid Wales, as well as the Border Counties. When I suggested this to the Bishop he seemed quite interested, until I explained that first he would need around one thousand pounds to equip The Deanery Centre with a decent piano, whereupon the subject was quickly dropped never to be raised again. There rarely seemed to be enough money to see through any of his grandiose ideas, yet one madcap scheme really did come to fruition. Bishop Vaughan decided to make his Deanery a venue for diocesan youth activities under the guidance of the charismatic young Minor Canon, Stephen Brooks. Soon it was decreed that around thirty unemployed youngsters from Swansea would come to live in the Deanery Centre for a week in the summer and spend the time pondering the significance of life. Then came the first bombshell: many months before I had booked the Deanery Centre to accommodate a number of young orchestral players from London's Royal Academy of Music who were coming to Brecon to help me with the Cathedral Singers performance of Elgar's 'Dream of Gerontius'; now I was told that I might have to look elsewhere. In the words of Queen Victoria: 'I was not amused'. The second bombshell was much more dramatic!

Because Bishop Vaughan so often thought big so he had set about bringing the Queen to Brecon to open his Deanery Centre and meet these youngsters from Swansea, also to attend a service in the Cathedral. Unfortunately for the Bishop, no sooner had the thirty or so youngsters from Swansea discovered that their week at Brecon was to be part of a religious happening, than their number rapidly diminished to around six, despite the obvious attraction of meeting the Queen. However, the Bishop was far from perturbed because by now he was busily planning the most magnificent service in his Cathedral to welcome the Queen. 'I want to start with Parry's 'I was glad' he said to Hazel and me, 'with trumpets and organ accompanying the choir'. That was fine by us, positively exciting until he let drop that he was planning for the Queen not to sit in the front of the nave – ('too much of a security risk' he mumbled), but (what a coincidence!) on a seat beneath the Organ Chamber, next to his Bishop's Throne. We were horrified and hastily pointed out that the Queen would be deafened by the noise of the organ but he waved away our protests saying to Hazel: 'Play the organ more quietly, my dear'. How ludicrous! Here was to be a Cathedral jammed full of people expecting to sing hymns lustily and Hazel was being told to accompany their efforts quietly on the organ so as not to deafen the Queen. As the day of the service drew nearer and nearer I wondered what to do. In the end, three days before the great day, I plucked up courage and wrote a letter to the Queen suggesting that she take some precautions against the inevitable noise of the organ situated immediately above where she would be sitting. Imagine my surprise therefore when by return, from Buckingham Palace, I received from her Private Secretary the following reply:

'Dear Mr Gedge,
    Many thanks for your letter of 18th July with its prudent warning about cotton wool. Her Majesty is much obliged to you for your forethought.
                            Yours sincerely
                            William Heseltine'

Meanwhile, at a meeting before the great day, the Bishop had informed the Residentiary Canons, Hazel and me that we were all to leave the Cathedral by the South Aisle door during the singing of the last hymn, so that we could line up in The Close in preparation for being presented to the Queen. I demurred and said that Hazel and I could not possibly leave the Cathedral until the service had ended whereupon the Bishop told us rather irritably, to please ourselves but that we might go down to the Deanery Centre after we had finished and if the Queen was still there we could be presented to her then. And so it came to pass, the service celebrating sixty years of the diocese of Swansea and Brecon which, according to the Service Sheet, started 'at approximately 5.00 pm' went like a dream. At the end, not during the final hymn but after the Welsh National Anthem had been sung by everyone present in the Cathedral, and the Blessing had been delivered by the Bishop, the Residentiary Canons left the Cathedral via the South Door, each to be presented to the Queen, while Hazel played the final Organ Voluntaries – J S Bach's 'Fantasia in G' and Henri Mulet's 'Carrilon Sortie', and I processed out with the choir. After I had seen off the excited choristers and Hazel had finished playing the organ, we made our way through the crowded Cathedral Close and down to the Passageway leading from what thereafter became known as The Queen's Room, in the Deanery Centre. As the Queen was still there my mind began to work furiously while I thought of something to say when we were presented, because I was terrified of becoming tongue-tied. Presently, the Queen's Private Secretary, William Heseltine, came along and shook our hands, giving me a knowing smile, then along walked the Queen. When Hazel and I were introduced to her, I muttered something about being grateful to her for maintaining St George's Chapel, Windsor and its music, explaining that my son went to school nearby with the result that when we visited him on a Saturday afternoon we often had to choose between Choral Evensong at St George's Chapel, or a soccer match at Queen's Park Rangers. She laughed and remarked that we would have to get our priorities right, whereupon as she began to move on up the passage she stopped suddenly, looked back and said with a smile: 'Oh! and thank you for your letter'. The expressions that crossed the faces of the Bishop and the Dean were priceless.

Bishop Vaughan was lavish in his praise of the music at his service: 'quite marvellous and certainly the best I have heard anywhere', he wrote in a letter four days later but by then an amazing weekend of more music had taken place. On the second day after the great service was the long awaited performance of Elgar's 'Dream of Gerontius' by the Cathedral Singers and the vastly augmented Gwent Chamber Orchestra in the Cathedral. Fortunately, the problem over accommodating visiting musicians in the Deanery Centre had been resolved because no sooner had the Queen left Brecon for home than the few unemployed youngsters also left for their homes thereby leaving space for the twenty or so young orchestral players who had been sent up from The Royal Academy of Music by my good friend David Robinson. Initially they had seemed to be a surly, suspicious lot but after a rehearsal in the evening and a drinking session in The George Hotel with the local musicians, they had begun to unwind and to enter into the spirit of Brecon hospitality; furthermore, after Hazel and I had sat up chatting with them until the early hours of the morning, some of them had dropped their guards and had begun to bare their souls. Indeed the more time we spent with them the more we came to know them and soon we became one happy family regretting only the absence of any clergymen to complete the pastoral work that unconsciously was being done.

Saturday was a day of ever increasing wonder. Sometime before, worried that the Cathedral Singers might not conquer 'The Dream', I had invited volunteers from the Hereford Cathedral Choral Society to assist as the work was often sung by this choir. Imagine my horror therefore, when after the afternoon rehearsal I heard a rather bumptious visiting tenor asking where he should collect his fee! Having never mentioned any such fee and not being good at confrontations, I melted away leaving Mary Kneen, the wonderful Cathedral Singers' secretary, to defuse the situation which she did in her most charming manner. The concert drew a 'full house' to the Cathedral and the atmosphere was highly charged, but all went off happily beginning with a full-blooded account of Hubert Parry's 'Blest Pair of Sirens', moving on to a sympathetic performance of 'The Dream of Gerontius'. By the end of the concert we were all drained but elated as another milestone had been reached in the history of The Cathedral Singers.

We celebrated as we always did, in The George Hotel, until Mrs Jones called 'Time!' whereupon we retired to The Deanery Centre to continue our celebrations. By now midnight had struck and eminent tenor soloist Ken

Bowen was responding to a challenge from local tenor Tony 'Topnote', husband of Cathedral Singer Gloria Bennett, as to which of them could hold the highest note for longest. Pandemonium reigned. Within an hour some of the assembled multitude had moved into the kitchen to brew up some coffee whereupon the door flew open and in swept Minor Canon Stephen Brooks clad in his pyjamas and dressing gown, white-faced with rage. While he was complaining loudly and angrily about our noise, using a few choice words as he did so, the door moved gently back to reveal Dotty, (Cathedral Singer Dorothy Phillips from Pontardawe) who said very gently but firmly: 'Stephen, I have known you since you were a little boy. Why don't you go back to bed!'. Without another word he stalked out of the room and left us to our partying. By 3.00 am the two bassoon players were being rather amorous on the lawn outside not realising that they were being watched by the Canon in Residence from his bedroom window opposite. At 5.00am, trombonist Rob Price revved up loudly in his car and took off through the archway in the Close taking with him two friends and a French lad named Thierry who was staying with us, to show them sunrise from the top of the Brecon Beacons, then his home in the Rhondda Valley at dawn. It was quite an occasion. So, too, was Sunday morning when choristers from Swansea churches came up to join the Cathedral Choir to sing all the C M Widor Mass for two choirs and two organs including the stunning Gloria that we had been forbidden to sing at the Ordinations. Great fun as that was, much of my efforts that morning were devoted to avoiding the clergy who, not surprisingly I suppose, were not kindly disposed to us at this moment; although on reflection, I still could not understand why they had made no effort to enter into the spirit of a weekend which had involved many of their own parishioners and young choristers from Swansea, not forgetting the cream of young musicians from The Royal Academy of Music. That afternoon at Evensong, choristers from Swansea and Brecon sang with great aplomb, S S Wesley's magnificent large-scale anthem 'Ascribe unto the Lord', and they too were elated by what they had done. Afterwards I and the much augmented Gwent Chamber Orchestra set about rehearsing for that evening's concert at which they played Joseph Haydn's Symphony no. 48 in C, 'Maria Theresia', Mozart's 'Jupiter' Symphony and Beethoven's 'Emporer' Piano Concerto which was magnificently played by Gwent pianist Christopher Knott. So ended the first of what was to become many twice-yearly weekends of music-making when the local orchestral players would be joined by others from London and elsewhere. For the last time that weekend Hazel and I sat up until the early hours of morning in the Deanery Centre listening to these young musicians talking about their aspirations. One indeed had succeeded in having a 'jingle' performed on ITV for which he had received £1500, but he would gladly have sacrificed it all to have his Symphony performed. On the next day as they made their way homewards, dear Dennis Townhill arrived with his charming wife, Mabel, from St Mary's Cathedral, Edinburgh, as he was to give an organ recital on that Monday evening. Afterwards we threw a party in our garden to celebrate

John and Mary Cynan Jones's Silver Wedding. Next morning the Gedge family received a postcard written on the previous afternoon:

> *'Five hours later and we're only in Bath! Had a good lunch but the hospitality and the locals are not a patch on Brecon. Thanks again for a lovely weekend, which we wont easily forget!! Have fun in Durham.*
>   *Love from Jenny Stinton and Sarah Moser'.*

Jenny in due course, went on to record all the Mozart flute concertos on a Collins label CD, and Sarah was the other half of the bassoon section over the previous weekend when Jenny had played first flute.

The reference to Durham pointed to the next Cathedral Choir singing holiday which was to be at Durham where the choristers were to sing services in the magnificent Norman cathedral that dominates that small and ancient city. Indeed within a few days we were travelling northwards in a Williams bus bound for Durham School where Sub Organist Kelvin Redford had procured for us lodgings in Poole House by virtue of his being an Old Boy of the School. Again we were blessed with good weather; furthermore, the school was conveniently sited near to the city and its Cathedral. So the youngsters spent many a happy hour at the local skating rink until one of them complained to the Management that he was being victimised whereupon all of them were banned from the premises. Immediately they transferred their attentions to the local swimming baths where they ducked this same boy so often that he complained to the Management there and again everyone was banned. By this time we were nearing the end of the trip so we entertained the youngsters ourselves by taking them to Beamish Open Air Museum which was so interesting that even they were fascinated. Afterwards a short detour took us to nearby Seaburn to meet Kelvin Redford's aged parents before we travelled on up to marvel at Hadrian's Wall. Later, when I saw how much of the wall the boys had brought back to Durham as souvenirs, I marvelled at how much of the Wall was still there!

It was not only the choirboys who had a good time but also the lay clerks; they took over the nearby 'Yew Tree', in Allergate, where they drank vast quantities of Vaux Ales and usually after Closing Time had been called, were locked inside to drink more. The Landlord was an ex-Warder of Durham Jail who became so enamoured by the assembled multitude's singing of Welsh Hymns and Arias that one night he telephoned his daughter in the USA so that she could enjoy them too! At the Cathedral the Assistant Organist, Ian Shaw, was no stranger as he had been an Organ Scholar at St John's College, Cambridge, when my son, Nick, had been a chorister there. One night he threw a party for the Lay Clerks which resulted in thirty-six empty wine bottles being piled up outside his back door. Early next morning my daughter, Harriet, was arriving by the overnight bus from London and Ian had offered to meet her, driving Kelvin's car; however, as the evening wore on it became more and more obvious that he was not going to be able to do this. He got as far as driving the said vehicle part of the way through the school grounds whereupon he flaked out, stopped and vanished leaving me to find the car some time later with its engine still running and its headlights still on.

Matters in the Cathedral could be great fun too. Richard Lloyd, the resident Organist, whom we had known well at Hereford when he had presided at the Organ there a few years before, still was matchless at improvisation. As we processed into Evensong on the Sunday afternoon he was happily playing away delightfully on the magnificent Harrison and Harrison organ and the choristers wallowed in this as they meandered along. Suddenly their ears pricked up as in the midst of this lovely music they heard distinctly but quietly the melody of the Welsh National Anthem, 'Mae hen wlad fy nhadau'. At our final Evensong on the following Wednesday we sang the psalms for the third evening, The Thomas Morley Responses, the famous Magnificat and Nunc Dimittis from Thomas Attwood Walmisley's Service in d minor and the lengthy anthem by S S Wesley, 'Let us lift up our heart'. Before the service the Lay Clerks had organised a lottery as to how long this Evensong would take, with the winner taking all the entry money as a prize; the estimates ranged from 57 minutes and 21 seconds (John Cynan Jones) to 83 minutes and 15 seconds (Maurice Parry). Of the twenty-six members of the party who had paid an entry fee, John Cynan Jones's son David came nearest; his suggested time of 63 minutes was just five seconds too much!

XLI

By now the new Dean had been at Brecon Cathedral for a year and he had quickly made his mark. The Very Reverend D Huw Jones had been Vicar of Rhyl, a North Wales seaside resort, and before that had been Sub Warden of St Michael's College, Llandaff, Wales's last remaining Theological College. During the time that had elapsed between Alwyn Our Dean's departure for St Asaph and D Huw Jones's arrival at Brecon, there had been another interregnum, a shorter one this time but time enough for the North Transept to be emptied of its pews and carpets, also to reduce the amount of furniture in the Sanctuary. Not for many years had it been possible to view so much of the Cathedral in so uncluttered a state. The new Dean had been installed on Saturday, October 2nd, 1982; after the service I found a stranger wandering around the Cathedral Close looking for his house. He turned out to be the Organist of Rhyl Parish Church, therefore I showed him to the Almonry and made sure that the Dean, his former Vicar, was there to greet him. A month later, quite unexpectedly, I received a telephone call from this same Organist, asking me how I was making out with the new Dean; I was most puzzled!

The Dean and his wife were nowhere near as content with living in The Almonry as Alwyn and Meriel had been; they wanted more room. Wanting more privacy also, they were not happy with Hazel and me continuing to park our car in the Tithe Barn opposite their front door as we had done for years. So we had to use our back yard which offered our vehicle no protection from the weather at all and this could be exceedingly wild. Further, in the interest of privacy, they had the big gates by the Almonry permanently closed and locked so to prevent people from entering the Close by walking past their home. Now these people had to use the stone steps further on by the West End of the Cathedral and while this could be no great hardship, it was the principle of the matter that upset them. Len Hatton, for example, had sung in the Cathedral Choir as a treble then as a bass for more than sixty years, always walking through those gates and past the Almonry to the Choir Room for choir practices and services; he was not amused. Eventually at considerable expense, the new Dean and his family were re-housed in Blackstone, a large house two-hundred yards away, up Pendre on the left, where bass Lay Clerk, Atlantic-Ocean-sailing John Evans had lived until the Ministry of Agriculture and Fisheries had ungraciously moved him away from Brecon to Reading. No sooner had the new Dean moved out of the Almonry and into Blackstone than the gates into the Cathedral Close were unlocked and thrown open once again to the general public.

Meanwhile, 'Dads' Army', a voluntary group of men that Alwyn Our Ex-Dean had formed to maintain the Cathedral grounds, had run into problems. In the past, on a Wednesday evening, they had helped themselves to whatever they needed from the Tithe Barn Shed and had got on with whatever needed doing. Now with the new Dean being more security-conscious, the shed was kept under lock and key leaving members of 'Dad's Army' to ask the Dean himself for whatever they required. One Wednesday evening the Dean heard sounds of a lawn mower being operated in the grounds whereupon he rushed out demanding to know how the person had obtained it only to be told curtly: 'It's my own, I brought it from home!'. Sadly, 'Dad's Army' fizzled out; so too did the Thursday morning army of ladies who kept the Cathedral clean and tidy, to be replaced by a part-time groundsman and a part-time cleaner, at more expense.

Soon problems arose over singing Latin Masses on Sunday mornings. In the dim distant past, when Ungoed Jacob had been Dean, the choir had only been allowed to sing L G Viadana's 'Missa L'hora Passa' if English words were used; these had to be written into the copies where they remain to this day, above the original Latin. Only later had Dean Jacob relented and allowed the original Latin words to be restored to use by which time, at Bishop Vaughan's request, C M Widor's great Mass for two choirs and two organs was being sung at Ordination Services, in Latin. Similarly on Whitsundays, the choir suddenly had been allowed to sing in Latin, Joseph Haydn's sublime 'Little Organ Mass'. The reason why I had asked if the choir could do this on Whitsunday had been quite simply because this great Festival had now ceased to be attached automatically to a Bank Holiday. I had hoped that by singing William Byrd's 'Mass for three voices' at 8.00 am and the Haydn Mass with string instrumental accompaniment at 11.00 am, the religious importance of this day might be underlined despite its no longer being accompanied by a national holiday. During Alwyn our Dean's time, the choir had begun to sing more of these Viennese Masses, one on Christmas Day and another on Easter Day for example, and others being sung on the first three Sundays in July to help make the month especially musical with concerts and organ recitals also taking place. So our mad choirboys had begun to pride themselves on singing these sparkling settings of the Mass in Latin, a language which to them was meaningless, it having recently been removed from the state school syllabus despite it being the basis of the very English language which they spoke all day, every day. The idea of singing these Masses in July had not been our own, we were merely aping St Paul's Cathedral where such music was being performed liturgically during the month to great popular acclaim, particularly from the countless tourists who found their way there at that time of year. Personally, I liked to perform these Masses liturgically because this was the reason why they had been composed; to me concert performances seemed ineffective as they always tended to fade away with a gentle 'Agnus Dei'. Yet Dean Jones did have a point when he argued against having these and other latin Masses, which are essentially of Roman Catholic origin, sung at the main Sunday morning service on a major Festival. After all, certain features in these musical settings are distinctly un-Anglican. The lengthy Benedictus is one, as in 'The Little Organ Mass' by Joseph Haydn, for example, this lasts for at least five minutes, if not more. As the Dean began to make known his diquiet, so rumours began to circulate that he might stop the singing of Palestrina's Missa Aeterna Christi Munera', which was much loved by the choir and which also has a lengthy Benedictus. Alarm bells immediately began to be rung which led the Lay Clerks to persuade Pat Evans, a member of the congregation who was also a Cathedral Singer and who was sympathetic to their cause to write a letter of protest to the Dean. Rather than reply privately to her letter, the Dean published an article in 'The Beacon', the Cathedral's monthly magazine. Headed 'Cathedral Music' it read:

'I have received a letter from a lady who bewailed the fact that she had heard that all the beautiful musical settings to the Eucharist sung in the Cathedral were to disappear and be replaced by congregational singing. One wonders how rumours of this sort arise and are spread – the human imagination is a powerful instrument! The immediate cause of this rumour I presume is the discussion I had recently with the Choir and the Cathedral Advisory Committee concerning future policy relating to Eucharistic settings.

This discussion took place as a result of a careful review of the matter which the Cathedral Chapter has undertaken recently. The problem with some of the Latin settings, especially those composed in the eighteenth century by such composers as Haydn and Mozart is that they were composed for a completely different service – the old Latin mass (no longer used by the Roman Catholic Church) and for a very different understanding of the nature of Eucharistic worship. These settings seriously distort the nature of the liturgy we use in the Church in Wales since they put the emphasis on unimportant features such as the Benedictus or separate the four actions of the Eucharist so that the essential unity is lost. To clarify this – the Ministry of the Sacrament, the second main part of the Eucharist, is based on the four actions of our Lord in the Last Supper when he took bread and wine, blessed them, broke the bread and distributed them. In our service the actions follow each other closely in the Offertory, the Great Thanksgiving, the Breaking of the Bread and the Communion. The unity of this four fold action is marred if a long Sanctus and Benedictus in a different language from the remainder of the service comes between the first action and the second.

The other question raised by these settings is that of the congregations role. When the Eucharist is celebrated it must be seen as the action of the People of God assembling together for worship. The celebrant has his particular role in leading the worship, the choir has its role in leading the singing and providing a musical vehicle for worship and the congregation has its part to play and to be as fully involved in the service as possible. The danger of these elaborate settings is that they reduce the congregation to a passive role – so that it becomes more of an audience than a congregation. This is, of course, what happened in the Roman Catholic Church in the earlier centuries and members of their congregations were encouraged to pursue personal and individual devotions with the Mass as a sort of background. The Roman Church itself reacted most strongly to this tradition at Vatican 2 and there is no church now which puts greater emphasis on congregational participation – hence the switch away from Latin to the vernacular languages of the peoples and a restructuring of the service to re-emphasise the congregation's role. The question raised by the use of these settings then is whether they cross the line between a service and a concert – whether the congregation's role becomes too limited. People are, of course, divided on this – some say that the music helps them to worship, others that it goes too far in the direction of a concert performance.

It is in the light of these considerations that the Chapter has made some slight alterations in the pattern of Eucharistic settings. On the great Festivals of Christmas, Easter and Whitsun when we have so many visitors who have come in the main to make their Communion on the festival, we want bright, joyous English language settings with which the congregation can identify itself more easily. We would also like to see a simple, modern, congregational type setting added to the repertoire which could be used from time to time. (for this to be truly effective we shall need some congregational practices and it is hoped to arrange these in the New Year). We do not wish to see the disappearance of the Viennese settings which the choir has made such a splendid feature of its repertoire and these will have their place in the July festival month and on certain mid-week Festivals such as Epiphany and Ascension Day. As can be seen, these changes are fairly minimal and the reports of the demise of good music have been greatly exaggerated. What we hope to achieve is a better balance in being true to contemporary understanding liturgy and the importance of congregational participation while at the same time giving the choir ample opportunity to maintain the high standards and the rich musical tradition which has been established here. For the role of a Cathedral Church in using and encouraging good music is another factor that has to be constantly borne in mind. Moreover, these changes and their effect will be reviewed after a year's implementation.'

So Dean Jones decreed that there be no more Haydn and Mozart Masses sung on major Festivals except when these occurred on a weekday as happened on Ascension Day and so often on the Epiphany, St David's Day and All Saints Day. Then there would be few people in the congregation to be contaminated by our music, and little or no heat – indeed one St David's Day, on a Saturday morning, with the temperature at a record low 38° F, the string players had to retreat to the Choir Room between the Gloria and Sanctus, in order to thaw out! Naturally, there were repercussions over the forbidding of such music at Christmas and Easter, occasions when the choir tried hard to make the day special. One of the Head Choristers, Malcolm Bennett, son of 'Tony Top Note' and Gloria of the Cathedral Singers, was so upset at not being able to mark Christmas Day and Easter Day in the way to which he had become accustomed that he screwed up courage to ask Dean Jones, 'why?' only to receive a very unsympathetic reply. As for me, I was moved to compose some music for the Holy Eucharist and the result was Brecon Mass No. 2, which in due course became known as 'Missa in Protestatis'. Its highlight was the

Benedictus which lasted eleven seconds during which time the choir sang all the words on one note beneath which the organ played grinding discords. This Mass received its first performance on Christmas Day, 1983, and the Dean was so pleased with his alterations that he wrote in the January 1984, issue of the Cathedral magazine, 'The Beacon', an article headed 'Christmas services' which began:

> '*Our services were well attended this year, showing a clear increase on last year's figures. We began with a fine service of Blessing the Crib on Christmas Eve in the Cathedral. The new position of the Crib enabled us to have a much better ordered service and the special service used for the first time focussed much more satisfactorily on the events of Christmas .....'*

Not everyone agreed with Dean Jones's assessment of the new 'Blessing of the Crib' service. Gone was the old informality and spontaneity as bubbling youngsters had gathered with their bishop around the enormous crib that had encompassed much of the West End of the Cathedral, to contemplate the miraculous birth; in its place, to be fair, was a well-ordered service in which certain aspects of the Christmas Story were considered. However, the two hundred or so excited youngsters now were expected to sit in tidy rows on the hard pews in the nave near to a smaller, more streamlined and neatly constructed Crib that stood in the place normally occupied by the Lectern. The scene now resembled a well-delivered public lecture where a group of students were invited to contemplate the miraculous birth of their Saviour Jesus Christ. If informality and joy were casualties, so too was the crib itself, with its backcloth of mountains no longer climbing up the West wall over which had traversed the three Kings on their camels, daily being moved ever nearer to their eventual destination, the illuminated manger where already the shepherds were presenting their gifts to the new-born babe lying in the manger, with Joseph and Mary kneeling in love, adoration and praise. Naturally by the Feast of the Epiphany, January 6th, the Kings had reached the stable ready to present their gifts of gold, frankincense and myrrh and in so doing, take up a central position on the stage. This crib had always been so lovingly and painstakingly created and carefully but informally stage-managed to make the maximum effect. Shortly after Christmas the following letter, sadly anonymous, was published in The Brecon and Radnor Express:

> '*Sir – What has happened to our Christmas Crib. In 1926 Mr Albert Tilley and Archdeacon George Wilkinson, at that time Diocesan Missioner, had a vision and with the help of Mr Tom Watkins created and built up with various gifts a quite remarkable Christmas Crib. Eventually as far back as 1956 it received press comments that 'there was none other like it in the whole of Wales! Since then, with the huge interest in motor transport, its impact on residents and many, many visitors has spread, and who can tell now how far afield?*

How many generations of children have looked at this, and in an age when visual arts are thought so much of, have had their interest, knowledge and imagination stimulated. Mr Edgar Hawkes and Mr Ossie Griffiths, and others who have followed, have kept up the tradition for now over half a century. Imagine our disappointment to find all this changed this year. It is to be hoped that there will not be a similar change to the Easter Garden, and that our Crib will be restored in its original setting next year'.

Unfortunately, not only was there a similar change to the next Easter Garden but worse was to accompany this. During Holy Week in the previous year, on Dean Jones's first Holy Saturday, The Cathedral Singers had sung J S Bach's 'St John Passion' at 7.30 pm. In Alwyn Our Dean's time the Easter Vigil had been introduced to follow this at 11.45 pm, ending with the first Eucharist of Easter in the early hours of the morning. Dean Jones did not take kindly to this idea, nor did he really want the Passion performance on Holy Saturday, he would have liked it on Palm Sunday or on the day before, Good Friday. I, too, would have liked it on Good Friday but could not afford the market price for soloists on that day and certainly would not have been able to obtain the services of international tenor Rogers Covey Crump as 'Evangelist' because he had a long-standing arrangement to sing this for Denys Darlow at St George's, Hanover Square on that day. However, on Holy Saturday, which I was only too ready to acknowledge was a less relevant day for such a performance, everyone from the soloists and orchestral players to the additional chorus singers, was available and at the much cheaper price that I could afford. Alwyn Our Dean had understood this and had realised that if all the special musical events could be spread around the many services over the Easter Holiday weekend, more use could be made of the musicians who had moved into Brecon to help make Holy Week and Easter more meaningful. Furthermore, he and I had hoped that many of the tourists who had flocked into Brecon for the holiday period, could perhaps be attracted to the Cathedral to provide a much needed source of additional congregation or audience and so become the source also of additional income. So Alwyn our Dean had fitted his Easter Vigil around the Passion performance and had made the service all the more dramatic and meaningful by starting it in darkness and ending it in a blaze of glorious light. Dean Jones, however, did not like the idea of Holy Eucharist in the early hours of Easter morning and arranged for his first Easter Vigil to take place at 5.45. pm in broad daylight with the result that the symbolism of moving from darkness into light was completely lost.

In theory, Dean Jones had been quite right: the Passion would have been better performed earlier in the week; it would also have been better having the Cathedral empty on Holy Saturday to symbolise Jesus lying in his tomb, until a great service of Easter Vigil, late in the evening, could have symbolised his resurrection and marked the start of Easter. Unfortunately, this is not an ideal world and in my seventeen years at Brecon Cathedral I had learned how to compromise. So, I had pondered, as had Alwyn, was it really bad to draw into the Cathedral on Holy Saturday for a J S Bach 'Passion', around one hundred and twenty performers of various faiths, and many of them locals, along with an audience of nearly three hundred people, some of whom would then be drawn into the Easter Vigil service that followed? Tragically, however, now that Alwyn had moved on, few, if any, of the Dean and Chapter seemed to realise that the visiting musicians actually wanted their musical offerings to complement the Cathedral services, nor did they seem to want to realise this. It intrigued me to find just how many of them had begun to turn against Alwyn while Hazel and I had made known our allegience to him by actually going to stay with him and Meriel up at St Asaph. Indeed was it a coincidence that on our first three visits there one of the Canons had chanced to telephone Alwyn and Meriel each time while we were there, after all we had made no secret of our impending stay? Yet it did sadden me that obviously I could not convince the Dean and Chapter of my sincerity about the proper observance of Holy Week in view of my years at Holy Trinity, Lambeth, at Southwark Cathedral, and above all at St Mary the Virgin, Primrose Hill, where the week had always been observed with great devotion. Even so it did come as a great shock when the Dean decreed that on the next Holy Saturday, the J S Bach 'Passion' could not be performed in the Cathedral. I was devastated, so too were the Cathedral Singers and the Gwent Chamber Orchestra; furthermore, his explanation that he wanted the Cathedral empty on Holy Saturday so that parishioners could make their confession, just did not ring true. As a youngster I had been brought up to make my Confession at Christmas and Easter and I had been at Brecon long enough to know that this sort of High Church activity was not part of the scene; also lurking in the back of my mind was the possibility that the real reason for emptying the building on that day had been to enable elaborate floral arrangements to be made all day in peace and quiet! Fortunately James Coutts came to the rescue.

James Coutts, Vicar of St David's, Llanfaes, on the other side of Brecon, was a very special priest of the persuasion to which my father and Archdeacon Timms had belonged. An Anglo-Catholic, quiet, gentle and learned, he served his flock with great humility and devotion. It was because of him that I had abandoned wearing my academic hood at services, also persuading the Lay Clerks to do likewise. I had seen the light during a diocesan service in the Cathedral when I was going through a bad time with the Dean and Chapter. On that occasion I had seen a great assembly of clergymen parading around looking very important, wearing their various colourful and imposing academic hoods, while standing in their midst was one whose shoes they were not worthy to unloose, namely James Coutts, humbly attired in a cassock and surplice with only a black stole around his neck. This made me think: my Cathedral Choir depended on a number of singers who had no academic qualifications of any sort and were not likely to attain any, therefore why should those in the choir who had these qualifications parade the fact that their fellow Lay Clerks were of lesser academic prowess, especially when many of these academic hoods had nothing to do with music or theology. Interestingly, not long before, James Coutts had figured in the thoughts of the Lay Clerks, Hazel and myself, when the Deanery of Brecon had become vacant on the appointment of Alwyn Our Dean to the Bishopric of St Asaph. We had argued that the time was right to make the town of Brecon into one parish, for with a population of barely eight thousand souls it seemed a luxury to have two parishes. What better way to unite them than by the minnow, St David's Llanfaes, taking over the shark, St Mary's the Parish Church of Brecon, whose Vicar was also Dean of Brecon Cathedral; than by the Vicar of St David's being allowed to unite his parish with that of St Mary's and so becoming Dean. Sadly, however, Bishop Vaughan did not make this controversial appointment so the chance to make Brecon into one parish passed by, much to our sorrow; worse still, James Coutts continually was ignored in the promotion stakes and in the end left the Diocese of Swansea and Brecon to become Vicar of Monmouth and, eventually, a Canon of St Woolos Cathedral, Newport, but not before he had come to the rescue of the Cathedral Singers. He put St David's Church, Llanfaes at their disposal and on Saturday 21st April, 1984, J S Bach's 'St Mathew Passion' was performed there to a full house with great success and a tinge of sadness.

Even more was to come. Sometime during these proceedings I received a letter from Dean Jones to inform me that the Cathedral Singers in future would have to pay £200 per annum for the use of the Choir Room for their weekly Tuesday evening practices. I was not happy at all about this as some of the Cathedral Singers travelled many miles at great personal expense to attend rehearsals and concerts and much of this work was to help the Cathedral. So I wrote to Bishop Vaughan to tell him what I thought about this request and said that in future I wished to be paid £5 for playing the organ at Diocesan Services and that the money was to be paid in the form of a cheque made out to the Cathedral Singers. Until now I had been paid nothing for my services on diocesan occasions with the exception of the Mothers' Union Festivals and I had been happy enough to do this voluntarily although in most other Cathedrals the Organist was paid for this extra work. This matter came to a head on the day before a Diocesan Women's Offering Service when a note was pushed through my front door letter box telling me not to attend. I was curious. At 5 pm, an hour before the service, I went to the Cathedral to unlock the North Transept door then I returned home. At 5.55 pm I crept through the door into the North Transept and quietly moved into the darkness of the Regimental Chapel to observe the person who was playing the organ; there at the console playing from my music, taken from my cupboard, was one of the Cathedral Canons who many years before had been Organ Scholar at St David's College, Lampeter.

XLII

Meanwhile, alongside these problems had arisen other problems; these concerned our home, Garth Cottage. For some while now Hazel has boasted about every room having running water – down the walls, but by the time Alwyn Our Dean had moved on and Dean Jones was preparing to move in, this had ceased to be a joke. In desperation, Hazel went to Bishop Vaughan to complain and to ask his advice, adding that if nothing was done to remedy the situation she would move out and return to live with her parents at Kidwelly. She pointed out that the only person who would be affected by this arrangement would be me as by now few of the Cathedral Canons seemed remotely interested in what we were doing musically at the Cathedral. To his credit Bishop Vaughan took immediate action; he enlisted the help of his friend Bill Rees, the local Health Inspector, who was also a Lay Reader and who often acted as his chauffeur. What Bill Rees saw so bothered him that he offered to have Garth Cottage condemned as unfit for human habitation. With this a distinct possibility the Chapter was forced to do something and, to be fair, the new Dean was quick to take action. He had Garth Cottage inspected by the diocesan architect, Cyril Hughes, and then invited him to draw up plans for improvements. Eventually the most grandiose scheme was submitted, which included the addition of an upstairs bathroom and another bedroom which would allow me room to have a study; not surprisingly, so expensive a scheme was dropped for the moment on the grounds of cost. However, the Dean and Chapter had another idea. Recently, somehow they had been given a house in Camden Road and we were invited to move into it. Hazel was quick to point out the inconvenience of such an arrangement, particularly with regard to the days when I had an early evening boys choir practice as I would arrive home from school at 4.20pm have a quick cup of tea, then run over to work with the trebles at 4.30 pm in the Cathedral Choir Room, something which would be impossible if we moved to Camden Road. In any case, as she pointed out, it really was so convenient living close to the job. Sadly the Dean and Chapter proved to be completely unsympathetic to these problems with the result that the members of the sub-committee set up to discuss the matter remained far from helpful. Fortunately we had allies in the Cathedral congregation, one of whom was a local solicitor, Jasper Selwyn, whose father had been Dean of Winchester Cathedral. He told us to sit tight and not to move out because if the Dean and Chapter chose to sell the whole site, as was rumoured, we had rights as sitting tenants which possibly could allow us to purchase the house at a reduced price. In any case, despite being the lowest paid Cathedral Organist in England and Wales, and having to help keep our son Nick at Eton College, my teaching job at Builth Wells High School had become full-time therefore we had decided that it was time to dabble in the property market and find somewhere of our own so that we could cope more easily with visitors.

So we purchased what we thought was a small Victorian cottage one-hundred yards up the road, no. 16 Pendre; it was cheap because it had long been empty and was in a terrible state. However, we had reckoned without our friend from the Cathedral Singers, Tony Wainwright; he came to look at our purchase, rammed his umbrella through the downstairs ceiling and muttered: 'Beams there'; tore some wallpaper off the wall to reveal some stone whereupon he left saying: 'I'll be back tomorrow morning with Beth and the boys'. So he was, and by lunchtime the Wainwright family had revealed three stone walls, a fourth half-timbered wall, along with twelve beams in the ceiling. Far from being Victorian, the cottage was at least two-hundred years old and furthermore, the lovely Brecon stone walls went up the stair-case too. Tony then fixed us up with Stuart Barratt, a builder from his home-town, Talgarth, to extend the tiny kitchen, presented us with an oak beam to put into the ceiling to make it look old, and gave us a smaller oak beam to put over the open fireplace which he had uncovered in the main room. Finally, Tony taught me how to point a stone wall which enabled me over the next twelve months to spend every possible spare moment restoring the three stone walls and the half-timbered wall so that by the time Stuart, Hazel and I had finished, we were in possession of the most beautiful, charming, centrally heated eighteenth-century cottage with a fully-fitted kitchen, a living room, a bathroom with a loo and two bedrooms. It was magical and our two children loved to escape to it when Hazel's mother and father came to stay with us at Garth Cottage, or when they had friends staying. Strangely, without realising it, we had paved the way for the Dean and Chapter to do something about Garth Cottage. When the time came that they had sufficient money to re-roof the house, to add a new bathroom, a utility room and a cloakroom where had formerly been a shed, also to replace the horrible modern fire-place with a lovely old slate one that we had begged from the Almonry for our Sitting Room; they used our builder, Stuart Barratt, and we moved into our cottage for three months to get out of the way. It was because Stuart's prices were so reasonable that the Dean and Chapter gave him the work yet so untrusting were they that they appointed another builder to check up on each stage of Stuart's work. When the final cost was revealed to us and we told Stuart the amount, we learned that it was somewhat more than he had asked for.

Sadly, while all this was going on it was unfortunate that I should fall out with Bishop Vaughan as he had been so helpful in this matter early on, but this was more by accident than by design. It came about in a strange way which has its origins in one of the interesting traditions of the Anglican Church. While a Diocesan Bishop may have his throne in his Cathedral, on the other hand he has no power there; he cannot even preach there unless invited to do so by the Dean. The only chance the Bishop has of wielding any influence there is by conducting an official Visitation; therefore, on Monday, April 30th, 1984, at 5.45 pm, the Bishop of Swansea and Brecon conducted his Third Canonical Visitation of The Cathedral Church of the Diocese. The procedure was outlined on the cover of the Service Sheet as follows:

'Sunday, the 29th April, 1984

1. The following announcement will be posted on the church door, and will be proclaimed during Divine Service.

'Notice is hereby given that the Lord Bishop of the Diocese will begin his Visitation in this Cathedral Church on Monday, 30th April, 1984, when all Persons liable to his Visitation herein, and all other persons having just Cause of complaint in respect of this Cathedral Church, are required to Appear personally before the Right Reverend Father in God, at the conclusion of Evening Prayer which will be sung at 5.45. o'clock in the afternoon'.

2. The Registrar of the Diocese will have prepared a list of all who have been Cited to the Visitation with their full names, degrees, and style. He will deliver a copy thereof to the Bishop.

Monday, the 30th April, 1984 at 5.45. pm
Reception of the Lord Bishop at the door of the Cathedral.
Evening Prayer will be sung.
The Bishop's General Charge.
Visitation of the Dean, Minor Canons, the Chapter Clerk, Organist, Members of the Choir, and all other officers or servants of the Cathedral.
Address by the Lord Bishop to the Chapter (to take place in the Chapter House).
The Visitation of the Cathedral Church, and the books and the Ornaments thereof to take place on the following day.'

Inside the Service Sheet were listed nineteen points concerning the correct procedure in the conducting of this Visitation; it was archaic, almost mediaeval in spirit. For me, it was also irritating because at the Evening Prayer, when the anthem had been sung, the Registrar had to 'preconize all who (had) been cited to the Visitation', which meant that the name of everyone present at the Service had to be called out individually, whereupon the person concerned had to bow to the Bishop and 'take his stand before the Throne'. Unfortunately, it was considered bad form for a name to be called out and that person not be present to respond, therefore I had to ascertain beforehand which choirboys and Lay Clerks were available on that evening, then submit their names to the Bishop's Secretary, so that they and only they could be sent an official 'summons' and have their names read out. At a time when spare time was scarce, this seemed an unnecessary chore. Even more irritating, however, was that while the Dean and Canons were allowed the luxury of sitting on chairs after they had been preconized, the choir and organists were required to stand behind them for the duration of the Bishop's Charge. This particular Bishop's Charge was of more than passing interest in view of the disputes over the Mozart and Haydn Settings of the Mass, as the Bishop recommended that 'the forms of worship used in the Cathedral should contain an element of discovery.' To this end he actually suggested 'some rearrangement of the Chancel and Choir around a Nave Altar,' (on the official draft of this Charge the word 'Altar' had been originally spelt 'Alter' and corrected by hand!). He also suggested 'the introduction of responsorial singing' and 'the use of movement, dance and drama' which, he ventured to explain, as if we didn't know, 'would require great expertise'. Among other suggestions made was one that 'Personal relationships must be nurtured', which in view of what was to follow, was of amusing significance. After the Charge had been delivered the assembled company was expected individually to pay respect to the Bishop before departing from the Cathedral, leaving him free to inspect anything that he chose within the Cathedral complex. Knowing that this could include the Choir Room and everything therein, I had sorted out the notice board, removing from it two cartoon post-cards. The origin of these harmless cards was quite simply a celebration on behalf of Orrie the Alto Lay Clerk, because at last, after many years of trying, he had procured a lady friend who seemed keen to join him in holy wedlock which, later, indeed she did. These cards, both the work of Pre-Raphaelite painters of Victorian origin, had been 'doctored' and set up by tenor Lay Clerk Malcolm Johns, who had found them at the town museum where he now worked. The first showed a young, earnest-looking young man kneeling at the feet of a naked young lady who was clasping her hands in a pose of pious adoration; from out of her mouth Malcolm had added the words: 'For God's sake, Orrie, wait until after Evensong'. The second showed a young lady clad only in a white nightgown, sitting alone forlornly on her bed; from out of her mouth Malcolm had added the words: 'Orrie! I only said I didn't think much of your Magnificat.' A third cartoon I had left behind on the notice board, thinking that Bishop Vaughan might have been amused by it. This had been cut out from a monthly magazine entitled, 'The Welsh Churchman' and it showed two ladies talking together with their Vicar standing in the background. Knowing how fond Bishop Vaughan was of 'The Peace' in the Holy Eucharist, also his fondness for greeting lady members of the congregation with a kiss, the caption had been altered on this cartoon from: 'Our Vicar does love his kiss of peace', to 'Our Bishop does love his kiss of peace'. Unfortunately, I had misjudged Bishop Vaughan's sense of humour. Far from being amused as I had thought he would be, he wrote to me this letter:

> 'Dear Mr Gedge,
>   I was conducted round the Cathedral buildings on Tuesday, in the course of which my attention was drawn to a cartoon on the Choir Notice Board, about which no doubt you are well aware, and on which in your own handwriting you had crossed out the word 'Vicar' and inserted the word 'Bishop'. I cannot understand that a person in your position as Choirmaster of the Cathedral should resort to this kind of ribald behaviour with your Choir. I am deeply offended and I would like to have your assurance that this kind of thing will never happen again.

Will you please come and see me at 4.30 on Friday, or if that is not possible, at 10.00 on Saturday morning, so that you have an opportunity to explain and apologise for this very strange behaviour.
Yours sincerely
Benjamin Swansea & Brecon.

I replied immediately:

'My dear Bishop
Thank you for your letter.
I am sorry you were offended by the cartoon. We removed two concerning young Christopher Morris who is in love, because we thought those might go just a little too far, but we honestly thought that you might appreciate the one left. No offence was intended, nor was the writing mine because there is in the choir a very good comedian who keeps us all amused.
I can come and see you on Saturday at 10 am.
Yours sincerely
David '.

At the following Thursday evening choir practice, I read out Bishop Vaughan's letter to the lay Clerks who fell about laughing in disbelief whereupon I learned to my amazement, that the offending cartoon had been the work not of Malcolm Johns but of Kelvin Redford, one of my Assistant Organists. He immediately offered to call on Bishop Vaughan on the next day at 4.30 pm, as requested. In view of the fact that Kelvin had been teaching at Christ College, Brecon for seventeen years and helping at the Cathedral for sixteen years, and that during the last eight of those years Bishop Vaughan had been Chairman of the Governors at Christ College and had been attending services at the Cathedral by virtue of his position as Bishop, it seems incredible that when Kelvin called at Ely Tower to make his apology, Bishop Vaughan not only failed to recognise him but sent him away telling him to telephone his secretary to make an appointment! This Kelvin did. When finally Kelvin managed to speak with Bishop Vaughan his explanation was accepted only after he had written the word 'Bishop' on a piece of paper so that the Bishop was able to compare it with the writing on the cartoon. There the matter rested with no hint of an apology to me.

However, the paths of Bishop Vaughan and the Cathedral Choir crossed again: not many months later, at the wedding of Lord Swansea's daughter in Llandeilo Graban Church, up on the hills above Erwood near to Builth Wells. The Cathedral Choir had arrived early having allowed plenty of time for the journey as 'snow had fallen, snow on snow'. While the choristers and lay clerks had taken over the Vestry at the back of the church, at the front Hazel, clad in a thick, black, winter coat and wearing a fur hat to keep out the bitter cold, had begun to make music on the harmonium. Obviously Kelvin did not appreciate Hazel's efforts because suddenly he appeared at the entrance to the Vestry, peered down the Church through his plate-glass spectacles, and, not realising who was playing this ancient instrument, muttered to me: 'When the hell is this old woman going to stop'. Moments later Bishop Vaughan arrived to take the service. 'David my boy', he said to me, 'Where shall I go?' to which I replied cheerfully: 'You had better come and join us', indicating the choirboys and lay clerks behind the screen at the back of the Church. 'How very gracious of you', he replied, then, turning to my daughter who was now nineteen years old, he said: 'Harriet, my child, I do hope you don't grow up to be like your father', to which she replied spiritedly: 'I hope I do.' Entering the little Vestry he spied the one table on which lay all the coats belonging to the Choir whereupon, without a word and with one sweep of an arm, he propelled them all onto the floor and proceeded to lay out his robes in their place. After the service, while the choir was departing from the Church, Hazel and I stood chatting with our son Nick, who was on holiday from school, when out from the Vestry came Bishop Vaughan. 'Who shall carry my case?' he asked Hazel; immediately she volunteered a scowling Nick who very ungraciously did as he was bidden. As we drove from the scene along narrow country lanes, we found ourselves behind Bishop Vaughan's car; presumably he was supposed to be attending the reception because when his car arrived at the venue he stopped. Surveying the scene from the warmth of his comfortable vehicle we could almost hear him thinking: 'Snow, bitter cold, a muddy field, a marquee on the bank of the River Wye...', so he drove off along the road and continued on his way to the comfort of Ely Tower, Brecon.

Another twelve weeks on and Holy Week was with us again; this time it was the turn of J S Bach's 'Mass in B minor' to be sung by the Cathedral Singers on Holy Saturday. It don't know why but suddenly I asked Dean Jones if the Singers could use St Mary's Church for the performance because much as I liked St David's, Llanfaes, the church was so much less accessible, being on the outskirts of the town whereas St Mary's was right in the centre. To my amazement, the Dean saw no reason why J S Bach's masterpiece could not be performed there and so it came to pass. Before that there was, of course, the concert on Good Friday in the Cathedral, with a programme that included a Mozart Piano Concerto and a Weber Clarinet Concertino, not forgetting the Tallis 'Lamentations', but for some reason the building was bitterly cold there being no heat of any sort, nor was there any heat in the Deanery Centre where many of the visiting musicians were staying. I was so unhappy about this that early next morning, Holy Saturday, when I happened to meet the Canon in Residence and Minor Canon, I complained that it was almost as if there was a conspiracy to make the organisation of such musical offerings as difficult as possible. Obviously one of these two clerical gentlemen told the Dean what I had said because quickly Dean Jones protested his innocence in a note which was delivered to me later that morning. This began:

'Dear David,
   The boiler was <u>on</u> for last night's event – I was very surprised to hear this morning that it was ineffective. Indeed I came down late in the evening to

switch it off. Testing it this morning I can only conclude that the cut off button must have de-activated it for some reason, it does occur from time to time. I assure you that this was completely accidental – and quite unbeknown to me – not part of any deep laid plot or conspiracy! It should have been reasonably warm for last night.'

Sadly the Dean chose this year to introduce a Service of Preparation for Easter in the Cathedral at 7.30 pm, which clashed with the performance of the B Minor Mass in St Mary's Church. Yet despite the problems there was much fun during that weekend although one question mark remained and that concerned the programme for the concert on Monday night. This was publicised as 'A concert given by the Gedge family and friends in aid of the Cathedral Concert Society – the funds badly need replenishing', but the trouble was that I hadn't really thought out a programme. I knew that many people would part with money willingly to hear me play the viola in public but that wouldn't be enough. By chance playing the horn that weekend, in the B Minor Mass, had been our young friend Peter Francombe, who also was involved in a weekend of Schubert Octet rehearsals with the Albion Ensemble in Raglan. Every time we met that weekend, he would ask me with an inane grin on his face: 'Dave, have you planned your programme for Monday night yet?', knowing full well that I hadn't. Suddenly, late on Saturday night he said; 'How would you like the Albion Ensemble to try out the Schubert Octet?' I was overjoyed as the last of my problems that weekend melted away. All I asked of Peter was a list of names so that when I announced this performance during Sunday evening's orchestral concert, I could give the names of the eight kind performers. This Peter promised to give me during the interval, and so he did, just as the augmented Gwent Chamber Orchestra was getting ready to play Mendelssohn's *'Italian Symphony'*. He must have known that I would not have time to read through the list because as I excitedly told the audience all about the Albion Ensemble coming to play the Schubert Octet on the following evening, he watched with a disbelieving smile as I took the list from my top pocket and started to read through the names:

'Betty Swallocks, Carey Hunt ...' suddenly the atmosphere became highly charged and I realised that something was wrong, so I stuffed the list back into my pocket, ignored the remaining six 'names' and turned my attention to the Mendelssohn Symphony.

XLIII

During this time BBCTV had decided to make yet another film of James Hilbon's sentimental tale 'Goodbye Mr Chips'. Part of the filming was to take place at Christ College, Brecon while the leading role of the lovable schoolmaster, Mr Chips, was to be played by Roy Marsden. Some years before I had been much impressed by this actor in the popular TV series 'Airline' at the same time I had commented to Hazel how his face seemed familiar. Later indeed he was to achieve notoriety as Inspector Dalgleish in a series of fine TV films based upon novels by the author P D James, but at this time he was 'up and coming'. However, it was while sitting, waiting to have my quarterly haircut in Dai Hopkins's barber shop at the top end of The Watton, reading one of the many rubbish magazines to be found there, that I learned how Roy Marsden had once been a Cathedral Choirboy. Now I was sure that I knew him. When filming got under way in Brecon I learned that most evenings he relaxed in a Wine Bar situated in the centre of Brecon, opposite the Wellington Hotel. Now it chanced that this Wine Bar was owned by the uncle of my Head Chorister, Kevin Phillips, so I asked the boy to let me know when Roy Marsden was there in order that I could meet him. One Friday evening Kevin telephoned me at 9.30 pm to tell me that the actor indeed was there – immediately I made my way to the Wine Bar where I found him sitting surrounded by a host of admirers who were hanging on every word that he uttered. Pushing a way through the assembled company I walked up to the acter and said 'Roy Mould', much to his astonishment. Just no-one knew that this was his real name and as he was now forty-two years old it was nearly thirty years ago that we had been fellow choirboys at Southwark Cathedral. As he had joined the choir later than most of the other choirboys and had been most proficient, he had been placed above some of us in the order of seniority and this had not pleased us. Furthermore, as he had been rather confident and well-spoken we had not taken to him too well and had nicknamed him 'Mouldy', although as time had passed we had warmed to him. So on this Friday evening in Brecon he and I talked about our choirboy days whereupon I learned something extraordinary. On asking him where he now lived I discovered that not only had he purchased a large, rambling house on the edge of Clapham Common, but that he had modelled it on my father's Vicarage. So he went on to remind me how when there were extra services on Saturdays at Southwark Cathedral he had numbered among the choristers who had stayed the night at Holy Trinity Vicarage, returning to the Cathedral on the next morning to sing the Sunday services. Apparently, what had made a lasting impression upon him had been the informality of life at the Vicarage, so much so that he became determined in later life to recreate this sort of atmosphere in his own home.

Not long after this, early in August 1984, The Cathedral Singers went on tour again, this time to Denmark and Holland. The first part of the tour had been organised by The Brahetrolleborg Choir from Denmark that had visited Brecon during the previous summer; the Dutch part of the tour was supposed to have been organised by Jan Smit whom I knew through my dealings with the choir of St John's College, Cambridge, when my son, Nick, had been a chorister there, because he had organised many trips for that famous choir. Unfortunately, however, at the time when we left Brecon in our coach, driven by Russ the Bus, his arrangements had yet to be completed, although only I knew that! Indeed, he had suggested to me that the Dutch part of our tour might have to be cut short, but how was I to tell everyone this? So as we crossed the English Channel in the ferry, I had that sinking feeling in my stomach which only Cathedral Tenor Lay Clark, Maurice Parry, seemed to notice because when I shared my problem with him, all he said was: 'I thought you were looking bothered; don't worry, we'll sort it out when we get to Denmark.' And so it was! We were staying in a beautifully appointed, modern Agricultural College, in a tiny village named Korinth, on the island of Fünen, where the kindly Principal, Christian Ermose, told Maurice that we could stay for another week if we so wished. This was manna from Heaven because not only was the accommodation comfortable and the food excellent, but the company was congenial and the countryside lovely; in no time at all everyone was having a wonderful time. Not far away in one direction was the town of Odense, birthplace of Hans Christian Anderson the famous writer of Fairy Tales, where The Cathedral Singers were booked to give a concert in St Hans Church as part of an annual 'Orgel Festival'. When we arrived there to rehearse on the morning of our concert we found the Danish Radio setting up recording gear and discovered that our concert that night was to be the basis of an half-hour broadcast of British Sacred Choral Music! Not far away in another direction was the delightful seaside resort of Faaborg where The Singers were given a Civic Reception, where gifts were exchanged, also where we sang in both Welsh and English, such hymns as Calon Lân, Cwm Rhondda, Blaenwern and Ar Hyd y Nos; later, a concert was given in the lovely town church. Further along the road was Svendborg with a population of thirty-nine thousand people, centre of South Fünen, where the town church had a fine carillon which the Organist, Hans Mollerup, played with great aplomb, indeed he had an international reputation for his prowess. At noon on the day of our visit he regaled us with the English and Welsh National Anthems along with 'what shall we do with the drunken sailor' and 'Jesu, Joy of Man's Desiring', all of which rang out over the town centre. On Sunday morning The Singers returned to St Hans Church, Odense, to sing the Kyrie, Gloria and Agnus Dei of the William Byrd 'Mass to Four Voices', at what to Lutherans constituted a High Mass; in the evening they provided Evensong at Brahetrollberg Kirche singing Adrian Batten's 'Short Service' and C Hubert Parry's 'My Soul, There is a Country far beyond the skies', plus two hymns in Danish! Here they encountered for the first time ever, a lady priest who turned out to be a gorgeous thirty-eight year old blonde – a sign of times to come, back in England and Wales. By now Hans Smit had got his act together with the result that the Dutch part of the tour proved to be as successful as the Danish part. This included a visit to Helmond where The Singers saw some extraordinary experimental houses, also a fascinating castle where they were given another Civic Reception. After this they went to Arnheim and learned about the famous World War II battle that features in the popular film, 'A Bridge Too Far'. This visit was of special interest to one of the basses, Jim Morris, who had been a Sergeant Major in the British Army; the many War Graves there were a particularly moving sight. One of the concerts was given in a church where the Parish Priest had helped a RAF pilot from Caernarfon escape out of Holland during the fighting; another concert was given in the hospital which had provided our accommodation and the programme was purposely 'lightened' so that it could be broadcast around the wards!

Back in Wales we experienced the first ever Brecon Jazz Festival, an occasion remembered by many with great affection because of the novelty of so many jazz concerts in such a short space of time, because of the wealth of street jazz, also because there was only one arrest! Subsequent Festivals were enlivened by the arrival of yobbos intent on standing or sitting around the town drinking alcohol at all hours of the day and night, misbehaving even urinating in the street; later the drug-pushers arrived much to the consternation of the police, yet the music went from strength to strength until the event became undoubtedly the No. 1 Jazz Festival in Britain with around a hundred concerts packed into the second weekend of August. All this was the brainchild of dynamic Liz Elston whose husband ran the large Ford garage beneath the Cathedral yet found time to be Mayor of Brecon; she included a Jazz Festival Service in her plans and where better a place to hold it than the Cathedral. Initially, I was horrified but only because I was ignorant of the joys of jazz because as a youngster I had been protected from it by my orchestral and heavenly church music activities. However, not surprisingly, Liz had her way and I was unwillingly thrust into the limelight as Musical Director of the Jazz Festival Service. I was clueless. There were three hymns which I tried to teach to the congregation with the aid of the Adamant Marching Band from Cardiff, and an unenthusiastic Hazel at the Cathedral Organ. It was just my hard luck that this was the one and only time a Music Critic chose to attend the Jazz Festival Service, especially as my experience of syncopation was limited to playing the viola part of Khachaturian's '*Sabre Dance*'. So my efforts were ridiculed by Robin Lyons who mentioned in The Guardian '*The Cleric*' (actually me wearing my cassock) '*who, with no sense of syncopation, tried to teach 'When the Saints' to the congregation*'! Fortunately I did not see this review for many years by which time I had learned by experience how to direct the music at this service with a little more aplomb, although Hazel still was an unwilling partner in such a venture. Furthermore, the Cathedral Lay Clerks had started to sing Compline in candlelight at 11 pm, in the gloom of a darkened Cathedral, on Friday and Saturday, and just occasionally there would be someone in the congregation who needed spiritual help from a clergyman. As often as possible these services ended with a jazz voluntary, always extemporised, on perhaps a clarinet, a trumpet, or a piano, which added to the unique atmosphere that had been created by the combination of monastic plainsong and the extraordinary beauty of the ancient mediaeval Cathedral bathed in candlelight. Eventually the youngsters in the Cathedral Choir made one more contribution to the Jazz Festival when they began to pick litter throughout the weekend, in an effort to keep the town more tidy. Usually they succeeded until late evening when their labours were defeated by the enormous volume of empty cans dumped by the army of young people who littered the town centre, nevertheless, the Choir Tour Fund benefited by a good sum of money.

Nine months later, on Thursday, May 23rd, 1985, at 3 pm, the Cathedral Choir sang a service of a different sort in a different place. The Court Page of The Times Newspaper said it all:

'Princess Anne was present yesterday in the Guards Chapel, Wellington Barracks, at the marriage of Mr Richard Plunkett-Erle-Drax, Coldstream Guards, eldest son of Mr and the Hon Mrs Walter Plunkett-Ernle-Erle-Drax, of Charborough Park, Wareham, and Miss Zara Legge-Bourke of Glanusk Park, Crickhowell ....

The Guardian Newspaper, in enlarging on this, put it differently:

...'Miss Zara Legge-Bourke, younger daughter of Mr and the Hon Mrs William Legge-Bourke of Glanusk Park, Crickhowell, Powys was this week joined in holy matrimony to Mr Richard Plunkett-Ernle-Erle-Drax, eldest son of Mr and the Hon Mrs Walter Plunkett-Ernle-Erle-Drax, of Charborough Park, Wareham, Dorset.

The ceremony was described in its full swooning glory in the social pages of the posher newspapers yesterday...'

Further on it was suggested that 'By leaping from two barrels to four Miss Legge-Bourke (had) already become a member of a rare breed. Not for them that ceaseless striving towards polysyllability over many years which enabled the former Hugh Warrand to emerge first as Sir Hugh Lucas-Tooth MP and finally as Sir Hugh Munro-Lucas-Tooth of the Teananich: your average Plunkett-Ernle-Erle-Drax is simply born that way ...' Yet in continuing, the anonymous writer declared that 'as Mrs Zara Legge-Bourke-Plunkett-Ernle-Erle-Drax', the bride 'would give incomparable pleasure to all who appreciate arbitrary melody of words.' Zara Legge-Bourke actually was the granddaughter of Lady de Lisle who had an estate at Tretower, near to Crickhowell, just down the A40 road from Brecon. If I remember rightly, when her mother and father had been married, Brecon Cathedral Choir had sung at the Service. So began a series of coincidences. Mr and the Hon Mrs William Legge-Bourke wanted Brecon Cathedral Choir to sing at their daughter's wedding even though it was in The Guards Chapel,

Wellington Barracks. Furthermore, with the Hon. Mrs Shân Legge-Bourke being Princess Anne's Lady in Waiting, not only did Princess Anne number among the guests but her daughter, Zara Phillips, was a Bridesmaid. Finally as the Bridegroom, Richard Plunkett-Ernle-Erle-Drax was a Lieutenant in the Coldstream Guards, the Regimental Band of the Coldstream Guards had to take part in the wedding service, joining with the organ, played by Hazel, in accompanying C Hubert Parry's, *'I was glad'*, and the three hymns *'Praise my soul the Kind of Heaven', 'Cwm Rhondda – Guide me O thou great Jehovah', and 'Jerusalem – And did those feet in ancient times'*. The day of the wedding was long and eventful. Leaving Brecon at around 7 am the Choristers and Lay Clerks in their Williams Bus, arrived at the Barracks close to Buckingham Palace at around 11.15 am. Almost immediately they settled in for a rehearsal with the Coldstream Guards Band which proved to be quite an event as the bandsmen created such a huge, lovely, sonorous noise. However, any hope of making music by mutual consent was destroyed by the antics of the Bandmaster. He began by having one of his minions bring on an electronic tuner whereupon he proceeded to establish his authority on the proceedings by going round the band to make sure that all the instruments were in tune, but the fact that his musicians had already done this therefore he was wasting his time, seemed to elude him. Then he led his band into *'I was glad'*, ploughing his way through the music, ignoring all the speed indications which so demoralised my choirboys that I resorted to relaying the beat to them in an effort to encourage them to make more noise. Suddenly the Bandmaster stopped, tapped me on the shoulder and said curtly: *'Follow me'*. Dutifully I followed him out of the Rehearsal Room whereupon he shut the door and launched into a tirade which ended with: *'Only one of us can be in charge'*. By now Hazel had come and joined us; she tried to tell him that her job and his job was to accompany the choir but he wasn't having any of this. *'I've conducted this for forty years'*, he thundered, *'I sang it at the Coronation'*, I retorted, at which there was a deathly hush whereupon he turned around, returned to the Rehearsal Room and continued with the practice. At the end, when he went to leave, the members of the Band stood up as was their wont, but then, as they left the room one by one, to a man, they all shook my hand or gave me a thumbs up sign, such was their joy at the outcome of my discussions with their leader. The wedding itself went like a dream and any worries that the Band had drowned out the choir's singing were dispelled afterwards in a letter from Bill Legge-Bourke:

> *'With the Band being so powerful maybe you felt you may have been rather overpowered, but so many people commented on the singing that quite clearly you were not – even though the eardrums may have suffered in 'I was glad…'*

He was so thrilled with the service that he promised to send the choir a video recording, which indeed he did. That August, when the choir was singing services for a week at Canterbury Cathedral, the Lay Clerks played the tape repeatedly when they were socialising in the evening, but only so that they could watch one of the basses, Derek Hill, collapsing in the heat, then they would play the tape backwards so that they could watch him being resurrected! The Canterbury trip was fun as all such trips were, the chief hiccup being the closing of the gates into the Cathedral Precincts where the accommodation was situated at 11.pm,which conflicted with 'Last Orders' at the local pub.

XLIV

At the time of the Cathedral Choir's expedition to The Guards' Chapel, Wellington Barracks, the parliamentary constituency of Brecon and Radnor was plunged into a famous By-Election after the unexpected death of the sitting Conservative MP, Thomas Ellis Hooson. Politically Tom Hooson is now remembered as the man who broke the Labour Party's forty year grip on this constituency when in the 1979 General Election he had taken the seat from the Labour Party with a majority of 3,027 votes which he then turned into a majority of 8,784 votes four years later. The Spring of 1985 had been a bad time for Margaret Thatcher's Tory Government as with 13.4 per cent unemployment coupled with general rural decline, the rival Labour Party had started to move ahead of her Party in the latest opinion polls while in the May local elections the Liberal Alliance had gained control of a number of traditionally Conservative areas. Not surprisingly therefore a big question mark hung over the By-Election in the constituency of Brecon and Radnor, so much so that a more than usual amount of interest was aroused. Indeed outside the Houses of Parliament many a politician was seen to be consulting maps to discover the whereabouts of this remote constituency, so to offer support to their Party's candidate.

As far as Conservative supporters were concerned, this was not the time for a Government auditor to decree that the rebuilding of Builth Wells High School, in the middle of the constituency, was not economically justifiable, on the grounds that bussing the pupils to Llandrindod Wells High School would make more economic sense; after all, they badly needed the support of the very people that had now been upset. The teaching staff in particular were furious; they decided to put the By-Election to good use by inviting the four main candidates to meet them. By chance I was unexpectedly able to bring about other valuable assistance. A BBC/TV producer had approached me unexpectedly at the Cathedral to ask if he could record the Cathedral Singers to make background music for a Newsnight programme about the By-Election – *'this would make a change from the usual Welsh-Male Voice Choir'*, he explained. Naturally I agreed but then was taken by surprise when during the recording session the Producer handed two sheets of paper to all the Singers who had voted at the last election: on the first sheet each person had to write the name of the candidate they had voted for back in 1983, while on the second sheet they had to write the name of the candidate who they proposed to vote for now. To everyone's amazement the result of this unofficial poll revealed a significant swing to the Liberal-Alliance party.

Having helped this Producer, I now asked him to do a favour for me: to come and visit Builth Wells High School, thereby possibly creating for the By-Election, a local issue. To my amazement he did just that. Much to the excitement of the pupils, TV cameras arrived at the school to take countless pictures and these made the place look frightful with yellow-stained lavatories, unkempt concrete floors in flimsy pre-fabricated classrooms, dingy corridors, not forgetting the jerry-built science block and the road running right through the middle of the school which had to be crossed in all weathers to get from one side to the other. It really could not have been more helpful to the cause and helped to bring the four main candidates with their supporters, rushing to meet the teachers. First to arrive was the Conservative candidate, Chris Butler, a former adviser to the Prime Minister, Margaret Thatcher. He was exceedingly generous with his promises and naturally favoured the rebuilding of Builth School was soon as possible, but then he was desperate to win votes so to hang on to the seat. The Labour Candidate, Dr Richard Willey, wisely was more cautious and merely promised to put every pressure on to make sure the Builth School rebuilding plans went ahead, even though he was desperate to win back the seat for the Socialists which was an uphill task since electoral boundary changes had deprived his Party of much of its stronghold in the South. The third candidate to arrive was Richard Livsey, the Liberal-Alliance candidate, who brought along with him Clement Freud the MP for Ely who was a household name through his appearances on TV advertising dog food. They were both sensible and helpful with their comments, indeed Richard Livsey said: *'My demand for a new school goes without saying'*, but he went further, *'It is our policy to keep communities alive. Education is central to this'*. The fourth candidate to the school was Janice Davies of the Welsh Nationalist Party, Plaid Cymru, who said something similar.

Unfortunately, such promises had been made continually since 1928, when the provision of a new school had first been discussed, therefore the teachers remained rather cynical about the promises made by the politicians. So they set in motion a plan to put up their own candidate because this was to be the last time that any candidate who polled so few votes as to lose his deposit, was to be relieved of £150, which with a staff of thirty amounted to £5 per teacher! Immediately the necessary forms were sent for, also a Register of Electors, the intention being to put up for a candidate, Bernard Jones, Head of the English Department and School Representative for The National Union of Teachers, a noted 'left-wing' rebel, on a 'Save Our School' ticket. Naturally, the other candidates were not anxious for this to come about as obviously it would divert a large number of votes away from the main candidates in the Builth Wells, Llangammarch Wells and Llanwrtyd Wells area of the constituency. However, they need not have worried as their worries and the teachers' endeavours were both overtaken by events. With this issue beginning to dominate the By-Election, officials at County Hall, Llandrindod Wells suddenly did an 'About Turn', hurriedly arranged some meetings and within a few days had agreed to build a new High School at Builth Wells at a cost of £2,000,000.

Meanwhile I had set myself up for ridicule in the school staffroom by being interviewed for BBC/TV in the garden of my home at Brecon, Garth

Cottage, and stating that I **had** to vote for the conservative candidate as his party was the only one that would guarantee support for the Cathedral Choir Schools. Actually I really did mean this because the other political parties had made it abundantly clear that they believed such schools to be privileged institutions whereas Hazel and I had struggled hard to put our Nick through such an education because we firmly believed it to be the best course for a musical boy and we certainly did not belong to the 'privileged class'. It has never ceased to amaze me how this By-Election put Brecon and Breconshire so firmly before the eyes of the nation because there was so much TV coverage showing vast amounts of lush and lovely countryside, even if one Presenter standing on the top of the tower of St Mary's Church did describe the proud and ancient town of Brecon, spread out beneath him, as a village! At this time there was no room in any inn as all accommodation in and around the town was full to overflowing and remained so for the remainder of the summer. One person unable to find a bed to rest his weary head one night was a certain Peter Boizot who Hazel and I had found after a Cathedral Singers rehearsal, wandering around the Cathedral as we were trying to lock up. We took him with us down to The George Hotel and as we chatted we learned that in his youth Peter Boizot had been a chorister at Peterborough Cathedral and later a Choral Scholar at St Catherine's College, Cambridge where our friend Peter Le Huray was Organist. So he went on to tell us how he had stood as a Liberal Candidate in an election at Peterborough, then he told us that he had come to Brecon to canvas on behalf of Richard Livsey. Eventually he set about looking for accommodation but found nothing whereupon we offered him a bed at Garth Cottage which he gladly accepted but then suddenly asked: 'What about my car?' Laughingly, we asked him if he had a Rolls Royce and indeed he had! Inside Garth Cottage that night therefore was Peter Boizot, founder of the Pizza Express chain of restaurants in and around London, also future owner of Peterborough United Football Club, while outside in the yard was his gleaming Rolls Royce car! Hazel and I laughed for much of the next day, at the thought of him canvassing for the Liberal-Alliance Candidate, travelling up and down the narrow byways and not much wider highways of Breconshire in this enormous Rolls Royce car. He and his fellow Liberals must have worked hard because when the result of the By-Election was announced at around lunchtime on Friday, 5th July, it was just as the Cathedral Singers had predicted in their unofficial poll: a swing of 16% to the Liberal-Alliance, thereby making popular, local Richard Livsey the new MP.

Some people described this as the worst Tory defeat for twenty-three years, certainly it brought about a reshuffle in the government but by the time Margaret Thatcher was busily involved with this, The Cathedral Singers were busily involved with final preparations for their performance of Claudio Monteverdi's magnificent 'Vespers', which by then had become known affectionately as 'Montevideo's Jesters'. Performing these was one of the great experiences of my life. When I had been planning this performance Rogers

Covey-Crump had said: 'Give me £1,000 and I will fix you up with soloists.' So he did and along came Lynne Dawson and Tessa Bonner to sing soprano, Wilfred Swansborough to sing counter tenor, the tenor Leigh Nixon, and the two basses James Morgan and Charles Pott. Added to these singers were the chitarrone player Robin Jeffrey along with the renowned Robert King and six members of his Kings Consort playing cornetti and sackbuts, plus a few members of The Gwent Chamber Orchestra. It was magical. Furthermore, it was also something of a re-union because both Wilfred Swansborough and Charles Pott had sung in the choir of St John's College, Cambridge, when Nick had been a chorister there while Robert King, a former St John's Chorister, had been studying for a degree there at the same time. The Cathedral Singers' Treasurer, Dr Harry Crann, former Chief Executive of Welsh Water, had been instrumental in obtaining some superb colourful posters with the result that these and the lure of the fantastic music produced one of the largest audiences ever seen in the Cathedral. It was such a memorable evening that I have never dared do another performance of Monteverdi's 'Vespers' for fear that it might not be so satisfying. Nothing like the noises of the cornetti and sackbuts had been heard here before, nor had anything like a chitarrone been seen here before, while the vitality of the chorus cross rhythm singing was electrifying at times. When the famous 'Sancta Maria' arrived I could see that Robert King was itching to add his infectious direction to the proceedings so we swopped places, I took over playing his chamber organ while he conducted with tremendous exuberance. It was very much a special occasion, the like of which has rarely happened again, so spontaneous was the fun of it all.

Often in Brecon as one project ended another started and so it was on this occasion. Even before the 'Vespers' had been performed I had been invited to take part in discussing a project that was to end in two performances of 'Everyman', a Morality Play, in the Cathedral. I must confess that with the By-Election and all the work involved in performing the 'Vespers'' also in taking the Cathedral Choir to sing at Canterbury Cathedral, my enthusiasm was at a low ebb. However, I had reckoned without the determination of the Producer, Vivienne Griffiths, who numbered among the characters to be found in the Cathedral congregation. She loved being involved in plays and for many years had been wrapped up in the activities of Brecon Little Theatre which had an excellent reputation for its productions. She loved the Cathedral too and whenever she read a Lesson at one of its services, she sounded as if she was on the stage at the nearby Guildhall. Her husband, Richard, had been Manager of Boots the Chemist for around thirty years before he had retired to make way for Maurice Parry who sang tenor in the Cathedral Choir. As an apprentice in Gloucester, Richard Griffiths could remember the famous Herbert Sumsion being appointed Organist of Gloucester Cathedral back in 1928. However, his main claim to fame was that he had actually served the even more famous Sir Edward Elgar in the chemist shop where had worked. Richard, who was very quietly spoken, loved to tell me how he and some friends used to enjoy rowing a boat up the River Severn; when they reached Sir Edward's house they would play an old 78 rpm record of 'Land of Hope and Glory' on a wind-up gramophone whereupon the great man would come out into the garden and doff his hat to them. Inevitably I was drawn into Vivienne's project, my job being to supply three 'monks' who at various times in the play would wander around the Cathedral singing plainsong. However, where was I going to find three monks' habits? Then suddenly I remembered ….some years before, in the days of Alwyn our Dean, he and I had been wined and dined by the monks of Belmont Abbey, close to Hereford, one lunch-time, and had enjoyed ourselves so much that on the way home we had both declared how we too could live such a life but for the absence of our womenfolk. As a result of our visit the monks of this Roman Catholic Benedictine Abbey had come to Brecon Cathedral one evening to sing Vespers during which their Abbot, who by tradition is a mitred abbot, had preached a sermon. Some weeks later, Alwyn our Dean and I had taken the Cathedral Choir to sing Evensong in Belmont Abbey one Sunday evening; afterwards everyone had supper in the monastery whereupon wine flowed freely and the choirboys were not a little merry! Now, needing monks' habits for the morality play 'Everyman', and remembering the gentle, kindly Abbot, Jerome Hodkinson, I wrote to him asking if he could lend me any dirty habits! By return I received the loveliest of letters, dated 17th September 1985.

> '*My dear David,*
>
> *Many thanks for your letter which came this morning. It was good to hear from you. If we can rustle up the necessary habits I will be delighted to lend them to you. You appreciate that there might be a problem and that the brethren might be reluctant to release any but their tattiest habits. (Most of our stuff is in any case fairly tatty!)*
>
> *I'll get one of the younger brethren to scout round and send you what he can find.*
>
> *I do hope your play is a success.*
>
> *Kindest regards to your wife and yourself,*
> *Yours Ever*
> *Jerome Hodkinson*'

Indeed, the play was a great success, with Maurice Parry, Michael Thomas and myself parading around the Cathedral dressed in our habits but with bare feet; a photograph on the Choir Room wall commemorates the event. Apparently these habits were authentic for the play because the hood had remained unchanged since the Middle Ages, so the Abbot explained in a later letter.

The year 1986 opened with the birth of the New English Hymnal. The Editor of this 'Rolls Royce' of hymnals, was none other than our good friend George Timms, who had moved on from being Vicar of St Mary the Virgin, Primrose Hill, to become Vicar of St Andrew's, Holborn and Archdeacon of

Hackney which entitled him to a stall in nearby St Paul's Cathedral. His glorious Vicarage, the creation of that notorious Victorian architect S. S. Teulon, had long provided Hazel and me with a most useful free car parking space in central London, also free accommodation for short stays there, should the need arise. Archdeacon he might have become but still he was Fr Timms to us, although really he liked to be known as Fr George, the same person who had endured my early attempts at being an Organist and Choirmaster, who nearly twenty-four years before had taken our wedding service in Kidwelly, and still he was surrounded by his company of cats whom he treated with loving care and affection. In recent years we had become accustomed to spending a week or so at his home in Minster-in-Thanet, a wing of a magnificent seventeenth-century house in Kent, not many miles from Canterbury. The idea was that we would minister to his cats while he went off in his smart car for a week of touring, but it never worked out that way; inevitably, he would return after two or three days to enjoy Hazel's cooking and our company as he was unmarried and had no family of his own. His historic and very lovely house was stacked full with treasures, many of them antiques. I remember asking him about some oak panelling which recently he had used to line the walls of the downstairs hall and passageways. He went on to tell me how while supervising the demolition of a redundant church in the East end of London in his capacity as Archdeacon, he had spied this panelling about to be put on a fire and had thought how lovely it would look in his own home, so here it came and indeed it did look very lovely, almost as if it had always been part of the house.

On our last few visits it had become obvious that he was preoccupied: it was his New English Hymnal that was consuming all his attention. We used to take bits and pieces home to check over, particularly the attractive Folk Mass that he was composing to the words of Rite A. When the book finally had been published I taught this setting of the Mass to some church choirs in Swansea and it was adopted by at least one church for its weekly Parish Communion Service. However, the very name, 'New English Hymnal' sadly mitigated against many churches in Wales adopting the book for regular use although, to my amazement, Dean D Huw Jones did adopt it for use in Brecon Cathedral. Interestingly Hazel and I had tried to persuade Fr Timms to prevail upon the publishers to produce a small number of books containing a supplement consisting of some Welsh hymns with Welsh and English words but, sadly, this was considered not to be an economic proposition, therefore it did not happen. Personally, much as I admired the New English Hymnal I was sorry to find that some of JH Arnold's plainsong accompaniments had been altered as had a few of Ralph Vaughan Williams accompaniments to some of the great mediaeval French melodies. However, it was good to find such hymns as 'Soul of my Saviour, sanctify my breast' and 'Sweet Sacrament Divine' in the book even if my favourite, 'The day is past and over' to a fine W H Ferguson tune, had been left out. Hazel went down to St Andrew's Church, Holborn, on Friday, January 24th, for the launching of The New

English Hymnal, when a choir from the Royal School of Church Music sang the Kyrie and Gloria from Fr Timms's 'Folk Mass', Timothy Dudley Smith's 'Child of the stable's secret birth' to Anthony Caesar's magical tune, along with Christopher Smart's 'Where is this stupendous stranger?' to an extraordinary tune, 'Ottery St Mary', by Henry Ley. Also sung were two of the new Responsorial Psalms, a hymn with words written by Fr Timms himself, along with several other items including 'Soul of my Saviour, sanctify my breast,' a hymn much loved by Anglo-Catholics like myself.

Three months later it was my turn to go to London, to a dinner attended by Southwark Cathedral Lay Clerks of twenty-five years ago. Much had happened at Southward Cathedral since 1961, and initially little of it had been musically good. Sometime back in the 1970s when Mervyn Stockwood had been Bishop of Southward, he had decreed that the money spent on the choir could be put to better use; as a result he had brought about the demise of the six paid Lay Clerks whilst vastly reducing the number of choral services. When this was proposed I had vague recollections of the Southwark Cathedral Old Choristers Association requesting past members of the choir to make a special effort to attend the annual reunion that year, so to show solidarity with the dismay at what was being proposed. Naturally I turned up. The proceedings that Saturday afternoon began as usual, with Choral Evensong but while a large number of Old Choristers were present, the Bishop, the Provost and the Canons were all conspicuous by their absence. Indeed, the only clergyman present was a Minor Canon who not only proceeded to sing the service but also chose to deliver a sermon during the course of which he told the assembled company to forget the past and accept change. After singing the final hymn the Old Choristers processed out with the choir and after the Minor Canon had said the Vestry Prayer at the West end of the nave, they spontaneously formed a circle around him and set about him verbally for what he had said. It was quite extraordinary. Interestingly, the Minor Canon was none other than Roger Royle who went on to achieve fame as the Presenter of BBC/TV 'Songs of Praise' and BBC/Radio 'Sunday Half-Hour' programmes. Afterwards, at the dinner that completed the proceedings, the only cleric to make an appearance was the much loved (except by my late father) retired Bishop of Southwark, Bertrand Fitzgerald Simpson; it felt as if the Cathedral musicians, past and present, had been cast out into the wilderness. For me, this had been a bitter blow as I had owed so much to what I called the Old Southwark Cathedral, when the choristers had been drawn in from the highways and byways of South London, and had been so well cared for by a succession of clergymen. In those days a family atmosphere had prevailed with Mr Barfield cleaning the brass and silver, with old Miss Reynolds looking after the linen and the surplices, with Mrs Thomas sorting out the music, with Mrs Dexter providing squash and tea after Evensong, and with Canon Cuttell masterminding the Cathedral Scout Troop and the Easter holiday and Summer Camp. Those had been happy days and they had greatly influenced my work at St Mary the Virgin, Primrose Hill,

Selby Abbey and Brecon Cathedral. Perhaps I was looking at it all through rose-tinted spectacles! Anyway, on Saturday, April 12th, 1986, I travelled to London to attend the twenty-fifth anniversary dinner of the 1961 Lay Clerks of Southward Cathedral which appeared to have been masterminded by the two altos, David Huke and David Hill, both of whom had resigned from the choir in protest at the changes, one to become a Lay Clerk at Hereford Cathedral, the other to become a Lay Clerk at St Alban's Cathedral. I was full of the joys of spring, also excited at the prospect of meeting old friends, many of whom I had not seen for a long time, but it all went horribly wrong and it was my fault. As we entered the dining room I noticed Roger Royle among the assembled company and wondered why. While the meal slowly progressed, so the thought gnawed at my mind that the only time we had met before was when he had dressed down the Old Choristers who had attended the Reunion Service some years before, in order to express their concern about the future of Southwark Cathedral music. This puzzled me so much that in the end I could contain myself no longer and went up to ask him; of what then passed between us I have no recollection although I do know that after I had returned home I had to write to him a long letter of apology. In this I poured out my love for Southwark Cathedral, its music and how it had affected my life, also how unhappy had been much of my dealings with certain of the Brecon Cathedral clergy. However, by the time our correspondence had drawn to a close we had become good friends, so much so that in the not too distant future we had arranged for him to preach at the Jazz Festival Service and with his natural bonhomie, very good he was too.

XLV

It was now that Norman Jones crept upon the scene. Around my age yet only recently ordained deacon then, a year later, priest, he had the appearance of a Dickensian undertaker, was very quietly spoken, seemingly inoffensive and ineffective. How wrong we were! What emerged was someone quite different: a priest with a strong spiritual commitment and a cast iron faith, who quickly developed a great love for the town of Brecon, for its Cathedral where he was Minor Canon, and all that its worship stood for, above all who understood the depth of the work that Hazel and I were trying to do with our crazy choristers, and who gave us unstinting support; in all this he was admirably supported by his adoring wife, Margaret.

Almost at the same time arrived Wynn Davies who in the past had taught modern languages, principally German, in high schools at Llandrindod Wells and Llanelli; now having been appointed to a similar job at Gwernyfed High School not far from Brecon, he was able to live in the town and sing bass in the Cathedral Choir. Not long after arriving he was persuaded to take on organising the Cathedral Servers, a thankless task as some of them could be notoriously unreliable in this department. A glutton for punishment, Wynn also joined The Cathedral Singers and this brought on the scene the amazing Audrey Doughty who was soon so much loved by Cathedral Choristers and Singers alike as to become known as 'Aunty Aud'. Wynn had lodged with her and her husband in Llandrindod Wells and had sung in the 'After Eight Singers', later called 'Cantorion', which she had helped to start and worked hard to keep going. Now, having sadly lost her husband to cancer, she threw in her lot also with The Cathedral Singers, travelling over to Brecon on the evening bus from Llandrindod Wells, staying the night at Wynn's bungalow, returning to Llandrindod on a bus the next morning, such was and still is the state of public transport in Mid Wales. A very dear lady, far older than she looked, she seemed to have perpetual youth on her side. A talented writer, her work first became known to me when she produced a magazine article about her journeys on the Llandrindod to Brecon bus and very amusing it was too. She went on to supply the Gazeteer for the Ordinance Survey Leisure Guide for the Brecon Beacons and Mid Wales; eventually she went on to produce the definitive history of the Central Wales Railway, the line that winds its way from (originally) Swansea Victoria, through Ammanford, Llandeilo, Llandovery, Llandrindod Wells, Knighton and Craven Arms to Shrewsbury, which was a fascinating volume.

Two more amazing choristers chose to throw in their lot with The Cathedral Singers at this time: Mostyn and Margaret Williams. Who would have thought that Mostyn had been a Bank Manager on the outskirts of London? Evidently other people had thought this too because in his first bank Mostyn had once been accosted by a customer who had demanded to see someone more senior whereupon he had replied in mock protest: 'But I am the Manager!' His wife, Margaret, had been a Primary School Teacher and had been also a Church Organist in her spare time. That they had come to live in Llanfynydd was, to us, tragic because the village was situated between Llandeilo and Carmarthen, forty miles from Brecon, with no good church music nor liturgy near at hand, nor, it seems, a church that wanted it; on the other hand the attraction there had been a small-holding where they could entertain two donkeys and a dog. If only they could have found something like this nearer to Brecon but that was not to be, therefore not only did they make the eighty miles round trip to and from Brecon every Tuesday evening to attend Singers rehearsals but whenever I had a Monday night rehearsal with church choirs in Swansea they attended that as well. Always Mostyn drove the car so that he and Margaret could sing the music that they loved, always at great speed and in such a way that only he could, and to which Margaret had become accustomed.

The summer of 1986, found the Cathedral Singers doing something that they had never done before: they went to East Anglia to sing Cathedral Services. The original idea of invading this corner of England had come from 'Russ the Bus' who had come to Wales from Norfolk and now wanted to show us the choicest parts of the county of his birth. Sadly, however, when the time to leave Brecon for Norfolk arrived, Russ was on his way to the continent with another trip, sent there by Morris Bros. of Swansea, entirely against his will. He was replaced by John who, thinking The Cathedral Singers were a typical church group, had hidden away in his luggage a bottle of whisky for his own comfort. After his first night in their company and with his bottle empty, he realised that this indeed was not a gathering of teetotallers and thereafter enjoyed himself fully! Although it had been the idea of The Cathedral Singers to sing services, nevertheless some of them being inexperienced in such matters were apprehensive, especially about singing the daily dose of psalms. Tony Wainwright, for example, asked me for some manuscript paper and proceeded to write out the words of every psalm to be sung on the trip, putting the relevant bass notes above. By the time he had finished, he was the proud possessor of a great wad of manuscript paper from which he learned what he called 'Spasms'!

We arrived in Norwich a few days before we were due to sing Evensong in the Cathedral so to give us time to do lots of practice and for The Singers to become familiar with divine service. The School where we stayed was a very happy-go-lucky affair, primitive but comfortable; its kitchen however, was a magnificent new stainless steel creation, the food was wonderful, and we wondered why when everything else about the place was so dowdy. Tony Wainwright soon found the answer. 'Hey, Gedge', he said in soft, confidential tones one night as we were enjoying supper, 'those two (pointing to the Headmaster and the Cook) are an item'. 'How do you know?' I replied. 'Well', he said, 'I've just seen the Head lift her bicycle in through the front door.' Later that night, Tony confided in me once again: 'There you are, I was right!

I've just peeped through the crack in the Headmaster's bedroom door and seen her prancing about!!'. Yet we had a very happy time there and were exceedingly well looked after. Most evenings we entertained ourselves in a local pub, but not until we had been there for a few days did we discover that we were actually in a 'Red Light' area of Norwich. Indeed, one of our sopranos, Pat Evans, whilst walking back up the hill from the Market Place to the school, unwittingly attracted the attention of a Kerb Crawler who wound down the window of his car to ask her how much she charged! The Singers sang just one Evensong in Norwich Cathedral and that was on the Thursday evening when to our horror, we found the Bishop of Norwich in attendance to collate and install two Honorary Canons who were supported by a large congregation; one was a Chaplain to the Queen and Vicar of Sandringham, the other was the Administrator of the Anglican Shrine at Walsingham. Despite being in such august company The Singers acquitted themselves well not only in the ceremonial that had to be observed but also musically, so that even the Verger on duty was duly impressed by their efforts.

The next day The Singers moved to Ely Cathedral where many years before my Great Uncle, Hubert Stanley Middleton, had been Organist. There they lodged in the Diocesan Centre where the accommodation was prim and far better organised but far less fun. However, they compensated for this by taking up residence in 'The Albert' public house during lunch times and evenings; there the resident elderly lady pianist willingly abdicated her place at the piano to various members of our party. So a riotous time was had by all. It was here that a travel-weary Aunty Aud had found us as she looked for somewhere to have a quiet drink after her day long train journey from Llandrindod Wells to Ely. When she appeared The Cathedral Singers had been starting to celebrate their first-ever unaccompanied Choral Evensong with not a note of organ music having been sounded as it was a (monastic, penitential) Friday evening. They had sung the Ebdon Responses, the Magnificat and Nunc Dimittis from Orlando Gibbons's 'short Service', also C V Stanford's lovely anthem 'Beati Quorum Via', yet the greatest challenge had been the Psalms for the Day as these had involved four changes of chant without help from the organ. Tony Wainwright had been quaking in his shoes as he ploughed his way through page after page of his manuscript paper containing the bass line of the 'spasms', but all had gone well and now The Singers were unwinding in jubilation. What was most impressive about this visit to Ely was the wondrous rapport that had been struck up quickly between The Singers, the Vergers and the Clergy, which eventually led to all the Brecon contingent being entertained to drinks on the Deanery lawn. It was such a happy visit, furthermore all the musical challenges at the Sunday Eucharist which included a psalm sung in procession also four short, awkward responses composed by the resident Organist Arthur Wills, and sung at various times during the service, not forgetting the Herbert Howells 'Collegium Regale' jubilate, all were overcome with great aplomb. The local congregation and clergy were particularly pleased to hear The Singers perform The Brecon Mass which Dr Wills had composed for a Diocesan Choral Festival at Brecon Cathedral some years before. A few days after this visit I received the following lovely letter from the Precentor, the Revd. Michael Tavinor:

> *'Dear David,*
>   *Thank you for your kind letter. I'm so glad that you enjoyed your visit to Ely – I'm only sorry that I wasn't here to hear you more. Everybody says how excellent you all were, so I'm sure your halos are shining!*
>   *Come and sing again when you can!*
>   *With every good wish,*
>   *Yours sincerely,*
>   *Michael '*

By then, The Singers had moved on to spend Monday in London where they gave a lunchtime recital in my old haunt, Southwark Cathedral, before returning to East Anglia and more High Jinks at Norwich. The City of Norwich had long held a special fascination for me because in days gone by, so my father had told me, the Gedges had come to Norfolk from Scandinavia with the Vikings, 'raping and pillaging'. Indeed my wife, Hazel, one day received a 'phone call from a lady who had seen her name listed in the Associated Board of The Royal Schools of Music Handbook as the Local Representative for Brecon, because she herself was a Mrs Gedge and she had wanted to find out more about the Gedges. When Hazel told her about the Gedges coming with the Vikings, raping and pillage, she exclaimed excitedly: 'That's it, my husband has just gone off with another woman!'. Anyway, back in the eighteenth century a certain Peter Gedge had started a newspaper in Bury St Edmunds, in next door Suffolk, called 'The Bury Post', then when his first wife died he had married the daughter of the Editor of 'The Norwich Post' and so was born 'The Bury and Norwich Post'. He and his first wife have fascinating memorials in St Mary's Church, Bury St Edmunds, close to the Cathedral, his epitaph reading:

> *'Like a worn out type he is returned to the Maker*
> *in the hope of being cast in a purer and better mould.'*

Being suspicious by nature, I have often wondered if there was a hidden meaning to this! Over the years many Gedges had become Vicars in East Anglia, indeed it was interesting to find as many as forty-seven Gedges listed in the current Norwich and Norfolk telephone directory although none now were Vicars. This tour had provided me with my first real chance to scour the land of my forefathers. So I took The Singers to wallow in the wonderful half-timbered towns of Lavenham and Long Melford in Suffolk not forgetting the surrounding lush countryside, but most of all it was Kings Lynn that I was looking forward to visiting. I had been there before and just wanted to enjoy again the great churches, the market place and what remained of its ancient port. Mostyn and Margaret Williams also had been there before therefore they excused themselves from this trip and went bird watching instead. That afternoon, having explored Kings Lynn in the morning, as The Singers trundled along the coast road in their bus in the direction of Cromer, they saw Mostyn and Margaret on some marshy ground busily engrossed in watching birds through their binoculars. Quite without thinking The Singers prevailed upon driver John to give a friendly 'honk' on the bus hooter whereupon birds flew off in all directions! The last afternoon and evening of this magical tour were spent in Walsingham where pilgrimages were made to the Anglican and Roman Catholic shrines. Afterwards we practiced in lovely, airy St Mary's Church where the strong, unmistakable smell of incense took me back to my days at Fr Timms's St Mary the Virgin, Primrose Hill, and where we were due to sing a High Mass that night. Between the practice and service we adjourned to a nearby hostelry and while having a quiet drink I spotted a stuffed bird on a windowsill. 'What is that?', I asked Margaret in all innocence and she also in all innocence, replied: 'A Lesser-Spotted Shag', at which everyone in the room fell about laughing. The High Mass at which we sang was indeed 'very high', more like what I had been brought up with at my father's church, Holy Trinity, Lambeth, but with a little more decency and order; unfortunately not all the locals took kindly to the bold, strident music of Arthur Wills 'Brecon Mass', although they were very polite about it. So ended one of the happiest Cathedral Singers tours and all too soon I was plunged back into the classrooms at Builth Wells High School. However, this was one of those enjoyable terms where many pupils and a large number of the staff were busily engaged in producing another Gilbert and Sullivan Opera.

These were heady days at the school with plans being drawn up for some new buildings and with preparatory work being done. There was also a newish Headmaster, Thornton Toy, who had been a Deputy Head at Newtown High School, where he had earned a reputation as a strong disciplinarian. His appointment had been interesting. The final two candidates had been the school's own Deputy Head, Roy Baynham, Head of the Physics Department, and Thorton Toy himself. Unfotunately for Roy Baynham, it seems that more Montgomeryshire representatives of Powys Education Committee than those from Breconshire, had turned up to choose the new Headmaster, therefore their candidate, Thornton Toy, was appointed. Diminutive in size, he had been known in Newtown as 'Dinky', after the small 'Dinky Toys' that were all the rage at that time, yet he was a kindly man, a Non-Conformist Lay Preacher, also he was very much a family man with a lovely supportive wife and two gentle daughters. Every day started with a school assembly and this meant a lot to him, indeed it had to have a religious content with prayers, also a hymn sung from a green hymn book that had been put together by an enlightened committee shortly after the Second World War, that contained an excellent selection of hymns in both

English and Welsh. In the past these daily assemblies had been held in either Alpha Chapel or St Mary's Parish Church the chapel having a rare Martin & Coates of Oxford organ, and the church having a Peter Conacher of Huddersfield organ. Early on in Thornton Toy's reign a magnificent new Sports Hall had been built next to the school with the result that school Assemblies were transferred to there and a school band was put together to accompany the hymn singing. To my joy, however, Thornton Toy agreed to my suggestion that a pipe organ would enhance these daily acts of worship and for £3,500, I managed to obtain from Percy Daniel & Co. Ltd., the firm that maintained the Cathedral Organ, a small one manual and pedals organ built by Vowles of Bristol, which was duly installed in the Sports Hall! Indeed such was the novelty of this scheme that Thornton Toy succeeded in obtaining financial grants worth £3,000 with the result that the organ only cost the school £500, and the Sports Hall became the only Sports Hall in Britain to contain a pipe organ! Roy Baynham did not stay on long at Builth High School as he took early retirement but I was sorry to see him go as he had been a good friend to me and a great support to all my musical activities; at the same time Eric Corfield, Head of the English Department and Producer of my operas, also chose to take early retirement. However, joy of joys, in the place of Roy Baynham came Frank Banks who had lived and breathed Gilbert and Sullivan operas all his life; what he did not know about them was not worth knowing. So he took over from Eric Corfield and with the blessing of Thornton Toy, the school pupils had continued to perform, every second year, their beloved Gilbert and Sullivan operas: 'Mikado', 'Pirates of Penzance', 'HMS Pinafore' and 'Gondoliers'. Frank Banks's dedication to these works was such that he would also take pupils with him to rehearse and perform them with the Kington Operatic Society. Under his enthusiastic and knowledgeable direction these performances had improved out of all recognition. Come the autumn term of 1986, and Frank Banks had decided to break new ground; 'Ruddigore' was his choice much to everyone's delight. As usual there was no difficulty in finding singers for the solo and chorus parts indeed it had never ceased to amaze me how the most unlikely pupils had taken great pride in joining in and, as a result, had continued singing in later life, always talking with affectionate pride about these school productions. My own ingrained snobbish opposition to these Gilbert and Sullivan operas had long melted away as I had watched generation after generation of pupils develop a surprising sense of basic harmony and melody through singing the choruses, so many of which are based on the three main chords on which many a pop song is based. To me, what was so magical about this production was the fact that I had been able to re-score the entire opera for an orchestra consisting of one violin, one 'cello, two flutes, four clarinets, one bassoon, three trumpets and a trombone of whom three had reached the standard of grade 8, while the remainder were of grade 5 standard. These pupils did remarkably well and I have remained proud of their achievements to this day. Sadly, however, Eric Corfield's replacement as Head of the English

Department did not share Frank Banks's and my enthusiasm for these Gilbert and Sullivan productions. In 'Dramascene – Powys Drama Teachers' Newsletter' he wrote:

Ruddigore – Wyeside Arts Centre, December 1986

'The annual school show has been less annual of late, it's often one of the first casualties of any teachers industrial action. However, in the eye of the current industrial storm Builth Wells High School performed Gilbert & Sullivan's 'Ruddigore' at Wyeside at the End of December.

Let me put my cards on the table straight away, I hate 'G & S'. As Wyeside's most astute critic said to me on the first night 'the kids are great, but the trouble with Gilbert & Sullivan is that musically and lyrically it's emasculated'. Actually he put it more directly than that. Yet if you are in the unlikely position of seeking 'street credibility' in Builth, then one of the best ways of achieving it, is to perform a Gilbert & Sullivan with energy and style; and as everyone who came to see the show, and that's over 500 people, all agreed that is exactly what this production had. The credit goes to Frank Banks, Builth's Head of Physics, now a teacher adviser with Powys for Primary Science, and David Gedge, Builths agelessly energetic Head of Music. An orchestra of twelve musicians working on music re-scored mostly for grade five and below, and a cast of 60 from a school of 420 pupils is some achievement.

The show looked good with excellent, very colourful costumes, and a bright set. It is, of course, an enormous advantage to be able to use a professional space lit by Wyeside Technical Manager, Paul Brown; even if that space is as limiting as Wyesides Castle Theatre. Ioan Hurford, the stage manager had to struggle with a difficult two change set, whilst Frank Banks had to get the large cast on and off through a single exit. Both succeeded.

As a script 'Ruddigore' seems to me to be rather a bland blend of Rocky Horror Picture Show and Phantom of the Opera – some nice touches from the producer here with visual references to the 'Lloyd Webber Show'. 'Ruddigore' has a few good tunes, although probably only two memorable ones, but it does have the advantage of being for a Gilbert & Sullivan, quite dramatic. The principals are required to act rather more than in most Gilbert & Sullivan's and Nigel Pugh, Richard Jarman-Harris, Meryl Jones, Pat and John Thomas, Nigel Bedwell, Gretta and Heidi Ashe all did a good job of characterisation.

I was particularly impressed with Nicholas Evans, a great voice and stage presence and Juliet Evans who overacted wonderfully in a part that required just that. So what have the pupils involved in the show learnt? David Gedge would be happy with 'team spirit' and 'part singing'; Frank Banks is content with simply letting another generation experience a 'G & S'.

These are probably not acceptable reasons for the 'fee-play' school of drama teachers, who might question the opportunities for pupils' personal developments in a formal production of a 19th Century comic opera. Yet need a school play be more than a pleasant social experience with some added life skills thown in? 'Ruddigore' does in fact allow more scope for role development than many modern musicals – and most school shows these days seem to be musicals. However, 'Ruddigore's' plot, setting and theme rely for much of their success on a recognition that this opera is parodying a succession of dramatic and musical genres. This fact was lost on most of the audience, and some of the younger cast members. However is any hard criticism of one of a school's major social activities unfair? The cast had enormous fun, the audience loved the show, and huge amounts of goodwill were generated. Does the school show need the theoretical, psychological and pedagogical scrutiny that the rest of the curriculum is subject to. Times are hard, but not that hard surely.

'Ruddigore' overcame my prejudices about 'G & S' and I enjoyed the show rather a lot. No, I wouldn't do a 'G & S' myself. No, I wouldn't pay ENOs inflated ticket prices to see their current 'G & S'; and yes, the Arts Council did the right thing in stopping the Doyly Carte subsidy. But for Builth in 1986 this production was probably perfection.;

Frank Banks's wife was not a happy lady after she had read this review. In a privately circulated reply she wrote:

The critique of 'Ruddigore' as performed by Builth Wells High School has caused no little indignation on the part of some who have seen both the article and the opera.

They are among the people referred to in the surprising remark about 'being in the unlikely position of seeking 'street credibility' in Builth'. Actually I am not altogether sure what he means by this, but I do not see, on the one hand, that a show which attracts large audiences in a small market town is necessarily by that token, one to be sneered at; not, on the other hand, that because many Builth people enjoyed 'Ruddigore', this means they cannot cope with other sorts of art including Drama with a capital D. I find it hard to believe that the writer deliberately adopts such a condescending tone; did I completely misinterpreted the meaning?.

One assertion contained within the article, I can without any such fear, categorically refute. From personal knowledge I can assure the critic that Frank Banks did <u>not</u> embark on the arduous business of producing 'Ruddigore' simply to let another generation experience a 'G & S'. He needed a great deal of persuasion before he agreed to produce Gilbert & Sullivan operas in the school, being only too well aware how difficult, in parts, are both the words and the music. The youngsters came to grips with both in a very creditable way, and the fact (which I do not dispute) that some of Gilbert's jokes were not understood by all the audience, does not, I believe, detract from the undeniable learning experience and broadening of education of many members of the cast and orchestra. (I would argue that both Shakespeare and certain modern playwrights have also written lines incomprehensible to the average member of the audience).

The Writer may feel that he has been 'kind' to the show, in giving due praise *to its producer and musical director, and admitting that to raise an orchestra of 12 musicians and a cast of 60 'from a school of 420 pupils is some achievement.' It is fair to point out that very few school shows are capable of involving so many, and in particular, 'Ruddigore' was (in my experience) most unusual in drawing in pupils who under other circumstances would 'not have been seen dead' on or near a stage. And they enjoyed it too!*

Does the school show need the theoretical, psychological and pedagogical scrutiny that the rest of the curriculum is subject to? YES, it does, and it is unworthy to suggest that 'Ruddigore' would not stand up to such scrutiny. All right, the opera itself is just an opera (though it is one which has stood the test of time in pleasing audiences, whatever you may think about the D'Oyly Carte – that is another argument!) But you have missed the point. Is a school production intended only for the elite, the minority able <u>and willing</u> to tackle the intensities of Drama as taught to English students since the 60s (when I was one myself); or could it be a vehicle for educating children not only linguistically and musically, but in the arguably more important areas of self-confidence and presence of mind, and even (dare I quote?) 'team spirit' in association with the team discipline? When non-academic youngsters can gain in all these, and enjoy every minute, and end up with the satisfaction of knowing that they have been part of a worthwhile group achievement, I believe this is more than enough justification for my idea of what a school show should be.

I hope Builth High School's next production, which I am sure will not be a G & S, will live up to the standards set by 'Ruddigore'. I look forward to seeing it.'

So, sadly, ended the Gilbert and Sullivan tradition at Builth Wells High School with the most enterprising production being reserved for the last. Then, as so often happens, the best of teachers, Frank Banks, was taken out of the classroom and placed somewhere where he could teach others to teach; with his departure went the last hope of more 'G & S' operas at the school. In any case, with the new school came new ideas about curriculums, examinations and school management; education was never to be the same again. Not surprisingly, this coincided with teacher unrest as is echoed in this letter which was published in the Brecon & Radnor Express, written by Dr Davies, a local General Practitioner, a great supporter of the school, whose three children all studied music to 'O' level and learned to play musical instruments, two of whom had sung in 'Ruddigore'.

Sir, - Many will remember the recent production of Ruddigore by Builth Wells High School at the Wyeside Theatre for the sheer enjoyment it gave them.

I would also like to point out that the school, although small, provided the entire cast, orchestra and props, and that the high standard of production was achieved in spite of the disruptions of rebuilding and the disputes of the past year.

Well done Builth High School.'

However, two entirely unexpected events brought 1986 to an end. Firstly, on Advent Sunday at the Cathedral, I was presented with a card signed by more than fifty members of the morning congregation. This bore the words: 'With very many thanks for all your work and music through the year'; obviously more people than I had realised were sympathetic to the problems of making music at Brecon Cathedral. Secondly, and most extraordinarily: recently the Cathedral Singers and Builth Wells High School Band had initiated a Christmas Carol Service for Builth Wells Rotary Club in St Mary's Church, Builth Wells at 7.pm on the Monday before Christmas Day. It had seemed such a shame to return home to Brecon straight from this service so early in the evening, therefore I wrote to the Lord Lieutenant of Powys, Mervyn Bourdillon, to offer the Cathedral Singers to sing carols for charity, at his gracious home, Llwyn Madoc, in nearby Beulah. Back came his unexpected reply to the effect that as The Singers already did so much for Breconshire, why did we not all have an 'evening off' and enjoy a leisurely supper at his home. So, with the Carol Service ended, The Cathedral Singers drove to Llwyn Madoc where to their astonishment, everyone sat down at long trestle tables while Mervyn Bourdillon's entire family served supper to them all; quite an extraordinary act of humility the like of which I have not again experienced.

XLVI

1987 opened auspiciously; a chamber organ was given to St Mary's Church, Brecon. Built in 1825, by Henry Russell, this elegant instrument had lived for more than a hundred years in Abercamlais, the second of the two large country houses on the A40 road to Carmarthen, five miles out of Brecon, where the previous Lord Lieutenant, Captain Garnous-Williams, had lived. It was fitting that this organ should come to St Mary's because during the latter part of the nineteenth century, members of this Williams family had been Vicars of Brecon. Originally this organ had stood in Penpont Church but when in the 1870s the Williamses had purchased the historic 1804 Flight & Robson organ for the church, the Henry Russell chamber organ was moved to the hall of Abercamlais where it had stayed until now. At St Mary's Church, Brecon, it proved to be a most valuable acquisition because apart from its regency-style case looking very lovely and its gentle, unforced tone sounding exquisite, in being mounted on a platform with wheels it could be propelled to where it was most needed. So the instrument provided gentle musical accompaniment for services in the side chapel, furthermore on Good Friday that year it was wheeled to the back of the church to support the children's singing at a special 'Stations of the Cross' service (things like that don't happen today!), then on the next day it provided the most perfect continuo noises for J S Bach's 'St Matthew Passion'. Most of the £3,150 that was needed for the organ's restoration was largely donated by the families of Jim Rowlands, in memory of his wife, and William (Billy) Weston, whose late wife Eira also had been a Rowlands, indeed, Jimmy, Billy and Eira had all been much valued members of St Mary's Choir and the Cathedral Singers. A third substantial donation was made in memory of Mrs Holbourne, an extraordinary elderly lady who had the distinction of being Laird of the island of Fula, off the coast of Scotland, and who used to 'winter' in Brecon because she thought the weather kinder! Her son and daughter-in –law numbered among the Cathedral congregation and were Patrons of the Cathedral Singers, while her grandson-in-law, Paul Jenkins, played viola in the Gwent Chamber Orchestra.

Around this time I became embroiled in the problems concerning the future of choir schools, as a result a letter of mine was published in the Times Educational Supplement. I had written this in response to an article which suggested that if the Labour party won the forthcoming General Election it might 'silence the Choir Schools'; the letter read:

> 'Gerald Haigh writes that 'choir schools are unashamedly élitist' (TES January 30) What rubbish! The only possible elitism is to be found in the quality of the music produced at these educational establishments, a quality greatly admired throughout the world of music.

My son was a chorister at St John's College, Cambridge, and therefore attended the choir school nearby. My wife and I struggled hard to keep him there because, as well you know, my salary as a school teacher and her salary as a visiting and private music teacher were far from elitist. However, we got by with help from various sources which we will be paying back for years to come.

Gerald Haigh accuses these schools of being 'absolutely literally cloistered from their 'surrounding communities' '. With more than 200 day boys and girls, how could this ever be the case at St John's? Then, as often as possible, I made visits coincide with Cambridge United home games so that my son and I could enjoy the fun at Abbey Stadium. Never did we regret this sacrifice of time and money as the years at Cambridge were both happy and stimulating. We made many friends among the parents and among the staff. Indeed, as a result of the attentions meted out by the latter, our son won a music exhibition to Eton College.

Another elitist school? How could it be with our son there? Musical standards were phenomenal: teachers on all orchestral instruments (one violin teacher is full-time), two symphony orchestras and a chamber orchestra, chapel choir and choral society, fortnightly concerts of an exceptional standard organised by the boys themselves. Powys County Education Authority cannot offer anything comparable for its secondary school pupils on a county basis.

Now the labour Party promises to destroy all this. Even the Alliance threatens to remove the charitable status from choir schools – so Clement Freud stated when he visited Builth Wells high school during the Brecon and Radnor by-election. How pathetic! For countless years the Church held the monopoly of education in Britain. The writings of Maria Hackett (1783-1874) indicate how low were the standards in most choir schools. Thus when the State entered the education field, many choir schools failed to compete and, as a result, went to the wall.

However, other such schools accepted the challenge and triumphed eventually over their state rivals. If the state wishes to destroy choir schools then it should supply something better.

Yet, how ridiculous to suggest that the demise of these schools will, in the long run, make little difference to the Anglican cathedral music tradition. On the contrary, it will devastate it.

In my spare time, I officiate as organist and choirmaster of Brecon Cathedral. My choristers all are voluntary, drawn mainly from the town. Hard as they work, they readily acknowledge the excellence of choirs at cathedrals and collegiate churches where there are choir schools. When not singing themselves, they listen to these choirs on the radio, tapes and records, even in their own buildings. What is obvious to them is that our choir cannot possibly maintain a comparable repertoire. However, when such choirs as that at St John's College, Cambridge, sing for around 20 hours weekly and their choristers learn to play two musical instruments, is that really surprising?

Without doubt, to destroy the great choir school tradition would destroy also the great tradition of cathedral music. This would be wanton vandalism of the *worst sort. Furthermore, once done it would be impossible to be undone. It is a tradition of which Britain should be proud for it is unique. There is nothing like it anywhere else in the world. Treasure it!'*

Soon, two events brought home to me the yawning gulf that separated amateur parish church and cathedral choirs from professional collegiate church and cathedral choirs, especially those that benefited from their own choristers' educational establishment. First was the service of Thanksgiving and Praise for the Diamond Jubilee of the Royal School of Church Music, on the evening of Sunday, May 10th, when some seven hundred choristers converged on Cardiff to sing a great variety of music in the company of a congregation numbering two thousand people, in St David's Hall. Most of the singers came from parish church choirs in the three dioceses of Llandaff, Monmouth and Swansea & Brecon, and they were led by their cathedral choirs along with the choir of the Roman Catholic Metropolitan Cathedral of Cardiff. In the weeks before I had rehearsed my Swansea choristers on six occasions in the expectation that choirs from the other two dioceses would have done likewise, but on that day I was horrified to discover the opposite, that most of the other singers had been left to make their own musical preparations and some were taking pot luck with the music. However, a lengthy two and a half hour rehearsal directed by Dr Lionel Dakers, Director of The Royal School of Church Music on the very day itself, fortunately cemented together the choirs' musical contributions to the proceedings, and while this resulted in a service which was both meaningful and impressive, it could so easily have been magnificent. Yet what was magnificent was the organisation of what went on at St David's Hall; this was entirely the responsibility of the Diocese of Llandaff RSCM committee and the work was done impeccably.

The second event took place nine days later, on Tuesday May 19th, at 5.30 pm in St Paul's Cathedral; understandably it became one of the highlights of my life. Brecon's little Cathedral Choir had been invited to join with the choirs of Manchester Cathedral, Norwich Cathedral and St Paul's Cathedral itself at the Three Hundred and Thirty-Third Festival of The Sons of The Clergy. What excitement! Each choir had to sing an anthem on its own, without organ accompaniment, then all the four choirs had to join together under the direction of John Scott, the Assistant Organist, to sing William Walton's 'Coronation Te Deum' beneath the great dome, accompanied by The London Brass, with Christopher Dearnley, the Cathedral Organist, presiding at the organ. Before the big day arrived I thought long and hard about what my choir should sing on its own and eventually had decided on something both easy and unknown so that if anything went wrong, no-one would know! The following review by 'Corno Dolce', published in 'The Organists Quarterly', tells the story far better than ever I could have done:

'If you've ever wondered about an announcement in the 'Church Times' round about May each year, that the Corporation of the Sons of the Clergy is to hold

its annual service, join the club. No, I hadn't a clue what it was all about either. With a title that long who needs a service as well? For years I'd visualised rows and rows of parsons' sons all displaying some sort of strange solidarity.

In a way it did start like that back in 1655. Around that time Cromwell (or Warty Olly as his detractors may well have dubbed him) went in for legalised vandalism in churches and other holy places and generally making life intolerable for the clergy ... those who remained loyal to the Crown that is. When he wasn't stabling his horses in the parish church and smashing works of art therein (before we got wise to selling them to foreign art dealers and making a bomb) he was bleeding the gentry and the clergy of their pennies. (Armies came expensive in those days too). The ensuing poverty prompted City Merchants, all of whom were sons of the Cloth, to set up a Charity to help impoverished clergy and dependants. (How our family slipped through the net beats me. The first words we learned at our mother's knee were 'overdraft' and 'No, you can't.)

So, for 333 years an annual service of Thansgiving has been held, for the most part, at St Paul's. Everyone who is anyone in the City from the Lord Mayor downwards is invited. Last year there were sixteen bishops, the Archbishop of York.... And me. (Oh .... And a few thousand others, but who's counting?).

When someone of Christopher Dearnley's stature invites you to join him in the organ loft, you don't sit and think it over .... you go. I do anyway. The experience exceeded my wildest dreams ... the pomp, ceremony, colour and the music ... wow, the __music__ ... out of this world.

What I hadn't expected was that no less than FOUR cathedral choirs take part. Each year three different ones join with St Paul's in what amounts to a Four Choirs Festival.

I slid into a temporary seat under the Dome waiting for the magic hour of 5. pm when I was to join that other CD by the organ loft stairs. Complying with the Maestro's instructions, I rose from my seat and tip-toed as delicately as a stone-crusher to the Choir Screen. Two stewards leapt at me, barring my way. I felt like a failed terrorist. They let me pass, however, when I cannoned (bishoped?) into our Diocesan boss who shot me a haunted 'Oh-My-God-not HER-again?' look and strode off to robe with his Lordy buddies.

Thus it was that CD Major, CD Minor and assistant-assistant organist Andrew Lucas (who gritted his teeth manfully when I called him 'Adrian'... his Norwich counterpart) in high spirits nipped up aloft to the console.

*The service began with the arrival of the Lord Mayor. St Paul's choir some 15 miles away at the West Door sang him in to '**Exultate Deo adjutori nostro**' (Poulenc). Then the great procession began .... A state occasion without HM. First the choirs .... Manchester, Brecon, Norwich and St Paul's, then came the dignitaries of the City, the cathedral and everyone except the cleaners. Vergers were popped in like bookmarks keeping the factions tidily apart. CD improvised with the impressive splurge you long to copy but can't.*

'How do you gauge when to slop?' I asked fatuously (You can't see too well up there). 'You get used to it', he said stating the obvious. Well, after 333 years you would, wouldn't you?

As the service progressed each choir sang in turn. Manchester, city of motorways, urban sprawl and industry fielded a huge choir, under Stuart Beer's direction, **'Beati quorum vir'** that spine-tingler of Stanford's. Little Brecon, the baby of the group, a choir drawn from the Welsh countryside where sheep outnumber would-be choristers by heaven knows what, sang **'Blessed Lord, who hast caused all Holy Scriptures'** a prayer-anthem by William Russell. For this little choir of quality, the excitement of an outing to the capital (of England of course) must have rivalled that famous one of Dylan Thomas', only without the beer ... (Manchester brought the Beer with them). David Gedge skippered Brecon ... a cathedral since only 1923 when it was upgraded from a priory church tucked away in a small pretty Welsh town.

Norwich came in to bat last. Here's an impressive choir from the dreamy city where churches outnumber Birds Eye peas and Colman's put the mustard into their lives. Under the direction of Michael Nicholas they gave us **'Faire is the Heaven'** lovely mystical words of Edmund Spencer set to music by William Harris.

Then came the climax ... The William Walton **Te Deum** sung by all the choirs with organ and the London Brass Ensemble who had earlier played pre-service music. John Scott held them all together like a four-in-hand driver who knows he's onto a winning run. It was a glorious sound. My goosepimple gauge went off the dial. From somewhere up near the painted ceiling amongst the cherubim and seraphim I heard CD major below murmur: 'Hmm! Well it worked even if we did only have one rehearsal together'. What sang-froid! I'd have been a quivery heap of jelly.

If I'd heard one word of criticism on my way out I'd have impaled the culprit on my forked tongue. As far as I'm concerned only Almighty God is empowered to judge an offering like that.

I reckon He was tickled pink'.

'Corno Dolce' had misjudged the Brecon choir and its beer; while the Lay Clerks may have travelled to London without any, they had certainly made plans to remedy the situation after the service. My friend, Graham Sorrell, the St Paul's Vicar Choral, who many years before had sung with me in the choir of Southwark Cathedral and who now sang the part of Jesus regularly in my J S Bach 'Passions' at Brecon, had advised the Lay Clerks to go to 'The Rising Sun' in Carter Lane, near St Paul's. No sooner, therefore, had we waved goodbye to the choirboys and their parents as they drove off in their 'bus at the start of their journey back to Brecon, than we were on our way to 'The Rising Sun' where for the next two hours we enjoyed our sausage and mash washed down with real ale. Afterwards, I was presented with a bill, not for fifty-one suppers as I had been expecting, but for fifty-nine and when I protested the Landlord assured me that that number of meals had been eaten;

obviously eight locals had seen us collect our meals one-by-one as each arrived at the serving-hatch and had taken advantage of gaining a free supper without anyone noticing. One final surprise was in store for the Lay Clerks. On the way home, as their 'bus arrived at Membury Service State on the M4 motorway, bass Lay Clerk Mike Thomas prepared to be dropped off to collect his car when it suddenly dawned on him that it was parked on the other side. Fortunately, this was the one Service Station which could be crossed with a walk of only a mile or so.

In the days that followed I thought back over how the Brecon Cathedral Choristers and Lay Clerks had got away with so much at St Paul's. By singing something simple, lovely and unknown, but with such sincerity of feeling, they had made many friends including the one that they needed most: the Dean of Brecon. He had been among the robed clergy at the service and afterwards, while the Lay Clerks had been slumming it in 'The Rising Sun', having a supper of Bangers and Mash swilled down with beer, he and his wife Gwyneth had been wined and dined in great style by The Corporation of the Sons of the Clergy, in The Merchant Taylors' Hall. There, many people had made special efforts to tell them how much they had appreciated the Brecon contribution to the service, indeed even the Lord Mayor of London had commented most favourably when the Dean and his wife had been presented to him. Furthermore, during the dinner, the distinguished guests sitting near to them had marvelled at how a town as small as Brecon could raise a choir of such calibre. At last we were 'in' with the Dean, for the moment at any rate, as he revelled in reflected glory.

Back home there was little time for me to revel in any glory because another BBC/TV 'Songs of Praise' had appeared on the horizon, this time in Builth Wells at Alpha Chapel. I had been asked to direct the musical proceedings and fortunately was able to have Hazel as Organist for the occasion. The organ there was not a particularly colourful instrument - its only claim to fame being that it was a rare example of the work of Martin & Coates, a little-known firm from Oxford, therefore I enlisted the help of some of the Builth Wells High School instrumentalists to liven up its musical noises. As usual the BBC had made some musical arrangements of its own without consulting me in any way. So the town Male Voice Choir had been lined up to sing but failed to materialise in any great numbers at any rehearsals; similarly, a young vocal soloist had been booked who turned out to be unable to sing what was required of her until helped out by some of my singers from the High School. At this time the weather was amazingly hot, making the rehearsals exceedingly hard work, yet the townspeople who turned up to rehearse then to sing at the recording, responded valiantly and patiently. So the result was a broadcast that was particularly satisfying, having interviews that were both interesting and well put together, and hymns that were for the most part well chosen and well sung, also the countryside around Builth Wells always looked stunning. However, perhaps the greatest achievement had been persuading this very conservative, basically farming community to sing the hymn 'O Jesus I have promised' lustily to a great modern tune by W H Ferguson. BBC(Wales) had been in charge of this broadcast and the Producer wrote to me afterwards saying:

> 'Just a word of thanks for the magnificent job you did with the congregation at the Songs of Praise recording and also for the hard work which must have been put into the practice for the school band.
>
> Will you please pass on my grateful thanks to the School Band and also to your wife Hazel for her excellent contribution.
>
> I am sure you will be very pleased with the programme and that it will be worth all the hard work ....'

At the Chapel, after the recording, he had also said: 'We must use you again', which to a financially hard-up musician is music to the ears, but as before, on a number of occasions, it was full of Eastern promise', easily said but never followed up, so I heard no more.

The effort involved in rescuing this 'Songs of Praise' in some of the hottest weather of the year, left me in no mood for the next fight. For some time school teachers had been in a state of turmoil because of the changes in their conditions of work that were being inflicted on them from above. Among the most controversial was the stipulation that they should all work for 1265 hours every year because in the past, by tradition, many teachers had worked voluntarily, in their own time, for a variety of activities. At Builth Wells High School, for example, many members of staff had happily given up their Saturday mornings to supervise sporting activities, while others had given up weekday evenings to assist local Young Farmers Clubs with their drama productions, not forgetting the countless ways in which they had helped me with my Gilbert and Sullivan operas. Now the recently appointed Headmaster, Ian Brown, was insisting that in order to comply with this ruling, all members of the teaching staff would have to remain in School on Tuesday, Wednesday and Thursday afternoons until 4.30 pm. While to him this opened up endless opportunities of extra-curricula activities and staff meetings, to me it meant the end of Wednesday Evensongs at 5.45 pm because I would not have time for an adequate choir practice before the service. Mr Brown was adamant: if an exception was made for me it would weaken his position with the other teachers. In desperation I wrote a rather strident letter to the Director of Education Robert Bevan, who, being an active Churchman, knew of my work at the Cathedral. To my great surprise he sent back a far more understanding reply that ever I had deserved:

> 'Firstly let me congratulate you and all concerned on what appears to have been a memorable occasion at St Paul's Cathedral.
>
> The new teachers' conditions and consultation within the educational world and many of the questions remain unanswered. The 1265 hours is, in many ways, the central issue and my personal hope is that the voluntary efforts of so

many teachers like yourself over the years will not be prejudiced by the rigid application of a new formula.

At this stage I feel it would not be appropriate for me to intervene in the particular problem you raise although I am prepared to consider doing so if that is your wish. I hope, however, that it will be possible for Mr Brown and yourself to work out some compromise which will enable you to continue with your voluntary work unhampered.

I have assumed your letter is written to me in confidence and, for that reason, I have not sent a copy of this reply to Mr Brown as I normally would have done'.

However, it was not Mr Brown who compromised, rather it was Brecon Cathedral Choir which kindly agreed to transfer its weekday Choral Evensong from Wednesday to another day. From September 11th, 1987, onwards Evensong was sung at 5.45 pm on Fridays and soon became the perfect way to end the working week.

At this time two parties took my attention. The first was Hazel's and my Silver Wedding, the second, however, had a curious history. One St David's Day evening a few years before, when some of the Lay Clerks had been warming up at the bar of The George Hotel after a Mozart orchestra Mass in the Cathedral when the temperature had been positively arctic, my aged violinist friend, Haydn Bond, remarked: *'David, I enjoyed that. I would like something like that at my funeral'*, whereupon the assembled company had visions of Haydn's coffin standing solemnly in the Cathedral between the choirstalls, with his violin and bow laid out on the lid on top. But with Haydn nothing was solemn so he continued:

'The present National Savings Certificates give a good return, so good in fact that I am sure that at the Budget later this month the Chancellor will stop them. Tomorrow I am going to send you £100 in the post; when it arrives, go out and buy £100 of these certificates, then when I die you won't have to wait for my will to be read out, you can go straight out, cash the certificates and have a party down here straight after my funeral.'

True enough, two days later, a cheque for £100 arrived in the morning post and I immediately purchased the certificates. Imagine my surprise therefore when during the summer of 1987, I received a 'phone call from Haydn who by now was reaching the venerable age of four score years:

'Hey, Dave', he said, *'Remember those certificates you purchased for the party after my funeral, well sell them now, I'm getting married again and going to live in America. The money will pay for the drinks at my farewell party!'.*

So it was that Haydn and an old family lady friend had decided to marry, then to set up home together in Fort Wayne over in the USA and a grand dinner was held one autumn evening at The Bear Hotel, Crickhowell, to give us all the chance to say our 'Farewells'. Haydn had been a wonderful friend to us all, not just as a violinist but also as a librarian on choir trips, not forgetting the fun he had always generated whenever we had been together. Who can forget Haydn parading around Canterbury Cathedral, properly attired in a Brecon Cathedral Choir cassock, setting out music in the choir stalls? With Haydn there was never a dull moment and our lives became considerably poorer with his crossing to the other side of the Atlantic Ocean.

XLVII

1987 ended as auspiciously as it had begun, with the retirement of Bishop Vaughan, the sixth Bishop of Swansea and Brecon. Born on December 25th, 1917, his names had included Noel; now on December 25th, 1987, he gave his final sermon as Bishop of Swansea and Brecon at the 11 am service of Holy Eucharist in his Cathedral. There had rarely been a dull moment during his episcopate and when the time came for him to relinquish this important office he was, in fact, the senior Bishop in the Church in Wales. Had he been a little younger he would, by tradition, have enjoyed a few years as Archbishop of Wales and become the first Bishop of Swansea and Brecon to be elected to this exalted position, but that was not to be; anno domini ruled against him. However, events played into his hands to allow him to demonstrate how it could have been, as there was a new Bishop of Monmouth to be consecrated and, being Senior Bishop, he was able to decree that this consecration be in his Cathedral. So he presided over one of the most grandiose consecration services that many people had ever witnessed with trumpets adorning the music and lavish hospitality for the august company that had been assembled to witness the occasion. It was somehow reminiscent of the mediaeval pomp that surrounded prince-bishops in days goneby. His farewell service for Swansea had taken place in St Mary's church, Swansea, and it had been a similarly grand occasion. For this he had decreed that the Cathedral Choir and the choir of St Mary's should join together but never did he consult either Choirmaster. If the St Mary's choristers had been upset by the intrusion of the Cathedral Choir, I for one would not have been surprised, but in the end Cliff Rose, Organist & Choirmaster of St Mary's Church, was exceedingly gracious about the entire affair. On the night of the service the Bishop had driven from Brecon to Swansea and on arrival at St Mary's Church had parked his car on the main road, convenient to himself but with no thought for anyone else. After the service had ended and he had revelled in all the speeches, glowing tributes and presentations, smiling and purring throughout, he had returned to his car only to find it adorned with a Parking Ticket which he handed graciously to his Chaplain to deal with, while he drove back to Brecon.

Yet for all his buffoonery, Bishop Vaughan had been a man of vision; it had just been his misfortune to have neither kindred spirits nor the necessary cash to put his ideas into operation. His scheme to transform the Old Deanery into the Deanery Centre next to his Cathedral, and make it a venue for Diocesan occasions, was a good one but he only got as far as installing a Resource Centre there and with the majority of his clergy living far away in Swansea not surprisingly it was rarely used. Wanting me to organise educational musical activities there, he conveniently overlooked the fact that I was teaching full-time to augment my Cathedral Organist salary with the obvious result that I could not find time to do this, especially when no money was available to pay anyone to do the work he wanted and, furthermore, there was no piano in the building neither was there money to purchase one. Not surprisingly, despite the cosmetic refit given to this ancient, extensive mediaeval pile in time for its opening by Queen Elizabeth II, soon it all began to look jaded, nor did the disputes between the Cathedral and Diocesan authorities over who paid for what, help the situation.

Sadly, Bishop Vaughan had not always taken the trouble to endear himself to his flock. Take his holidays as an example. January in his diocese of Swansea and Brecon, could be a cruel month with appalling weather, even heavy snow but instead of sharing this discomfort with his flock he would often be sunning himself out in the West Indies in the company of the flock with whom he had begun his Episcopal ministry as a Suffragan Bishop. Yet this was nothing new. Apparently when he had moved on to become Bishop of Belize, the arrival of the hurricane season always seemed to coincide with his annual holiday visit to his homeland, Wales.

Yet one of his grandiose schemes which was greeted with much ridicule, did, however, appeal to me. Always conscious of the fact that Swansea hankered after a Cathedral of its own, Bishop Vaughan had taken the next best course and raised St Mary's to the status of a Collegiate Church. Personally, I thought that there was a lot of sense in this because in many ways St Mary's Swansea was not unlike Southwark Cathedral. Initially there was an extraordinary and little-known co-incidence in that St Mary's nineteenth century church and Southwark Cathedral's nineteenth-century nave were both designed by the same architect, Sir Arthur Blomfield, son of the famous Bishop of London who had masterminded The Cathedrals Act of 1840. More importantly, however, both buildings were surrounded by industry, even if this was different in each place. At Southwark it was offices, a fruit and vegetable market, warehouses, also ships unloading in the Pool of London; at Swansea the church was surrounded by shops and offices while a thriving port was situated nearby. At neither places were there many houses to supply people to make up a local congregation for divine services on Sundays, therefore some sort of weekday mission was vitally important with services taking place when the workers were around. Almost twenty years before, the visionary Archdeacon Harry Craven Williams, Vicar of St Mary's, had planned to create scholarships for choirboys at Ffynone House School, in the hope of establishing weekday choral services. What a pity he had not succeeded because an abiding memory of my days as a chorister at Southwark Cathedral was of the great church being lit up in full view of the countless hordes of people pouring across London Bridge from the City of London, making for their trains home to various parts of South London from the railway station close by, while we sang Evensong on their behalf. At St Mary's, Swansea, Bishop Vaughan went so far as to appoint a number of specialist clergy to positions in his Collegiate Church: the Chaplain to Swansea Prison, for example, also the Swansea-based Chaplain for the Mission to Seamen, not forgetting the local Chaplain to the Deaf and Dumb along with the diocesan Chaplain for Leisure and Sport. The idea was to form a College of Priests who could work together and pool their ideas but, sadly, no real enthusiasm was aroused for this project even though Bishop Vaughan had brought to Swansea as Vicar of St Mary's, the charismatic Don Lewis and his lovely wife, Ann, daughter of a former Bishop of Bangor, whom Hazel and I grew to love dearly. Perhaps Swansea was not ready for such a novel and far-seeing venture or perhaps the Bishop himself should have led the venture from the front rather than expect others to implement his scheme for him; perhaps someone should have been sent to somewhere like Southwark Cathedral to see how such a ministry could work. Unfortunately, the Bishop too often did not see his projects through to the end, after all had he not paid for me to spend three days in Taizé and then failed to make any use of what I had learned there about worship songs and chants.

I remember calling at Ely tower one afternoon to see Bishop Vaughan about some matter, and walking into his study just when he was talking with the stain-glass artist, John Petts, about the Cathedral, with two of the Canons and an artistic clergyman also in attendance. Listening in, to my horror I discovered that the Bishop was talking 'big' again, this time about putting colour into his Cathedral. He was suggesting the installation of a red carpet all the way down the nave and up into the chancel, much to the delight of John Petts and the artistic clergyman while the two Canons sat in silence, looking glum. I, on the other hand, protested loudly and vigorously, expressing my disgust in no uncertain terms, asking why they could not see nor appreciate the gentle, natural colours in the local Cathedral stone. John Petts immediately rounded on me and suggested that I visit St Mary's Church, Kidwelly, to see how he had added colour there by means of floor coverings. Unfortunately for him, of course, I knew Kidwelly Church intimately, as I had been married there, as Hazel had spent her childhood worshipping in it, as we both worshipped there now in our holidays. So I was able to point out that while his colour scheme might work there to a certain extent, as the colours were reasonably muted, a bright red carpet certainly would not work in Brecon Cathedral as it would be out of character with the building and would amount to sacrilege. So the matter was dropped there and then, never to be mentioned again by the Bishop, furthermore one of the two silent Canons, who chanced to be related to the Bishop by marriage – Canon John Davies, Rector of Llandrindod Wells, gripped my right hand warmly and congratulated me for making a stand! This, however, was not the Bishop's only foray into the artistic scene. For a time he had a vision of putting a hanging Rood back into his Cathedral, at the very place where the great Golden Rood would have hung in the days that preceded the Reformation. This was a laudable scheme, one which normally would have gladdened my heart, were it not for the fact that the Bishop wanted it carved in black British Honduras mahogany while his chosen craftsman, also from the West Indies, was planning a modern figure but with only half a body hanging from half a cross. Fortunately the project turned out to be rather more costly than was anticipated and died a natural death, no more to be mentioned. Yet Bishop Vaughan had one more surprise for his diocese before finally he departed from the scene; he married his secretary, Magdalen Reynolds, the ceremony being conducted by the Bishop of St Asaph, Alwyn our former Dean, shortly before he retired.

On Tuesday, January 26th, 1988, the Electoral College met in Brecon Cathedral to elect a successor to Bishop Vaughan as the seventh Bishop of Swansea and Brecon. Why The Independent Newspaper sent along a photographer and reporter to cover what was a routine event I do not know, however, beneath a magnificent photograph of the five Church-in-Wales Bishops processing past the Choir Stalls then turning left into the Havard Chapel, was printed this article:

'The electoral college in the diocese of Swansea and Brecon met yesterday for only the seventh time since the Church in Wales was disestablished. Its task was to choose a successor to Bishop Benjamin Vaughan, who reached the retiring age of 70 on Christmas Day.

The electoral college comprises clerical and lay delegates from the six Welsh dioceses; the five serving bishops, with six clerical and six lay delegates from the vacant see, and three clerical and three lay delegates from the other five dioceses – 47 electors in all.

The Archbishop is elected by the bishops from within their own ranks. When Parliament disestablished the Church in Wales in 1920, it was yielding to Prime Minister David Lloyd-George's illiberal antagonism to Tory Anglicanism – egged on by his Welsh Nonconformist farming constituents. By appropriating the Church's endowments at the same time, he believed it would be mortally weakened.

But the Church survived, it is said, by becoming what it had not been hitherto – the church of the people. By talented husbandry of property and investments it has prospered.

As a democratic and representative body it now elects its bishops, rather than having them imposed by the Queen.

But some old habits die hard. The five serving bishops pictured above wear convocation robes in a style inherited from Canterbury. In a scene of remarkable pantomime secrecy, first we were told we could take pictures of the election, then we were told to leave, then we were recalled, but by the time we got there it seemed that they had changed their minds again.

But at least the democracy worked. By the end of the afternoon, the statutory two-thirds majority had delivered a bishop-elect: the present Archdeacon of St David's, Dewi Morris Bridges, 55, who must formally accept the appointment within 14 days ....'

In continuing the story, The Western Mail, Wales's National Newspaper, in true Welsh fashion, made sure that its readers knew the origins of the new Prince of the Church:

'The son of a miner will take over soon as Bishop of Swansea and Brecon.

The Ven. Dewi Bridges was born in Beaufort, near Ebbw Vale, and as a youngster used to cycle across the mountain to the cathedral in Brecon, the centre of his new diocese.

Describing himself as 'moderate in his churchmanship', the 54-year-old Archdeacon of St David's and Rector of Tenby was nominated by the 47-strong electoral college in less than a day of private conclave at Brecon Cathedral....'

What neither The Independent nor The Western Mail could give their readers were the snatches of information that leaked out unofficially from some of the forty-seven electors in the days that followed the election, despite their having been sworn to secrecy. This, of course, highlights one of the problems of the democratic election of bishops opposed to the Crown Appointments that occur across the border in England. Piecing together the information that came to the surface after this particular election left one with the following synopsis: Firstly, there was no obvious candidate for the bishopric of Swansea and Brecon; Secondly, the new Archbishop of Wales, George Noakes, who was also Bishop of St David's, needed an Assistant Bishop to help him but unfortunately there was no money to pay one; Thirdly, if the Archdeacon of St David's became Bishop of Swansea and Brecon that would leave vacant the Archdeaconry of St David's; Fourthly, if the vacant Archdeaconry of St David's was annexed to the proposed Assistant Bishopric it would provide a stipend for the Assistant Bishop; Fifthly, so the Archdeacon of St David's was elected Bishop of Swansea and Brecon, thereby leaving the way clear for the Dean of Bangor, Ivor Rees, to be appointed Assistant Bishop of St David's. Is this how it really happened? We shall never know, but it was plausible!

Back on January 27th, the correspondent in The Western Mail had mentioned the new Bishop's attitude to the problems surrounding the ordination of women deacons to the priesthood, Bishop Dewi Bridges had said that

'this was a problem which Welsh Anglicans would have to face'

Then he had continued:

'the Welsh church may, however, have to wait for a lead from the Anglican communion as a whole, and this year's Lambeth conference.'

These Lambeth conferences were important because they took place every ten years and provided a valuable opportunity to bring together all the Bishops of the worldwide Anglican Church. The next such Conference was scheduled for the following Summer but, sadly, Bishop Dewi Bridges was unable to attend it. Soon after his enthronement he had been diagnosed as suffering from ME, therefore in need of considerable rest, so much so in fact that there were some in the Church in Wales who suggested that he might have to stand down. However, the Bishop weathered this storm and eventually took control of the

Diocese of Swansea and Brecon which he then led for almost eleven years, during which time he ordained the first women priests at Brecon Cathedral.

Meanwhile, illness had struck nearer home. For some time Hazel's father had been experiencing problems with his heart, at the same time her mother had been lapsing into unconsciousness with increasing regularity. For him it turned out to be Angina to add to the tinnitus which caused him considerable discomfort; for her, sadly, it was the start of Altzheimer's Disease. To help them Hazel had cleared her Thursdays of any piano lessons and regularly drove down to Kidwelly to do the shopping and any other necessary jobs like washing clothes and cleaning Bridgend House. However, it had become painfully obvious that while her father could fend for himself, after a fashion, her mother could not, indeed she needed constant care and attention. So mum and dad squeezed into Garth Cottage with us as we turned our sitting room downstairs into a bedroom for them, putting two single beds there, while we converted Nick's bedroom upstairs into a small, snug sitting room for us. Hazel's dad hated Brecon, it was the last place he wanted to be in; he badly missed Kidwelly where he had been born and where he had spent all his days, he especially yearned for the lovely Priory Church, the majestic castle, also the River that flowed close by Bridgend House. Not surprisingly he became a very difficult patient. Hazel's mum, on the other hand, was reasonably happy and was quite content to be here although she was becoming increasingly vague and forgetful. Yet life had to go on and for Hazel and me this was a busy time, although on reflection it was always a busy time! The Cathedral Choir was about to go to Denmark and although Hazel was supposed to be on this trip it became increasingly obvious that she would have to stay at home to be with her parents. So I returned to the Isle of Funen, near to Odense, but this time with the Cathedral Choir and another good time was had by all. Having so many youngsters with us a visit to Legoland was included in the itinerary; there a display board containing Lego letters suddenly was found to bear the statement 'Brecon Cathedral Choristers are here'. Indeed on joining a day trip to Copenhagen some of them had managed to cause the customary mayhem. As the train crossed a stretch of water on a ferry and instructions were issued telling passengers not to leave their carriages, one of them, feeling sick, promptly did just that only to experience great difficulty in getting back onto the train when dry land was reached, as all the doors had been locked. On arriving at Copenhagen Station most of the Cathedral Choir party made a mad dash to the 'bus that was to take them into the city centre, in the hope of avoiding being on the same bus as the troublesome choristers. As on the previous Cathedral Singers trip, the Agricultural College in Korinth provided accommodation and there, as usual, the life and soul of the party was Tony Wainwright who, being a doctor, was of especial value. One evening before supper he had placed his violin on top of the piano in readiness to play 'Happy Birthday to you' for a Birthday Boy, only for someone to put his strings in reverse order when he was not looking, with the result that the melody was unrecognisable.

Back at home, Tony Wainwright took charge of dad even to the extent of enlisting him as a patient despite his Medical Practice centering on Hay-on-Wye and Talgarth, but this allowed him to get dad into Bronllys Hospital, there to get to the bottom of his heart complaint. As time went by, he and his nurse-wife Beth became a constant source of help and support to Hazel over the problems she was experiencing with her parents. Perhaps it was fortunate that at this time Tony Wainwright's weekly violin lessons with me had been abandoned because they were rowdy affairs. These had been going on in the Music Room at Garth Cottage for the past few years and had resulted in Tony successfully passing some Associated Board of The Royal Schools of Music Examinations. However, the last exam. he had taken, grade 3, had cost him considerable time and effort, in particular the final lesson on the night before, which had resulted in pupil and teacher consuming half a bottle of whisky before retiring to the Cwm Inn nearby for some supper. The next morning as a nervous Dr Wainwright parked his car in the yard outside GarthCottage and got out clutching his violin case, he found another gentleman also alighting from a car, who muttered in passing: *'Lovely morning'*, to which Tony retorted: *'Glad you think so, I'm doing a violin exam'*. He had unwittingly met the Examiner!

XLVIII

I have no doubts at all about God working miracles and have long considered Brecon Cathedral Choir to be one of his miraculous creations. Indeed it has continually irked me that people who were in a position to realise this and to give a hand ministering to the young choristers, never made the slightest effort to do so. Christmas Eve 1988 found me, as usual, with them all at Ely Tower singing carols to the new Bishop and his wife. Afterwards, as was customary, they were rewarded with some tasty refreshments and all seemed to be going on happily. Unfortunately, one particularly thuggish choirboy seemed not to be satisfied with his lot and later was discovered by Mrs Bridges helping himself to more goodies from her 'fridge, whereupon a distinct chill descended upon the proceedings. Never again were the choristers invited to Ely tower on Christmas Eve although, to be fair, the bishop from then onwards, always gave me a £10 note to put into the Collecting Box as the choir lined up in the downstairs vestry for the Blessing of the Crib service. I had tried hard with this particular boy but he was a difficult lad, powerfully built and handy with his fists. Sometimes he used young Ben as a punchbag which was unfortunate as Ben was a slightly built, sensitive lad with a lovely voice. He lived up on a council estate with an older brother who was into leathers and motor bikes, and a caring mum who was a kindly lady, fond of life, who looked after Ben with loving care and devotion. Many was the time that I had to crawl around to her front door to grovel with apologies for Ben being beaten up by one of the more thuggish choirboys, usually after a game outside the Choir Room following a choir practice; always she would smile and say: '*I doubt if he will come back*', yet always he did. Ben adored animals and one summer befriended a young rook that he had found in the Cathedral grounds, which only had one wing and therefore could not fly. Strange to relate, he found a similar bird a year later and I often wondered if it was the same one; once again he took good care of it. Shortly after Christmas that year of 1988, I was asked by the Swansea Philharmonic Choir if I had a choirboy who could sing the part of Young Nicholas in their performance of Benjamin Britten's 'St Nicholas' at Swansea's Brangwyn Hall. So I took Ben down to Swansea where he sang with great aplomb 'God be glorified' seven times, on one note, which is the sum total of Young Nicholas's offering in this popular work. A photograph hangs on the wall of the Cathedral Choir Room to commemorate this event along with a second photograph that commemorates another performance given by Ben a few months later. Two London opera singers, Brendan Wheatley and Bridget Gill, had started an annual fortnight's summer course for aspiring opera singers, which was based at the most unlikely villages of Merthyr Cynog and Upper Chapel, a few miles north of Brecon, at the foot of the Eppynt Hills which rise to little over a thousand feet. Benjamin Britten's '*Albert Herring*' was the opera performed in the summer of 1989, and Ben was given a minor part, of a village boy in Norfolk where the opera was set. How he revelled in the rehearsals especially as he missed so much school, furthermore, the cast made such a fuss of him that he was blissfully happy. In the performances Ben shone and he thoroughly enjoyed the experience of being an opera singer but for me one opportunity regrettably was lost. This is the opera which immortalised my father as it is set in a Norfolk village where the local Vicar is a Mr Gedge. Brendan and Bridget had visions of my son, Nick, singing this part, after all he was my father's grandson, but this was not to be.

Nick had come a long way since taking up his Music Exhibition at Eton College back in 1982, ending up as 'Keeper of the Orchestra'. This had made him responsible for setting out, then collecting in, the music copies and dealing with other associated jobs, also it had put him among the College officials. As well as having viola lessons he now had singing lessons because his immediate ambition was to return to St John's College, Cambridge as a Choral Scholar, although he dearly wanted a gap year. So on his University Entry Form he had set out these aims:

1st Choice:	St John's College, Cambridge.	Choral Scholar, September 1987
2nd Choice:	St John's Colege, Cambridge.	Choral Scholar, September 1986
3rd Choice:	King's College, Cambridge.	Choral Scholar, September 1987
4th Choice:	King's College, Cambridge.	Choral Scholar, September 1986

Meanwhile he had taken the Associated Board grade 8 examinations and achieved good distinctions, actually obtaining more marks for his viola playing than for his singing, furthermore, he had won a place in the National Youth Orchestra of Wales. However, singing was his first love and he had begun to attend Ralph Allwood's holiday singing courses with a view to furthering his chances of winning a Choral Scholarship back at St John's College, Cambridge. It was at one of these courses that he had met Kate Robinson and a long, torturous and tumultuous courtship followed, lasting several years, before she finally ended up as Mrs Gedge (junior). Happily he had gone on to achieve suitable 'A; level grades and so was able to take up his first choice of becoming a Choral Scholar at St John's College in September 1987, and this allowed him the gap year that he had wanted so badly. What did he do with it? He spent much of it as a student-teacher back at his old choir school in Grange Road, Cambridge, working alongside dear Michael Peacock, the much admired Housemaster of his chorister days, earning some useful pocket money. Sometimes returning to work in your former school can end with disappointment; not so for Nick, however, because during this short stay of a few months at the school, he had been even more blissfully happy.

Through these singing courses Nick had gone on to make many more good friends among his fellow students, most of whom had been potential solo singers. So, surreptitiously, Nick had begun to transform the soloists scene at Cathedral Singers concerts in Brecon Cathedral, with experienced and confident amateur soloists being replaced by inexperienced and less confident future professional soloists. By Holy Saturday, 1988, this had brought to Brecon young William (Bill) Purefoy, a counter-tenor Choral Scholar at Magdalen College, Oxford, when the Cathedral Singers had given him his first professional solo engagement to start him on a career which eventually led a few years later to his numbering among the soloists at the Proms in the Royal Albert Hall. Now in 1989, there turned out to be quite a challenge because on Holy Saturday that year, it was the turn of J S Bach's 'St John Passion' to be sung and, for once, Rogers Covey Crump was not available to sing the vital Evangelist part, having been booked to sing at a prestigious concert in New York. (It had always been a policy of mine that if a regular soloist received a more lucrative offer elsewhere then he or she had to take it because I could not afford to pay full fees yet they had to make a living). To replace Rogers, however, was a nightmare because he is one of those singers who never, just never, sings an incorrect note, furthermore, having perfect pitch, he can maintain his Evangelist part no matter what is going on around him. This was brought home to me forcibly when not long before, the first time the Henry Russell Chamber Organ had been used at St Mary's Church, Brecon to accompany his recitatives, the instrument was so wildly out of tune at the start of the rehearsal that I had to send for an Organ Tuner to come over there and then to remedy the situation. While the Singers and Gwent Chamber orchestra were singing and playing away the poor tuner had to minister to the chamber organ, yet no matter what the cacophony of sound, Rogers had never sung a wrong note. His replacement for The St John Passion on Holy Saturday 1989, was another young Choral Scholar from Magdalen College, Oxford, Andrew Burden, son of my friend Lewis Burden, who used to sing with me in the choir at Southwark Cathedral. Even at that time, Andrew was an accomplished singer with a great future before him but unfortunately he had reckoned without the music desk on the chamber organ doing strange things to the continuo player's music copy. So at one crucial moment the organ continuo music disappeared from view whereupon the Organist guessed at the chord but guessed wrongly with the result that Andrew, through no fault of his own, was completely thrown off course. In a situation like this, Rogers would have raised his eyebrows and, with a wry smile, continued as if it was all part of the fun, but then this was Andrew's first performance of the taxing Evangelist part consequently he did not have Rogers' years of experience behind him and, not surprisingly, he got rattled.

One of the pitfalls in the St John Passion is the extraordinarily complex tenor aria at the centre of the work. Again the tenor was an untried Choral Scholar of Magdalen College, Oxford, with a lovely voice who has gone on to great musical heights; on this occasion, however, he was somewhat tentative which was not really surprising, yet the quality and potential shone through. It didn't help, therefore, when a few days later I received a letter from two members of the audience – a husband and wife who have since become great supporters of my work at Brecon, which demolished this performance of the

'*St John Passion*', reserving grudging praise only for the efforts of William Purefoy and my Nicholas, also for the chorus. The letter made no mention of soprano Eldrydd Cynan Jones, daughter of John and Mary Cynan Jones who had been good friends to Hazel and me for many years. I considered Eldrydd to be one of my 'finds' as she had come to the fore back in 1985, when my old friend from Royal Academy of Music days, the well-known soprano Sally Le Sage, had come to Brecon as soprano soloist in J S Bach's '*Mass in B minor*'. Unfortunately, I had not reckoned with Sally being such a purist so imagine my surprise when she refused to sing the second soprano aria, saying that it was pitched too low for her voice. At this point the rehearsal ground to a halt as I tried to persuade her to change her mind but to no avail, whereupon up from the chorus came Eldrydd offering to sing the aria which she then proceeded to do most beautifully. From that moment onwards she became the regular soprano soloist as her beautifully straight voice was ideal for the music of Bach and Handel. Indeed, one of my most treasured tape recordings is of her and my son Nicholas singing the duets in J S Bach's Cantata 140 '*Sleepers, wake!*' at one of the Cathedral Sunday Evensongs in Advent. Naturally, when the Cathedral Singers performed the '*Mass in B minor*' again in1988, there was no argument about her singing the soprano arias – both of them. The next year in the '*St John Passion*', to my mind she sang as beautifully as ever, but this time we did something new with the aria, '*I follow thee with gladness*'. I had in the senior school at Builth Wells High School, a girl who played flute in the National Youth Orchestra of Wales, Kate Studman, who was hoping to make a career in music. As she was also an exceedingly good recorder player, I dared her to play the elaborate solo flute obbligato part in this aria on her treble recorder and she took up the challenge. This she did exceedingly well (although the two hostile letter-writers complained that they couldn't hear her very well) but as the aria progressed, so I watched her face become more and more pale. Quite by chance, I had done Kate Studman an enormous favour. Later that year when she sat her 'A' level music examination at school, I went along to the exam room to collect a harmony and counterpoint paper to examine the questions. Only then did I see her at the far end of the room, playing on an imaginary recorder, and I wondered why. On looking closely at the Paper, I realised why, because there in the 2-part counterpoint question was the opening phrase of this very flute solo part that she had performed back on Holy Saturday, with the instruction: '*add the next few bars to the bass line in the style of J S Bach*'. Not surprisingly, therefore, Kate was thinking back to the performance of the '*St John Passion*' and trying to remember as many of Bach's actual notes as she could, so that she could write them down on her answer paper.

One of my regular gifted soloists was Douglas Jupp who always sang such minor roles in the Passions as Peter, Pontius Pilate, Servant and 'An Officer'!. A gentle, intriguing character, he earned his living as an Official Receiver and in his spare time was also Treasurer of the London Choral Society. He often expressed astonishment at how we managed to put on our performances so cheaply but truth to tell, several performers were friends of the family and therefore played or sang for what we could afford, consequently, while a Passion performance might cost Brecon Cathedral Singers around £4,000, it would cost his more professionally-run London Choral Society somewhere in the region of £18,000. On the other hand, people in London were prepared to pay much more in the way of admission prices for their music than people in Brecon, yet the Cathedral Singers constantly had to guard against pricing themselves out of the local music market. Unexpectedly there arose an occasion in the future when Douglas Jupp was able to give us the benefit of his professional knowhow. In the days when Jeff was running 'The Bull's Head', which eventually had become (and still is) the Choir 'local', I just could not get him to quote a price for refreshments during a weekend of concerts one July. Eventually Jeff took me to one side to explain that business lately had been so bad that he was awaiting the arrival of an Official Receiver. I immediately took the matter in hand and put him in touch with Douglas who was able to sort out the problem so that Jeff hung on to his pub while we hung on to our meals.

There was an unexpected sting in the tail of the 'St John Passion' performance back in 1989. As usual when this had concluded many of the visiting musicians went up to the Cathedral to help with the Easter Vigil either by singing in the Cathedral Choir or by playing trumpet or trombone in the C V Stanford *Te Deum in B flat*. The service which announced the arrival of Easter, usually had been a thrilling occasion, but in this year of 1989, there was an unexpected hiccup. A few weeks before I had received through the post a book of Holy Week music recently composed to modern texts by Richard Shepherd. I liked his music for the '*Exultet*' very much and asked the Dean if we could sing it at the Easter Vigil next Holy Saturday; after studying the text and its music the Dean agreed that we could. So towards the end of the service the choir sang Richard Shepherd's '*Exultet*' and with great aplomb, but no sooner had we finished than the Dean suddenly read out the text of the traditional '*Exultet*'. I was puzzled; why had he done this? I did not have long to wait to find out because as soon as the '*Te Deum*' had been sung and the Easter Blessing pronounced, as soon as the choir had processed out from the Cathedral into the Vestry and the Dean had said the Vestry Prayer, than he rounded on me and in front of all the assembled choristers demanded to know why we had sung the new version of the '*Exultet*'. A dreadful row followed and as the Dean and I moved closer together it was fortunate that the Minor Canon, dear Norman Jones, who understood the situation, stepped between us and said gently to me: '*David, go down to the Bull's Head.*' This I did, then after 'Last Orders', I with most of the assembled company moved back up Priory Hill to continue partying in The Refectory, next door to Garth Cottage, where during the weekend, some of the younger musicians slept on camp beds. I didn't waste much time puzzling over what had just happened because experience had taught me not to; true, since the 'Sons of the Clergy' service, the Dean had softened in his attitude towards the Cathedral Choir to the extent that the Choristers had won back their Haydn and Mozart Masses on such major Festivals as Christmas, Easter and Whitsun despite their long Benedictus movements, but what had happened that night had only been a return to past times, although I did feel aggrieved that the Dean had managed to forget that I **had** consulted him over the 'Exultet'. Anyway there was Easter Day to enjoy and despite the clocks being moved on an hour because of it being the last weekend in March, some of the Lay Clerks and their friends still had to be at the Cathedral by 8 o'clock in the morning to sing William Byrds' '*Mass to three voices*', after which there was always a bottle of Malt Whisky to enjoy. By 10.00 am the choir had to return to the Cathedral along with some of the orchestral players to rehearse the Mozart Mass for the 11.00 am Holy Eucharist. Always the Cathedral was packed for this service and extra chairs had to be brought in. It began with the choir and clergy processing round the Cathedral singing R. Vaughan Williams's splendid hymn '*Hail thee, Festival Day!*' and it thrilled me in particular to hear the congregation making such a valiant attempt at singing this. Lunch followed at The Bull's Head after which back at the Cathedral, Evensong was sung at 3.30 pm, often by a choir numbering some forty singers. With that number of voices crescendoing throughout the first page of Samuel Sebastian Wesley's anthem, '*Blessed be the God and Father of Our Lord Jesus Christ*', (without which no Easter at Brecon Cathedral is complete) a massive climax always was reached on the second page at the words, '*by the resurrection of Jesus Christ from the dead*' – at '*Christ*' Hazel inevitably brought into play 'full organ' for the first time, leaving me with an equally massive shiver running down my spine, so exciting was the sound. Easter Day ended with the customary orchestral concert at 8.00 pm, so timed as to allow people to attend chapel or church Evening services although fewer and fewer seemed to do this, while it also played havoc with the party arrangements because although an extension could be obtained on Good Friday an extension could not be obtained on Easter Day when already there was the earlier Sunday closing time to contend with. However, after this particular concert of Haydn's '*Symphony No. 24*' (in which the Minuet opens with the first six notes of the Welsh song, '*The Ash Grove*'), a Mozart Violin Concerto, also Schubert's popular fifth Symphony, which the two letter writers admitted was the only music that had given them 'the usual pleasure', there was a special party. This year, 1989, on March 12th, Nick had enjoyed his 21st birthday (a landmark in those days) while I had enjoyed my 50th birthday, but being a Sunday we had both been working, he at St John's College Chapel, Cambridge, me at Brecon Cathedral. So on this Easter Day, after the orchestral concert, we celebrated our special birthdays by having a great party in the Old Deanery and a great time was had by all.

Meanwhile, during some of the time when Nick had been at Eton College, daughter Harriet had been a few miles away at London University's Royal Holloway College, studying for a B.Mus. degree. This could not have been more convenient because it made it possible for Hazel and me to visit them both at the same time. So we got to know kindly Dr Lionel Pike who was in charge of the Chapel Music at the Royal Holloway, editing the music of Tudor composer Peter Phillips in his spare time. Whilst at the Royal Holloway College Harriet had helped Dr Pike to organise Chapel Choir tours in various parts of Europe and these inevitably had involved Russ the Bus from Swansea. In one of her first jobs after University, Harriet had worked for Novello & Co. Ltd., a long-established and well-known London firm of music publishers, and so had become involved in the professional music world. However, in the year between leaving school and going to university, Harriet had worked for a year in Paris and had made herself so accomplished in the French language that she could claim quite legitimately to be bilingual in French and English. In due course Harriet was prevailed upon to organise a Cathedral Singers tour in France which was scheduled for the summer of 1989, so we now had this to look forward to.

School term ended on Friday, July 21st and the plan was for the Cathedral Singers to leave Brecon that night. Harriet's organisation was immaculate: a pub extension organised so that the two buses could be loaded from 12.30 am in order that the time of departure could be 1.00 am at the latest. Furthermore, there was to be no mad scramble for the best seats as Harriet had attended to this and had issued everyone with a detailed itinerary which included the instruction: *'Please board the coach to which you have been allocated. The number of each coach will be displayed in the front windscreen'*. Such efficiency was unheard of in the annals of the Brecon Cathedral Singers. By 5.00 pm on Saturday, July 22nd, we had arrived at our hotel, *'Climat de Paris'* thirty minutes south of Paris. Much of the first night was spent on the top floor which had been allocated to us for rehearsals but we had such a riotous party there that by morning that privilege had been withdrawn; from then onwards all our rehearsing had to be done on the lawn outside the hotel where we sang to the accompaniment of jet aeroplanes coming in to land at D'Orley Airport nearby at regular intervals. The next day, being a Sunday, Harriet had arranged for the Cathedral Singers to sing at the 6.00 pm Mass in the Sacre Coeur, in the famous Montmartre district but it took longer than anticipated to get there and to park the coaches. Hurriedly, we made our way into the church, asked for somewhere to change and were ushered into a large room. Such was our hurry that it hadn't dawned on me how everyone was changing in the same place and suddenly I found myself standing alongside a topless soprano! The service was hilarious. A few years before, Vatican II had brought about a complete re-think about traditional Roman Catholic Liturgy with the result that the Ordinary of the Mass (Kyrie - Gloria -Credo - Sanctus - Benedictus - Agnus Dei) was no longer sung to plainsong or traditional music settings, instead a Cantor led the singing of the popular Taize-like chants with the congregation joining in as best it could. For this Mass the Cathedral Singers had been presented with very detailed Service Sheets and were doing their best to join in the congregational singing at the correct moments, therefore imagine my consternation – I was having enough trouble following the French instructions, when a voice from out of the crowd of tourists that was still noisily milling around the building, suddenly whispered in my right ear: '*Are you the lot from Brecon?*' When I nodded assent he continued: '*We saw your bus outside; we're from Llanelli*', and with that said he melted away back into the crowd. Fortunately for the Cathedral Singers, the music at the service wasn't all congregational as they were allowed to contribute motets by William Byrd, Mozart, C V Stanford and Vaughan Williams, along with the Gloria from Palestrina's Miss Papae Marcelli. So the week was packed with goodies: champagne tasting, a visit to Reims, Choral Evensong at St George's Church, Paris when all of S S Wesley's anthem, *Ascribe unto the Lord*', was sung, also trips to Fontainbleau and Versailles, not forgetting the one hour concert at magical Chartres Cathedral. Harriet led us into this Cathedral clutching her thick file of papers and letters under an arm but was most disconcerted to find that although we had been allocated an hour's rehearsal, someone had organised a Mass during this hour and she could do nothing about it. The Cathedral Singers were amused to find the Cathedral plastered with posters advertising them as:

'Brecon Cathedral Singers
(de Londres)

which presumably had come about because all of Harriet's correspondence had been sent from London. Later in the week, at a concert in St Michael's Church, Paris which is the British Embassy Church, 'Russ the Bus' was delighted to hear again the Mendelssohn '*Christus*' extracts, including his beloved '*There shall a star from Jacob come forth*', which by now had become known as 'Russ's Anthem'. However, the highlight that day had occurred earlier when a reception had been given to the Cathedral Singers by John Gray, British Ambassador to the OECD. Here we had learned that the Organisation for Economic Co-operation and Development includes all Western Countries plus the USA, Japan, Canada, Australia and New Zealand and that it had been established in 1961. The object of the OECD apparently is to identify economic and social problems facing its members and then to formulate policies for dealing with them. The Organisation works through some two hundred committees and working groups which meet two or three times a year and are supported by a large secretariat of highly qualifed people. John Gray's job was to keep the OECD in touch with a wide range of British government departments in London, so what was his connection with the Cathedral Singers? The answer was quite simple: he and his wife not only had a 'bolt-hole' in Llanddew, on the outskirts of Brecon, but also their accountant, Dave Millar, numbered among the Cathedral Singers basses. Be that as it may, the Reception gave the Singers a chance to experience a lavish and more glamorous way of life, also to meet a kindly man who had been much admired for his courage in adversity when he had been British Ambassador in the war-torn Lebanon.

Highest of the many delights was the second week-end which had begun with the Cathedral Singers arriving at Paris's fabulous Notre Dame Cathedral to sing at the 6.30 pm Mass on the Saturday evening. So excited had they been at this prospect that they were devastated to discover that they were actually advertised to sing the Sunday 11.00 am Mass. However, Harriet was equal to the problem; armed with her great file of letters she demanded to see someone in authority and within minutes had proved that the Cathedral Singers indeed had been booked to sing at the 6.30 pm Mass that night thereby leaving Notre Dame choirless on the Sunday morning. The Saturday evening Mass was amazing. There must have been around two thousand people in the congregation along with another two thousand or so people wandering around the Cathedral, making no attempt to curb their noise. As at Sacre Coeur, the liturgy was led by someone whom I now called irreverently the 'cheerleader', who used a microphone throughout to make himself heard above the general hubbub, and sometimes who led the congregation in the singing of Taize-like chants. Nevertheless, the Cathedral Singers were allowed to sing the Kyrie, Sanctus, Benedictus and Agnus Dei from the Palestrina Mass, also at the start of the service they had sung the hymn 'Love Divine, all loves excelling', to the famous Welsh tune 'Blaenwern', and at the conclusion they had sung with great enthusiasm, two verses of the famous hymn, 'Cwm Rhondda'. Then to their astonishment, the hymn tune pealed out again loudly, from the Great Organ at the West End of the Cathedral, exactly as it had been sung, even though whoever was playing the organ, had heard it only twice, whereupon he proceeded to make the melody the basis of a magnificently extemporised toccata as only a French organist could. If I had known that this was coming I would have arranged to record it. The finale occurred on the next morning when the Cathedral Singers sang the mid-day Mass at Saint Sulpice where C M Widor (of Toccato fame) had numbered among the past Organists. At 11.30 am the Cathedral Singers and a string quartet comprising Heledd Hall and Rhiannon Davies (violins), Michelle Moody (viola) and Harriet ('cello) had given a prelude-recital of music by J S Bach, William Byrd, W A Mozart and Henry Purcell, before contributing to the Mass – which again was led by a 'cheerleader', Palestrina's 'Missa Papae Marcelli'. So had ended a most memorable trip as on the next day, after a very early breakfast, eighty-eight tired but happy Cathedral Singers and their supporters left Paris, making for Dunkirk and the ferry to Ramsgate, then driving through Kent to London, the M4, the A449, the A40 and so to Brecon and some sleep!

XLIX

Normally, after such a scintillating trip as the one to Paris, the last thing I felt like doing was returning to school in September. However, this September was different because Princess Anne was coming to open officially the new High School that Builth Wells had won out of the 1985 By-Election and by chance this turned out to be the Princess's first official engagement since the much publicised break-up of her marriage to Captain Mark Phillips. Actually, my school musicians had been already ensconced in their new quarters for some considerable time, as the music rooms had been among the first to be brought into use. After the slum accommodation of the past this now was luxury indeed: a large teaching room with huge windows looking out onto the lush green playing fields, a sizeable store room leading off this, also two instrumental teaching rooms next door, each equipped with a new upright piano. In the main teaching room, however, was a lovely old German grand piano that used to belong to George Bradley, the Ironmonger-Organist of St Mary's Church, Builth Wells; his daughter, Anne, and son, John, who both sang in the Cathedral Singers, had kindly asked me to provide a home for it in my new empire and who was I to turn down such a generous request? The first time my senior Musicians had marched into my new Music Room they had straightway marched out on the other side into the Store Room saying: 'This will do.' 'What do you mean?' I had replied immediately, somewhat put out, whereupon they explained to me that they intended turning the Store Room into a Common room for the Senior Musicians – a Sixth Form Snug. What a good idea! So, after a visit to a carpet remnants sale in Builth Church Hall, the Store Room was carpeted, equipped with an electric kettle, filled with some easy chairs and a sofa, also a few table lamps were purchased from a junk shop and installed to provide soft lighting, then, last of all, Hazel and I donated the little, old Kelvinator 'fridge that we had purchased back in 1962, when we had first been married – after twenty-seven years it still fulfilled its function admirably.

From that moment onwards, the 'Back Room' as it became known, became a second home to the senior school musicians and it was a privilege that they treasured and defended for the remainder of their time and my time at the School. Indeed, the first musicians that had come into those rooms turned out to be the most hardworking set of pupils that I had ever had the good fortune to work with. Presumably they treasured the new facilities in a way that later arrivals could not, because up until now they had experienced the appalling working conditions that had been their (and my) lot in the past, consequently, they appreciated greatly their change of fortune, as did most of their parents. So in the years ahead these enterprising pupils went on to provide singers and instrumentalists who with some help from local members of the Cathedral Singers, went on to perform Christmas Music from Handel's

'Messiah', part one of Haydn's 'Creation', Vivaldi's 'Gloria', and, best of all, a concert performance of Purcell's 'Dido and Aeneas'; furthermore, in their breaks, lunch hours, also after school, they played vast quantities of Chamber Music. Before long, at the end of one summer term, the music department could boast of seven pupils who had passed the grade 8 examination which was no mean feat for a country school where a goodly number of pupils came from small hill farms. In all this they were aided by an excellent team of peripatetic teachers which included Susan Pryce who taught the flute and clarinet, Clare Walker then Amanda Corderey who were bassoon players, violinists Ruth Lowther then Michelle Moody, also 'cellist Alan Davies. Next onto the scene came North Powys Piano Technician, Martin Backhouse, who first had displayed his expertise by transforming a wreck of a Rogers piano from the old school into an instrument of great beauty in the new school. Not long afterwards he told me of a Primary School Headmaster who was so short of space in his school that he was prepared to swop a grand piano for an upright piano. Was I interested? You bet I was as the grand piano turned out to be an old Steinway – the Rolls Royce of pianos, which had a lovely action and an even lovelier tone. I hastily parted with my commonplace Fazer upright in exchange, knowing that I could replace it in one of the Practice Rooms with the rebuilt Rogers upright.

On Monday, September 25th, 1989, a helicopter deposited Princess Anne on Builth Wells High School Playing Fields. As she crossed the school courtyard, accompanied by her entourage of other distinguished guests, she was serenaded by the school band, with music copies clothes-pegged to the music-stands to prevent them blowing away in the breeze, while the sun shone to create a perfect autumnal day. In the space of a few minutes the Princess saw all that the new school had to offer: the fine stonework outside capped by a superlative Welsh slate roof for which an extra £30,000 had been added to the £2¼ million budget; the equally fine brickwork inside which, sensibly, had not been covered with plaster and therefore could not be rendered unsightly by dirty fingers; then there were the numerous brick containers built into the interior walls and filled with many varieties of plants to soften the school interior, which had been adopted by the school musicians and therefore now were looked after by them. I hope that this incredibly beautiful building impressed Princess Anne more than the two physics pupils who asked her if she would like to bang a hammer against some equipment wired to some gauges which measured the speed of sound, because she simply replied: 'Not particularly', then walked off. Nevertheless, the day was a memorable one and as she left the school the Princess received a standing ovation. For me, now, only one irritation still remained at Builth Wells High School and that was simply the fact that despite running the Music Department, organising the schedules of the peripatetic instrumental teachers and making sure that their pupils attended lessons, doing all the 'O' and 'A' level teaching, also preparing all the concerts, I was still paid only a basic wage whereas all the other Heads of Music Departments at High Schools in

South Powys were being paid Scale 1 or Scale 2 allowances which gave them annually an extra £1,000 or £2,000 Responsibility Allowance. Not for some considerable time was this situation remedied.

In this deliriously happy and positive climate not only did instrumental music flourish but also so much else in the school, which proved the point that in giving young people decent working conditions there is no end to what they could achieve. When the table of 'A' level results in British schools appeared in the years 1991 and 1992, there in the first two hundred and fifty were the pupils of Builth Wells High School. Two of these pupils, the Deakin brothers, William, who played the bassoon and Tom, who played the clarinet, both of whom achieved the much coveted grade 8 with distinction, also achieved distinction in another way. They succeeded in having a photograph of me published in a pop magazine called 'New Musical Express' because one of the 'in' pop groups at that time was called 'Wedding Present' and the lead guitar player was another David Gedge, a much younger one, from Birmingham. Alongside my picture was written:

> 'Spare a thought for poor old DAVID GEDGE. No not Housewives'-Choice type corporate moptop David Gedge – we're talking about Welsh music teacher and choir master at Brecon Cathedral David Gedge. It must be a bitch. All those indie-wank choirboys shouting 'Sing us a few bars of 'Why Are You Being So Reasonable Now', Dave!' and then being expected to deposit a huge wad from your RCA advance in the collection plate! Let's hope this brief taste of NTFZ fame makes like a little easier for Mr Gedge. Thanks to Will and Tom for sending in the snap....'

It was at around this time that news had filtered through telling how the Builth Wells High School building had been given a prestigious award by the Civic Trust. This was no mean achievement as these awards are not given lightly, indeed the school had to be visited twice by a panel of judges which included a person of high professional standing in the architectural world. Not surprisingly, Powys County Council had taken justifiable pride in the fact that its Architectural department had been rewarded for creating a school which could sit happily in a row of late Victorian houses in a street that was sited in an important conservation area. To this day, a plaque on a wall in the entry hall proudly commemorates this award.

However, all was not rosy. On Saturday March 10th, 1990, the school had been rocked by a devastating event. Among my third-year pupils was a talented clarinettist, Lizzy Davies, who was a quiet, unassuming, hard working pupil. She had a younger sister, Joanne, who positively bubbled, and who on St David's Day in the previous week had made her mark on the School Eisteddfod. They lived on a farm that could only be reached by crossing the Heart of Wales railway line that went through some of Wales' loveliest countryside, from Llanelli through Llandeilo, Llandovery and Llandrindod Wells to Shrewsbury, that carried just eight trains daily – four each way. On that Saturday Joanne was being driven home to the farm in a Land Rover and as she opened the gate that crossed the railway line she was struck by a train and killed. How she hadn't been aware of the approaching train remains a mystery. Maybe its noise was masked by the noise of the Land Rover engine or maybe she was just being her usual carefree self, whistling or singing away, completely oblivious to what was going on around her. Who knows? She was just twelve years old. A week later I played the organ for her funeral service in St Mary's Church, Builth Wells; afterwards everyone went to the lovely, remote churchyard at nearby Maesmynis, where her body was laid to rest. It was all very poignant and distressing. Four years later, Joanne's parents still had not recovered from her death, therefore much of the responsibility for running the farm had been taken on by Lizzy, yet in the term that she took her 'A' level examinations she still had the strength of character to take and pass her grade 8 clarinet exam. Now happily married, she works as a Vet in Brecon.

Meanwhile tragedy had struck again almost two years to the day, on March 3rd 1992, when Steven Woollaston was killed in a car crash on the notoriously bad, bendy section of road between Builth Wells and Llandrindod Wells. Steven was just fifteen years old at the time and was a popular member of both the school and local Youth Club. His funeral service was a very different affair from that of Joanne. Being on a Monday – a school day, made possible the attendance of pupils and allowed some to take part in the service. As a result the School Band was invited to play two songs, one of which was associated with Steven's beloved Liverpool Football Club. So my 'A' level pupils and I sat down to make the necessary arrangements of the relevant music and write out parts for the available instruments. The Liverpool song, 'You'll Never Walk Alone' was no problem but the second song, 'I only called to say 'I love you' was a different matter. Someone got hold of a copy, brought it into school and we orchestrated it, but when the School Musicians played what we had written, nobody recognised it! Obviously, this was one of those songs where what was performed bore little resemblance to what was printed in the copy which so often is the case with pop and light music. So we went back to the 'drawing board', found someone who knew the song well, re-wrote our music to their satisfaction and eventually everyone was happy. The Funeral Service was a highly charged, emotional affair and the school musicians did themselves proud keeping their composure despite the intensity of the occasion. So the Band played along with the organ in a packed St Mary's Church for the opening hymn, 'The Lord's my shepherd', which was sung to the ever popular tune 'Crimond', along with the alternative Welsh National Anthem, 'Cwm Rhondda' – 'Bread of Heaven' , which ended the service; in the middle the musicians played the two songs whereupon there was scarcely a dry eye in the building. Again it was all very poignant and distressing, leaving Steven now to be rembered by a public seat placed at the side of the Groe path that runs between the High School and the gently flowing River Wye, which is used daily by countless residents of Builth Wells and pupils of the school.

Two tragic deaths of school pupils within two years was bad enough but worse was to follow. On the morning of Friday, October 1st, 1993, as the boys, girls and staff arrived at school as normal, there were hushed murmurings about a pupil having been murdered on the previous evening. This seemed just too far fetched yet by the end of the Morning Assembly everyone knew the truth and there was much sobbing. As this sad day progressed, out tumbled the following details. A young former pupil, who by chance, had recently been working with his father doing some maintenance jobs on Builth Wells High School, and who lived nearby in Garth, had spent the previous day roaming the countryside around Llanwrtyd Wells armed with a gun, determined to shoot himself. When eventually he realised he could not do this, he decided to search for someone else whom he could despatch from this world to the next. So he proceeded to knock at the doors of houses in the area in search of a victim, but nobody answered, either because the occupants were not at home or, as it later transpired, because at one of these houses the elderly inhabitant was deaf and therefore failed to hear him. Eventually he had knocked on the door of Tan y Graig, one of a row of three houses, a mile outside Llanwrtyd Wells on the Abergwesyn road, whereupon the door was opened by a seventeen year old girl who had just returned home from Builth Wells on the school bus. Straightway he had propelled her back into the house, closed the front door, forced her to lie down on the floor, placed a cushion over her head, put his gun to the cushion, then had shot her dead. It had all taken a few minutes yet what a terrifying few minutes for the girl who by chance and bad luck, had become his unwilling victim. Emma Page was her name, a delightful girl who was one of nature's innocents, happy and carefree, vivacious and attractive, so intelligent and bright that only recently she had been offered a place at Oxford University. In her early days at Builth Wells, anxious to seize every opportunity available at the High School, she had even had a few trumpet lessons but laughingly she and I soon had both realised that this was not for her. She and her mother, Anna, had lived together at Tan y Graig and now, left alone, her mother was utterly devastated. Llanwrtyd Wells is a small and very tightly-knit community with an active church and a compassionate Vicar, Brian Bessant, who trained as an artist and is now a Canon of Brecon Cathedral, therefore he was equal to the tragic situation; so too was Builth Wells High School and its Headmaster, Ian Brown. Both the Church and the School took in Anna to give her comfort and attempt to divert her mind away from the terrible tragedy, involving her in their activities and giving her new interests. In particular the Form 6 pupils – Emma's contemporaries, were marvellous; they rallied round Anna, sharing with her their memories of Emma, laughing and joking about what she got up to at school, so much so that as the day of Emma's funeral came nearer, I began to worry. Music meant so much to Anna that she wanted the senior musicians to play before and during the service; how would they cope emotionally? I need not have worried as they were marvellous. While they wept and grieved with their fellow pupils, when their turn came to play their music they became true professionals and performed beautifully for Emma. The report of the funeral published in the Brecon and Radnor Express, said it all:

> *'A most poignant and moving funeral service was held recently for Emma Louise Page, daughter of Anna Page, who was so tragically murdered at her home on September 30th, aged only seventeen.*
>
> *The tiny church of St David's Llanwrtyd, within sight of Emma's home at Tan y Graig was packed to capacity, and many more stood in the rain in the churchyard, as relatives, friends, fellow students and staff gathered to pay their last respects to Emma who had just entered the Upper Sixth at Builth Wells High School.*
>
> *The service, which was relayed to those unable to get into the church, was conducted by the Rev. Brian Bessant, vicar of Llanwrtyd. Many of Emma's friends and relatives took part. Four of Emma's fellow A level students, Philip John, Ben Cook, Darren Hamer and Iain Hunter and two of her cousins, Rhiannon and Caronwen Davies read some of her favourite poetry: Mr Bernard Jones (Head of English BWHS) read the last piece of creative work that Emma had written, a poem entitled 'Wales 1993': Bible passages were read by Mrs Jayne Taylor (former French teacher) and Mrs Margaret Lewis (Emma's English teacher for the last six years). A moving tribute to Emma was compiled and read by Mr J Bale, (Deputy Head BWHS) and in his address Rev. Bessant spoke of the considerable contribution Emma had made to the community of Llanwrtyd Wells during her short life.*
>
> *A selection of music was beautifully played and sung by the school orchestra and friends, led by Mr David Gedge (Head of Music BWHS). A group of flautists played a delightful rendering of 'Bugeilio'r Gwenith Gwyn'.*

At the request of Anna Page bunches of garden flowers were placed in the church, and contributions were made to the Blue Cross Animal Relief Fund, one of Emma's favourite charities.'.

Shortly afterwards, the following message was published in the Brecon and Radnor Express:

> *'Anna Page would like to thank her family, friends and the people of Llanwrtyd Wells for their love and support after the tragic loss of her beloved daughter Emma; all the people who sent such touching and heartfelt messages of sympathy, flowers and contributions to the Blue Cross; the Headmaster, Staff and Pupils of Builth High School for the time and care they took to make the Funeral Service so beautiful; Reverend Bessant, family Doctors, Wyn Price and the Dyfed Powys Police for their compassion and sensitivity.'*

For the third time in as many years, it was all very poignant and distressing.

L

One of the joys of teaching at the High School was the daily car journey to Builth Wells in the morning and the return journey back to Brecon after school. Most often I used the back road down the lovely, green Honddu Valley up onto the bare Eppynt Mountain, then down 'Tumble Down Dick', the 1 in 4 hill on the other side, past Llanddewi'r Cwm Church into Builth Wells. When snow lay thickly on the ground, as it sometimes did during the winters of my earlier years in Brecon, then I travelled on the main A470 road, some of which runs alongside the River Wye. I wrote-off one car on this road simply because I kept close to the left side, as I always did on the narrow mountain road. On this occasion, one bitterly cold morning, I struck a patch of ice which had not been touched by either salt or morning sun, and found myself heading towards a minibus carrying children to Llyswen Primary School; this I managed to avoid only by hitting a hedge, whereupon over went the car. When a policeman arrived from Builth Wells to sort out the problem, he approached the wrecked car singing: 'With cat-like tread, upon our way we steal', because his daughter had been involved in my recent school production of Gilbert and Sullivan's 'Pirates of Penzance', which includes this chorus. More spectacular was the occasion when I was hurrying back to Brecon for a funeral, travelling on the back road which seemingly had been cleared of snow and ice. Approaching the village of Lower Chapel and keeping well to the left as usual, I touched more hidden ice and immediately found myself driving through a hedge on the right, rolling down a hill to finish upside down, six feet from the River Honddu. At the time I was listening to a Mozart Flute Concerto on the radio, so I waited until the movement had finished before hauling myself out of the wreck and walking back up the hill through what soon became known as 'Gedge's Gap', then down the road into Lower Chapel, where I telephoned the Minor Canon, Norman Jones, who immediately offered to drive to my rescue. Unfortunately, minutes later, I spotted a local lady walking towards the telephone box I had just left, and, feeling embarrassed at what I had done, I hid. As the local walked by, so Norman drove by in his car, but not until he reached Upper Chapel did he realise that he had driven past me; back he came to find me and drive me to the funeral.

Sometimes on this back road, I used to give a lift to a dear old lady who worked at a country house named Castell Madoc; in return she used to bring me up-to-date with the latest scandal. Further along, in more recent times, on the other side of Upper Chapel, I often picked up dear Pat Hern who lived with her husband, Lloyd, in a cottage next to the turning for Garth and Llangammarch Wells, who taught English at Builth Wells High School. A few yards further on stood another cottage, which was shrouded by trees and surrounded by a high fence; Pat was convinced that this was a 'safe house', possibly used by people on the run from such trouble spots as Northern Ireland. What convinced her of this was the scarcity of any visitors there, also the fact that if ever a car was parked there it was always covered over, with the number plate rendered invisible. Early in 1992, it is conceivable that Salman Rushdie holed up here for six months, certainly Pat thought so. Salman Rushdie had recently published his 'Satanic Verses' which had resulted in the Iranian Moslem leaders ordering his execution for blasphemy against their faith, and a million dollar bounty had been placed on his head. Having come to Britain for protection it was rumoured that Salman Rushdie and his wife were hiding in a remote Welsh cottage in the Brecon Beacons with not even local police aware of his presence. A Western Mail reporter claimed that this cottage was between Brecon and Builth Wells and that it had a round-the-clock police guard supplied by New Scotland Yard. Certainly sightings of the writer in the pub at Pwllgloyw were claimed, also his wife later admitted to having been shopping in Brecon. However, whereas the reporter claimed that the cottage was situated in a lane that ended by the River Honddu at Lower Chapel, Pat was convinced that it was situated next door to her cottage. One day she had approached a small coloured child playing outside the cottage only for the child to rush back inside; furthermore, Salman Rushdie's wife later mentioned the thousands of sheep and the unsuspecting soldiers on manoeuvres on the bleak Army training ranges. This sounds much more like the Mynydd Eppynt just beyond Upper Chapel, where both the SAS and regular soldiers regularly trained, notably for the Falklands War.

As well as giving a lift to Pat Hern I also gave a lift for a year or so to Tracy James, a girl who had moved from Erwood to Brecon but who wanted to continue studying at Builth Wells High School. One morning a tyre was punctured on top of the Eppynt and I had to do a hasty repair job. Pat had alighted to give me some help but only when we slowly began to jack-up the car did we realise that Tracy was still sitting down inside the car, whereupon we suggested to her that it might make matters easier if she too got out!

Back in the good old days, Breconshire had adopted a very positive attitude to the state of its roads in the deepest winter and kept forty-seven special vehicles to combat the dreaded snow. However, when the new county of Powys came into being Brecknock was forced to share its snow-ploughs with Radnor and Montgomery with the result that the roads in Brecknock were never again so safe. The effect of this snow on Builth Wells High School also was interesting. Invariably, the first signs of heavy snow would result in the prompt arrival of the school buses to take the country children home as some of them had long distances to walk when they left the bus. As for the staff, Headmasters Mr Davies and Mr Toy invariably sent home those teachers who travelled to and from school by car; Ian Brown, on the other hand, held the view that all members of staff should live near to their place of employment, therefore, no matter how grim the weather, he usually refused to let any teacher leave until the end of the school day. Hazel once telephoned him during a snowstorm to ask him why I was not on the way home when the A.A. had advised motorists not to travel unless it was absolutely necessary. When he began his customary speech about members of staff living near to their school she interrupted him, told him that Mr Davies and Mr Toy had a much more sensible attitude to the problem, then promptly rang off! However, Ian Brown's attitude changed as soon as I started giving lifts to Tracy James. At the first signs of heavy snow I was allowed to drive off back to Brecon because the safety of pupils was of paramount importance. Needless to say, the staff took a dim view of this 'official' attitude as it appeared to put the safety of pupils above the safety of staff.

No matter what the weather, one of the joys of driving to and from school was being out of reach of a telephone, also it allowed me time to think and to plan. I needed this because one problem with my life was the enormous extent of my work: full-time teaching, part-time Cathedral Organist with choir practices after school on Monday, Wednesday and Friday, Tuesday night devoted to rehearsing the Cathedral Singers (Choral Society), Wednesday night to rehearsing the Gwent Chamber Orchestra at Ebbw Vale, Thursday night to rehearsing the Cathedral Lay Clerks, Friday evening to Choral Evensong after which many of the Lay Clerks had supper together at the Bulls Head, an important social event which led to the formation of The Friday Night Club. Furthermore, sometimes on Monday night, after I had rehearsed the Cathedral Choristers in the Choir Room, I would drive down to Swansea to work with Archdeaconry of Gower choristers who now met regularly to rehearse for the Diocesan Choral Festival early in May, for the Ordination Service late in June, also for the Carol Service early in December, all events which were of great value to these singers. With such a heavy workload – all the evening work on Monday, Tuesday and Wednesday done voluntarily and without payment, so much administrative work concerning concerts at Brecon had to be taken for granted with the necessary work done by clockwork from one year to the next. So there was a fixed schedule of orchestral and choral concerts, always over the Easter weekend and the second complete weekend in July, which allowed the many orchestral players and singers to know when their services were needed without any doubt over the date. Why, therefore, was it necessary for there to be problems over the Easter weekend of 1990? For once I had actually met with the Dean, the Minor Canon, Norman Jones, and the Verger, Tom Toft, to sort out in advance the Easter arrangements. So I discovered that the Upper Room of the Refectory had been hired out permanently; this had always been useful for people wishing to escape from the riotous party after the concerts and retire early to bed. In addition, the main room in the Refectory had been let out to the Guild of Spinners and Weavers on Holy Saturday afternoon, forgetting the fact that the Cathedral Singers and the Gwent Chamber Orchestra always had tea there between their rehearsal and their concert. At this meeting it had also been decided that the girls in the orchestra and Cathedral Singers who required accommodation, should sleep downstairs in the Old Deanery.

However, shortly before the Easter Weekend, I received a curt note from the Dean:

> 'Tom tells me that you are still under a misapprehension re. the availability of the Deanery Centre for overnight stays. I thought I had made it clear when we talked last week that the Management Committee has decided that it is not possible – indeed I mentioned this decision as long ago as last July. This obviously affects arrangements not only for Easter but for visiting choirs in July and August.'

How such a misunderstanding arose I know not, other than the fact that it was girls only who had been assigned to the Old Deanery, and the fact that the Upper Room of the Refectory now was no longer available, makes me think that we had actually been trying to segregate the sexes of the sleepers! As it turned out, everyone had to sleep downstairs in the Refectory, both male and female, from Good Friday until Easter Monday, moving everything out on the Saturday for the Guild of Spinners and Weavers, which actually was most inconvenient. Nevertheless, the musicians did not allow any of this to spoil their enjoyment of the weekend as one participant sent me a card soon afterwards saying:

> 'Thank you so much for a wonderful Easter weekend, it was more than a pleasure to be part of the celebrations.'

Now that I was in my twenty-fifth year as Organist of Brecon Cathedral I had begun to think hard about the future. I had passed my fiftieth birthday and was slaving away trying to create something that I hoped was musically good at the Cathedral yet what chance was there that this would continue after I had retired. With my teaching job at Builth Wells High School now full-time there was no guarantee that this would be available for my successor, and with the Organist's salary at the Cathedral still the lowest in England and Wales, something had to be done. So I made two attempts to obtain the position of Director of Music at Christ College, the oldest public school in Wales, which was situated in Llanfaes, the other side of Brecon. My first attempt failed not surprisingly, because I refused to put Christ College first in the order of priorities; I reasoned that in the future the combination of these two jobs would produce candidates of the highest calibre so why should Christ College not make a preparatory sacrifice. My second attempt failed because my good friend Jonathan Leonard applied for the job so I lost interest while he secured the appointment and soon arrived in Brecon to transform the musical scene at Christ College, also to join in some of our musical activities at the Cathedral.

It was at around this time that I did make one small contribution to securing funds for my eventual successor as Cathedral Organist. Many, many years ago, when Ungoed Jacob had been Dean, the Chapter (Canons) had refused all the pay rises that I had requested, whereupon the Cathedral Singers had offered to make up the difference in the form of a small monthly salary. However, now that I was being paid as a full-time teacher, I persuaded the Cathedral Singers' Treasurer, Dr Harry Gann, to put my Cathedral Singers pay into a separate account and let it accumulate, so that when I retired it would be possible to pay my successor a salary of some sort to augment his Cathedral Organist pittance! The Cathedral Singers also were making other plans for the future because in the next year, 1991, they celebrated twenty-five years of bringing great choral music to Brecon. Three concerts with orchestral accompaniment were planned instead of the usual two, furthermore, the committee agreed to take a financial plunge with the summer concert, by laying out £2,500 on three 'star' soloists for a performance of Elgar's 'Dream of Gerontius'. Our friend, Hugh Thomas, had kindly agreed to do the negotiating and he set about trying to persuade the mezzo-soprano Alfreda Hodgson, tenor Arthur Davies, and bass Gwynne Howell to join us at fees that we could afford! He had some advantage in that he had worked with these three singers on previous occasions, therefore he and they knew each other.

Also at this time, Hazel received some recognition for the fact that over the past twenty-three years or so, she had hosted the Associated Board of the Royal Schools of Music instrumental examinations in Garth Cottage. This had involved looking after the visiting Examiner, attending to the needs of the candidates, who often were quite nervous about what they were about to do, also ensuring that our piano was in tune and in good order. So, at last, she was appointed Honorary Local Representative for the ABRSM, and her 'perk' was attending an annual dinner in a 'posh' London hotel with all expenses paid, which was just reward for overseeing annually three examination sessions, which could last up to three days each, in our own house.

Meanwhile, the Cathedral Choir was preparing for its next jaunt. This one was very dear to the heart of Sub Organist Kelvin Redford who having studied at Trinity College, Dublin and then having taught in a Dublin preparatory school for a year where his main claim to fame had been playing the organ at a service which had been conducted entirely in Irish, now wanted to share that fair and fascinating city with the Brecon choristers. While a student, Kelvin had befriended the University Organ Scholar, John Paterson, who later was ordained a priest in the Anglican Church of Ireland. Now he had become Dean of Christ Church Cathedral, Dublin, therefore Kelvin organised a long weekend of choral services for Brecon Cathedral Choir early in August.

Christ Church is a very lovely Cathedral, heavily restored by the eminent architect George Edmund Street, towards the end of the nineteenth century. He had been very daring. For example, he had retained the north side of the Early English nave which leans outward by a few inches, but had built a copy on the south side which stands upright. Most daring had been his decision to demolish the mediaeval chancel and replace it according to its older, Norman foundations, leaving a smaller Quire and apsidal Chancel which, however, matches exactly the area of the ancient crypt beneath. The Chancel, Transepts and Nave he had unified by creating a magnificent stone vault and by covering the floor with richly decorated, coloured tiles. It was a truly magical building with a fine acoustic and it boasted a superb, modern, mechanical-action organ built by the eminent Irish organ builder Kenneth Jones, of nearby Bray. Kelvin was in paradise playing on this machine and when after our final Evensong a photograph was taken of the choir, he could not be prised away from playing one voluntary after another. So a photograph taken of him seated at the organ earlier in the weekend was duly cut out and pasted onto the choir photograph, showing him and the organ above the choir, suspended from a tree, outside the Cathedral. For me, what was especially magical was only visible outside; an ornate bridge stretching across the main road, which linked the ancient Cathedral to what turned out to be the Synod Hall, built in a matching style obviously to more designs of George Edmund Street. This was a reminder of the more affluent Victorian days in the history of the Anglican Church in Ireland, when young C V Stanford roamed the streets of Dublin, attending 'Paddy's Opera' on Sunday afternoons, as Choral Evensong was called at nearby St Patrick's Cathedral. Sadly, however, the Synod Hall was now surplus to requirements and was up for sale. Just around another corner stood an elegant statue of Molly Malone who apparently really did exist, selling her cockles and mussels in Dublin's fair city. Nearby, and in a shameful state of neglect, was the Music Hall in Fishamble Street, where Handel's immortal 'Messiah' had first been performed. Near to these two important landmarks was Kinlay House where the choristers and lay clerks stayed; an extraordinary place, rather like a youth hostel but with residents coming and going all through the night, many of them students connected with the theatre. A motley crew, we fitted in well with them as the house seemed to be completely mad; indeed, one morning as we all descended from our rooms down the stairs to the dining hall for breakfast, we noticed that a fine series of old photographs showing old Dublin, had been unscrewed from the wall and stolen! The Lay Clerks had a fine time in any number of Dublin bars making the acquaintance of real Irish Guiness and Murphy's; Paul Jackson became so enamoured of the former stout that he drank sixty-nine pints of it! furthermore, while in O'Shea Merchant's Quay, he put money into a collecting box only to discover that he had contributed towards Sinn Fein funds!! One evening we all settled into a rowdy bar near to the Cathedral, to sing Folk Songs, led by my son, Nick, and his friend, counter tenor William Purefoy, who in addition to his singing also played the trumpet in a jazz group named 'The Honkin Hepcats'. William put his trumpet mouthpiece into a chair leg and managed to produce noises reminiscent of a strangled trumpet with which to lead the singing. All went well until we sang the 'Londonderry Air' whereupon a deathly hush descended on the premises; the use of the word 'Derry' was alright in Republican Dublin but what we had not realised was that 'Londonderry' apparently marked us out as Protestant

Northern Ireland sympathisers. Only that day members of the Republican Sinn Fein had been littering Dublin hostelries with leaflets in support of the 'Birmingam 6' who were on trial for bombing a pub in Birmingham, therefore not surprisingly, the Publican was not a happy man!

Throughout our time in Dublin the Dean of Christ Church was so kind and supportive. Not only did he pay for our Sunday lunches but also on the Sunday evening he took us on a tour of the lovely countryside around Dublin and its bay, even purchasing chips for the youngsters. Interestingly, visitors to the Cathedral out of service time had to pay an admission charge of 50p and in charging this the Dean and Chapter were among the first to make such a controversial innovation, reasoning that this was necessary if the Cathedral was to be run properly yet remain financially solvent. Kelvin and I chatted often with the Dean that week about such matters and in the course of our discussions we learned how, in the winter, he kept his Cathedral warm throughout the week by never letting the temperature drop beyond a certain level, yet heating costs were no more than if the building was heated only at the weekends when the sudden influx of heat would create down draughts that were not pleasant, this being what was done at Brecon Cathedral. So we persuaded the Dean to write down all the facts and figures to prove this point which, incidentally, had been a point that Hazel's father had been making over and over again but which had always been ignored. When we arrived back in Brecon we gave these figures to the Dean, Huw Jones, but, strangely, there was no change in the heating policy, indeed, when Kelvin and I enquired about the whereabouts of these figures it appeared that they had gone missing. However, that was in the future; for now, when the young Cathedral choristers arrived back in Brecon they embarked upon a new venture: picking litter at the Brecon Jazz Festival, something they have continued doing to this day, thereby earning valuable income for the Cathedral Choir Tour Fund, in addition to providing a valuable social service which has been greatly appreciated.

LI

The year 1991 began with a special service in the Cathedral on the Eve of the Epiphany, January 5th. This marked the start of the 'Decade of Evangelism', the idea being that the final years of the twentieth century should have a special significance to members of the Anglican Church throughout the world. So, during the service, a representative from each church in the diocese received a candle which was to be lit and displayed in that particular church during the season of Epiphany. The next day, I received a card from the Bishop, Dewi Bridges:

> 'Dear David,
>
> Please accept my sincere thanks and be so kind as to convey them to all concerned for the service on Saturday. The response was most gratifying in spite of the dreadful weather ………'

Later that month, with the grim Gulf War gathering momentum, the BBC decided to televise a service from a church with military connections. So, at very short notice, a service was broadcast from the Cathedral at 9.30, on the morning of Sunday, January 27th, with the Cathedral Choir and Cathedral Singers providing both choir and congregation. The Church Times had this to say about the Service:

> 'Prayers for the Gulf (BBC1 Sunday) is the now renamed This is the day and came from Brecon Cathedral. The Dean conducted the service from the chapel of the South Wales Borderers. In a beautifully constructed address he noted: 'Far from glorifying war, the chapel is a reminder of the cost and tragedy of war.'

As the Cathedral Choir had sung a psalm, three hymns and a short anthem, while the Cathedral Singers had led the congregational singing, the BBC Producer Iwan Russell Jones, who had been in charge of the programme, wrote to me afterwards:

> 'Dear David,
>
> Just a quick note to thank you and your wife for your contributions to the broadcast from the Cathedral. I'm extremely grateful for all your musical input and ideas; they helped to make an excellent service.
>
> Please pass on my thanks to the choir – both of them.'

Then came the customary 'promise' to which I had become used but which never seemed to materialise:

> 'I hope we'll have an opportunity of working together again sometime in the near future.'

Meanwhile, these world-wide events were to a certain extent overshadowed by an issue which had been troubling the Anglican Church for some considerable time: the ordination of women. Some Anglicans argued that unity with the Roman Catholic Church was a much more important issue; they were of the opinion that this would be set back many hundreds of years if women were ordained. However, the supporters of the movement for the ordination of women thought otherwise and pushed on relentlessly with their campaign. When the congregations of the parishes associated with the Cathedral, namely Battle, Llanddew, St Mary's and the Cathedral, were asked to vote on this issue, they did so in this way:

Church	YES: for the ordination of women	YES: but not yet	NO	Undecided
Battle	8	1	5	0
Llanddew	16	0	2	3
St Mary's	53	3	5	1
Cathedral	51	6	19	3
TOTAL	128	10	31	7

Furthermore, these voting patterns were echoed throughout the diocese of Swansea and Brecon. While 58 clergy voted in favour of the ordination of women, 38 voted against; similarly, while 1397 of the laity voted 'for', only 604 voted 'against'. Later at the Diocesan Conference, Bishop Dewi Bridges along with 54 of the clergy voted for the ordination of women while 42 clergy voted against. Similarly, 82 of the laity attending this conference favoured the ordination of women while 46 voted against. Indeed there were similar opinions expressed in the dioceses of Bangor, St Asaph and St Davids, but not in the dioceses of Llandaff and Monmouth where both the bishops along with a majority of the clergy opposed the ordination of women. So the scene was set for a fascinating conflict. Interestingly, only one member of the Chapter of Brecon Cathedral ever found the time to discuss this vitally important issue with the Cathedral Lay Clerks and that was Canon Eric Wastell, Vicar of St Gabriel's, Swansea, a noted Anglo-Catholic church in the diocese. Joining the choirmen at one of their Friday night suppers in the Bull's Head he talked knowledgeably and enthusiastically against the ordination of women and was most persuasive.

Easter that year was special; it marked Hazel's and my twenty-fifth year in Brecon and as usual, during the weekend some lovely music was performed. On Good Friday, New Zealand pianist Georgina Zellan Smith, whom Hazel had admired when a student at the Royal Academy of Music, played Beethoven's magical fourth piano concerto. On Holy Saturday, but sadly, still in St Mary's Church, the Cathedral Singers with the Gwent Chamber Orchestra, performed J S Bach's monumental 'Mass in B minor'. On the evening of Easter Day, back in the Cathedral, as well as Haydn's Symphony no. 51 in Bflat and Mozart's 'Jupiter' Symphony no. 41 in C, there was an opportunity to hear Mozart's concerto for two pianos, a rarity indeed – a second Bechstein grand piano being borrowed from Wyeside, the Arts Centre in Builth Wells. The weekend ended on Bank Holiday Monday with Georgina Zellan Smith returning to give a recital of piano music by Beethoven and Chopin.

By now Hazel's mum and dad had been living with us at Garth Cottage for three years, deteriorating in health all the time, dad frequently suffering from depression, mum sinking further and further into the abyss of the dreaded Altzheimer's Disease. Fortunately, Powys County Health Authority were very supportive, supplying Carers to help Hazel look after them, furthermore, every six weeks Hazel's Mum and Dad were taken into care at a local hospital for two weeks, thereby giving her a much needed rest. Fortunately, such a routine respite had coincided with the Easter weekend which had made our life easier while we coped with the ten choral services and four concerts. On the Wednesday afternoon after Easter, Hazel and I visited Mum and Dad at the Mid Wales Hospital in Talgarth. Just as we were about to leave, Dad told Hazel that he had not felt his left foot for a few days. Hazel mentioned this to a nurse and in due course Dad was taken to Nevill Hall Hospital at Abergavenny where his foot and ankle were examined and gangrene diagnosed. It now became a question of how much of the leg would have to be amputated. Hazel visited Dad often at Nevill Hall Hospital but on Saturday, Sub Organist Kelvin Redford asked us out to supper to celebrate our twenty-five years at Brecon, so on that day she reluctantly curtailed her evening visit. At 7.25 pm Kelvin collected us from Garth Cottage in his car to drive us to the Wellington Hotel for the celebratory meal. Strangely, as we were driving along The Struet I spotted our friends, Treorchy Male Choir Conductor John Cynan Jones and his wife Mary walking along the pavement, then further along, were also tenor Lay Clerk Mel White and his wife Iris, but although this seemed odd, I thought no more about it. However, when Kelvin led us into the Ballroom at the Wellington Hotel we found ourselves surrounded by more than a hundred of our friends and other people closely connected with our lives who had gathered together to celebrate our twenty-five years at Brecon. This had been masterminded by Kelvin who had taken the best part of a year in making the preparations without so much as a whisper reaching Hazel and me. A most memorable evening followed during which there were speeches and I was presented with a CD player and a tape deck; afterwards many of us talked and drank until late into the night. It was magical.

A few days later, dad's left leg was amputated and that was the beginning of the end for him. The evening afterwards, a kindly member of the hospital's auxiliary staff breezed into his room as he lay quietly in his bed with Hazel sitting alongside him. 'Hello John', she said cheerfully, ' had your leg off have you.' Poor dad! He belonged to that generation where only close friends and relatives called you by your Christian name otherwise it was always 'Mr Davies'; even I had never called him John. Nor did he want to be reminded about his missing leg. Soon he was back in Brecon, at the War Memorial Hospital, where Hazel and I visited him often; sadly he seemed disinterested in life. One evening when he was lying in his bed, we took mum to see him but she spent most of the time trying to pull down the sheet to see where his leg had been. She had long given up thinking of him as her husband as she now lived in a world of her own; indeed not long before, back at Garth Cottage, when dad had climbed into her bed to be close to her for comfort, she had started shouting at him that he was not her husband. After a life of adoration during which he had worshipped her every move, this was a bitter pill to swallow; no wonder his spirit was broken. Dad lingered on during the remainder of the month but as his eighty-first birthday approached, April 28th, he lapsed into unconsciousness. On that day, a Sunday, as the 11.00 am Choral Eucharist was drawing to a close, I was called away to the hospital to sit by his bedside as the end seemed near, but he lingered on. The Dean, having discovered what was going on, called in to say prayers; when he recited one in Welsh, dad's eyelids flickered which reminded us that not only was Welsh his first language but also that the last sense to leave a dying man was that of hearing. I returned to the Cathedral for Choral Evensong when by chance the anthem sung was:

'If we believe that Jesus died and rose again, e'en so them also which sleep in Jesus will God bring with him. Therefore, comfort one another with these words.'

words, which a nineteenth century Organist of St Paul's Cathedral, John Goss, had set to music so beautifully for the funeral of the great Duke of Wellington. Afterwards I rejoined Hazel at the hospital; she had been there all day, always in the company of close friends Mary Cole or Beth Wainwright. Late in the evening dad seemed uncomfortable, then he started groaning, obviously in pain, although all the time he was unconscious. Hazel called for a doctor and fortunately it was friendly Sandy Cavenagh who made him comfortable again. As midnight passed Hazel, who throughout her life had always been close to her father, sensed that the end was near. Quietly she whispered into his ear and the struggle gently subsided as he passed from this world to the next. Hazel and I went home from the hospital to sit in our kitchen and listen to the 'Angel's Farewell' from Edward Elgar's 'Dream of Gerontius', music that many years before Hazel had played on the Cathedral Organ at the funeral of dear Dean Gwynno James who had appointed me to Brecon; it just seemed right and proper. Dad's funeral took place in his beloved St Mary's Church, Kidwelly on Tuesday, May 9th. First, however, his coffin was taken to Bridgend House to stand in the sitting room whilst his family had tea in the living room. In due course the coffin was moved to the Lady Chapel in St Mary's Church and after a short service there, Hazel played a J S Bach Chorale Predule on the lovely old 1762 Thomas Warne organ, much to the disgust of the Verger who had never before heard music at such a service. The actual funeral, like that of his father, grandpa Davies, was said according to the 1662 Prayer Book with no music – except for three lovely J S Bach Chorale Preludes. Before the service I played 'Liebster Jesu' – 'Dearest Jesus, we are here'; in the middle of the service Hazel herself played the choral prelude which J S Bach had composed as he lay dying: 'Before thy throne herewith I stand'. When the service came to an end, Kelvin Redford played 'God's time is best', - the opening Sinfonia from J S Bach's Funeral Cantata 106. Afterwards the coffin was taken to the crematorium at Narberth whereupon his ashes were brought back to Kidwelly and laid to rest in the family grave close to the church porch. It was a beautiful day and everything went according to plan, the arrangements being meticulously organised by local Brecon Undertaker, Colin Griffiths, who was a tower of strength.

There was little time to reflect on all that had happened over the past few weeks because before the month was out, we were helping to entertain the Friends of Cathedral Music who had decided to hold their Spring Gathering at Brecon Cathedral during the weekend of May 24th – 26th. They came to Brecon from Avon, Buckinghamshire, Cleveland, the Cotswolds, Derbyshire, Herefordshire, Yorkshire, Aberystwyth, Birmingham, Bristol, London, even Glasgow and, more miraculously, Ohio in the USA, all wanting to experience what went on at Brecon Cathedral. Some stayed in Brecon, some stayed nearby, slightly more than one hundred of them, finding accommodation wherever they could, be it in a hotel, a guest house, at a B & B, in a private house,or in a caravan site. Forty arrived on Friday in time for Choral Evensong, then joined the Lay Clerks for supper at The Bull's Head which is where many friendships began. Saturday morning found them at an organ recital in Christ College, but by 12 noon they were back in the Cathedral, their numbers now swollen to eighty, listening to a lecture-recital on the Bevington Chamber Organ, its connection with the Kilvert Diaries fascinating them. Afterwards almost everyone walked down to St Mary's Church to delight in music on the Henry Russell Chamber Organ. They learned about how Charles Wesley, the hymn-writer, had married a Breconshire girl by whom he produced two eminently musical sons, some of whose music was played on this elegant instrument. After lunch they all returned to the Cathedral for a talk by me on my twenty-five years here as Cathedral Organist. After this there was an unexpected bonus when some singers from Brecknock's twin town in Germany, Blaubeuren, called in at the Cathedral and sang to them, whereupon the Canon Chancellor, David Walker, gave a talk on the history of the Cathedral. Tea in the Deanery Centre followed with some FCM members apprehensive, because in the year before this had been a disaster despite the venue being a Birmingham Hotel. However, fears were soon dispelled as the visitors could not cope with the feast provided by the Brecon ladies, with the result that they all returned to the Cathedral for Evensong with their hunger and thirst well and truly satisfied. There they were delighted to find the Bishop in attendance because some of them had the quaint idea that he had travelled all the way from Swansea as he could not possibly live in Brecon. The Bishop, in turn, discovered a quaint FCM custom: when he went to the Great North Door to bid the members 'Good-Bye' at the conclusion of the service, not one person stirred until the organ voluntary had ended! Later that evening the Cathedral Choir and Gwent Chamber Ensemble gave a concert: J S Bach Cantatas 140 and 159, G F Handel Organ Concerto op. 4 no. 4, also W

A Mozart Piano Concerto in A, K414. Supper followed back in the Deanery Centre when the assembled company was delighted and honoured to be joined by the Lord Lieutenant and Mrs Bourdillon, both of whom had also been present at the concert. On Sunday morning some hundred members of FCM attended Choral Eucharist, singing lustily not only all the hymns but also the Merbecke Gloria and Creed, enjoying a specially appropriate sermon by Canon Walker. Some guests now had to start their journeys homewards, others stayed for lunch at the Bull's Head and returned to the Cathedral for Evensong after which enough food remained at the Deanery Centre for them to have some tea before they too set off for home. A few lingered on, some to join a few of the Lay Clerks in supper at The Old Ford where they ate while they chatted happily as they watched the night draw on over the lovely Brecon Beacons. A perfect end to a fascinating weekend which found Hazel and me introduced to lovely Dr Rosemary Smith of St Mary's Cathedral, Glasgow, who from that day to this, every year, has sent us a beautifully hand-produced Christmas Card. Her letters are equally beautifully written; the one which arrived soon after the weekend included the observation:

> 'Among other things which will remain memorable are the food and Kelvin's ties.'

Many more letters arrived from various parts of the country from satisfied members of the FCM. One from Kirkby Stephen, Cumbria, said:

> 'I have been to scores of meetings but Brecon is no. 1 in the Charts (I believe that is the expression!) everything was splendid.'

Another from Dartford in Kent, said:

> 'It was very good to meet you at last – at the FCM at Brecon a few weeks back. Congratulations on your excellent choir and many thanks for the warm hospitality. (Incidentally a member of your choir named Trevor kindly chatted with me for a long time in the pub. Real courtesy which I appreciated. Please thank him.)'

Someone from High Wycome commented on the 'warm welcome, lovely meals, fine music, an entertaining talk, and the privilege of worship in lovely surroundings, and a liturgy which is relevant and does not jar,' this last point being a reference to the Church in Wales' much admired 1984 Prayer Book. One bonus from the week-end was meeting again Jamie Milford who thirty years before had numbered among my Head Choristers at St Mary the Virgin, Primrose Hill. His letter pinpointed one of the strengths of Brecon hospitality. He and a friend had been accommodated by Mary and Brian Cole who, it seems, had treated them 'like family'. Tony Harvey, one of the leading lights in the FCM, was fulsome in his praise for 'a wonderful weekend' and continued:

'We are all most grateful for such a warm welcome and a fascinating and interesting programme.'

However, his letter to Kelvin Redford was ecstatic:

'It was indeed a fantastic weekend thoroughly enjoyed by everyone both musically and socially. It will be a long time before we have such a delightful event. The ingredients were just right – even the weather was kind.'

It was not long after this that our dear friend Canon David Rutter died. Always so helpful to us, he had become Harriet's adopted Godfather after the death of Chris Tanner. Never had he forgotten Hazel's and my wedding anniversary and punctually on August 18th, a card would arrive at Garth Cottage all the way from The Precentory at Lincoln Cathedral. How sad for a life that had begun in such happiness and full of such hope should have ended in such sorrow and such controversy. David's problem was that loving the Book of Common Prayer as he did, he arrived at Lincoln Cathedral just when new Anglican Liturgies were being introduced. Unwilling to compromise in such matters, believing this to represent a lowering of the high standards which cathedrals existed to uphold, also being convinced that forsaking the Book of Common Prayer could lead only to disaster for the Church of England, he preached one of the most memorable sermons ever heard in Lincoln Cathedral. He said simply:

'Dean Dunlop, the man of taste, rejected this service. Dean Peck, the man of prayer, rejected this service'. It has remained for the present Dean to introduce it. In the name of the Father, and of the Son, and of the Holy Ghost. Amen.'

Not surprisingly, this led to considerable conflict with the Dean and the rest of the Chapter, which was further exacerbated when he helped the newly formed Lincoln branch of the Prayer Book Society not only by offering a room in the cathedral precincts for the inaugural meeting, but furthermore by ultimately becoming its Chairman. From then on life in the Cathedral Close at Lincoln had deteriorated, helped along by other controversies which were not of his making. This had resulted in Danny Danziger devoting the entire contents of a scandalous book, to nothing but Lincoln Cathedral and the people who worked in it, when in fact the intention originally had been to produce a book about the city of Lincoln and its people. Sadly by this time David Rutter was almost totally blind from diabetes, spending his time 'praying, thinking and brooding'. When the then Dean, The Very Revd. Brandon Jackson, tried to persuade him to retire, telling him that he was a sick man and not capable of carrying out the duties of Precentor in consequence of which the cathedral was suffering, he, in reply, predicted that he would die in office. And so it was. In what turned out to be his final sermon, he startled the cathedral congregation by reading out the contents of his will which included a request that there be no funeral nor memorial service for him in Lincoln Cathedral. David Rutter died on the evening of Sunday, June 16th, but perhaps it was only right and proper that a Solemn Eucharist was held in Lincoln Cathedral in thanksgiving for his life and ministry on Sunday, July 7th. The service followed the text of the Book of Common Prayer, the Mass was sung to C V Stanford in C and F, the motet was Elgar's 'Ave Verum Corpus Natum', and the hymns were 'When all thy mercies, O my God', 'When morning gilds the skies', and 'O Thou who camest from above'. Two psalms were sung, 101, to a chant by Philip Marshall, Organist of Lincoln Cathedral, and, as the choir and clergy departed at the conclusion of the service, 150, sung to Talbot's magnificent chant, as is the custom at York Minster. It was all as David wanted and he had chosen the music, yet what a sad ending to his twenty-five year ministry at Lincoln Cathedral.

Doubtless David would have approved of the Cathedral Singers' 25th Anniversary Summer Concert in Brecon Cathedral on the following Saturday. Opening with C. Hubert Parry's 'Blest Pair of Sirens' which during rehearsal had become known as 'Blest Pair of Nylons' or simply as 'Blest Pair', the main work that followed was 'The Dream of Gerontius'. Being the second time the Cathedral Singers and Gwent Chamber Orchestra had performed this masterpiece of Sir Edward Elgar, everyone was better prepared for its complexities. For once the Singers had spent a lot of money on top-class soloists; Hugh Thomas had acted as the 'broker' for this and at a cost of £2,500, had finally engaged mezzo-soprano Alfreda Hodgson, tenor Maldwyn Davies and bass Alan Opie. Meanwhile, my son Nick had lined up an impressive array of his singing friends to make up a fine Semi-Chorus. At the performance, not only were the soloists and semi-chorus superb, but also the Singers and orchestra 'rose splendidly to the occasion', as was stated in The Brecon and Radnor Express on one of its rare visits to a Cathedral concert. Sometime afterwards, Mike Smith, Managing Director of Novello & Co. Ltd., publishers of much of Elgar's music, wrote:

> 'Listening to Gerontius in the Cathedral was a very moving experience – a contrast to the first night of the Proms a week later despite the presence of Willard White et al..'

Alfred Hodgson wrote in a letter to Hugh Thomas:

> 'I thought the performance had a special quality and the day was filled with warmth and friendliness.'

which was all the more poignant when it is remembered that this lovely singer succumbed to cancer soon afterwards.

LII

While teaching at Builth Wells High School, I had always tried to involve the senior school musicians in Cathedral Singers' activities. 1991, therefore, seemed a good year for Annabelle Mills to carry out a survey on the Cathedral Singers in this their twenty-fifth year, for part of an Advanced Level Music Examination Project. It was interesting to discover that Singers originated from such places as:

> Alton-Staffordshire; Birmingham (3); Blackpool; Brecon (7); Bristol; Builth Wells (2); Bury, Lancashire; Caerphilly; Cardiff; Cheshire; Cray (2); Crugybar; Cwmdu, Powys; Dowlais; 'Eastern England'; Erwood; Essex (3); Germany (2); Glasbury-on-Wye (2); Gloucester; Gwent (2); Hampshire; Harrow; Heol Senni-near Sennybridge; Herefordshire; Hertfordshire; Holland; 'Home Counties'; Huddersfield; Kidwelly (2); Leicestershire; Llanelli (2); London (10); Maidstone; Merthyr Tydfil; 'the Midlands'; Monmouth; Montgomeryshire-Radnorshire Border; Newport-Gwent; Nottingham; Portadown, Northern Ireland; Port Talbot; Pontardawe (2); Radnorshire (2); Rhondda (2); Wiltshire and Yorkshire.

So thirty-seven Singers were Welsh, thirty-four were English, while the remaining four came from Germany, Holland and Northern Ireland. I was particularly interested in the fact that only seven singers came from Brecon and sixteen came from the old county of Breconshire. Even more interesting were the choirs to which Cathedral Singers had belonged in the past:

> Aberhonddu & District Male Voice Choir – Brecon (3); Alexandra Choral Society; Amersham & Chesham Bois Choral Society; Arnold Foster Choir – London; Arthur Martin's Boys Choir – Northern Ireland; Bach Choir – London; Baroque Singers – Mid Glamorgan; Berkhampstead Choral Society; Bishops Stortford Choral Society; Brianne Singers – Dyfed (2); Builth Wells Choral Society (2); Builth Wells Male Voice Choir; Bury Choral Society-Lancashire; Cairo Choral Society-Egypt; Cantorion-Llandrindod Wells (2); Cheadle Hulme Singers; Christchurch Choir-New Zealand; Cradoc Singers; Cray Male Voice Choir; Crowthorne Choral Society; Dee & Clwyd Choir; Delhi Christian Chorus; Dowlais United Choir; Dunvant Male Choir; Durban Symphonic Chorus-South Africa; Durham Singers; Hatfield Chorus; Hawes Operatic Society (2); Hay Mixed Choir; Hazel Grove Male Voice Choir; Henlow Singers; Karlsruhe Oratorio Choir; Kidderminster Choral Society; Lanchester Choral Society; Lanchester Male Voice Choir; Leicester Cantata Choir; Lerwick Choral Society; Malvern Choral

Society; Margaret Roach Singers; Missenden Singers; North Yorkshire Chorus; Padarn Singers; Plough Chapel Augmented Choir – Brecon (5); Portadown Male Voice Choir – Northern Ireland; Princes Risborough Choral Society; RAF Choirs at Bassingbourne and Nicosia; Rhayader Male Voice Choir; Richmond Operatic Society; Riedlingen Choir-Germany; Royal Choral Society-London; RSCM Nicholson Singers; St Andrew's Singers-Enfield (2); St David's Convent School & Christ College Choral Society –Brecon; St Ola Singers-Shetlands; Sine Nomine-Brecon; Stanley Civic Choral Society; Talgarth Male Voice Choir; Thurrock Choral Society-Essex; Treorchy and District Choral Society; Watford Choral Society; Welsh National Opera Chorus (2); Wensleydale Choral Society (2); Winslow Opera Group; Wokingham Choral Society; also Ystradgynlais Male Voice Choir.

Twenty-four Cathedral Singers sang in church choirs at some time including:

Arundel RC Cathedral; Belmont Abbey-RC.; Brecon Cathedral (4); St David's Church, Brecon; St Mary's Church, Brecon (5); St Mary's Church, Builth Wells; Glasbury Church; St Mary's Church, High Wycome; St Mary's Church, Holmbury; St George's Cathedral, Jerusalem; a church in Karlsruhe – Germany; Holy Trinity Church, Llandrindod Wells; Mauritius Cathedral; St Mark's Church, Mombasa; a church in Riedlingen – Germany; also Worcester Cathedral.

Twelve Cathedral Singers sang in College Choirs including:

Aberystwyth – University College Choral Society & Madrigal Singers;
Cambridge University Music Society; The Royal Naval College in Greenwich;
Goldsmith's College – London University; also the London Student Chorale.

Four ladies sang at some time in Women's Institute choirs and two more ladies sang in Townswomen's Guild Choirs. Membership of choirs at some of the more exotic places was due sometimes to War Service or to National Service. Bass, Jim Morris, for example, never tired of telling people how when he was a Sergeant Major in World War II, he had sung in a performance of Handel's 'Messiah' in Cairo Cathedral, conducted by Clifford Harker, a future Organist of Bristol Cathedral. He was particularly proud of the fact that the audience was so numerous that it stretched out from the Cathedral and down to the banks of the River Nile.

If Cathedral Singers had originated from many varied places so they travelled to many more varied places, indeed one of the joys of being a Cathedral Singer was the regular trips abroad. Now as the schools' summer term ground to an end, they prepared to visit Brittany. First, however, for me at Builth Wells High School there was the Royal Welsh Show on the other side of the River Wye at Llanelwedd. There some pupils were involved in picking litter in the early hours of the morning which raised a few thousand pounds for school funds, while others made music on the Powys County Council stand to entertain the general public in the afternoon and earn a few 'brownie points' with the Education Authority. As this went on almost up to the day of departure, I was left ill prepared for the Cathedral Singers trip to the extent that I was preparing for the bus to Plymouth Dockyard knowing neither where the party was performing nor what music it was singing! An hour before departure time I loaded some music into four boxes, put these on the bus, then away we went, down the M5 to Plymouth and so on to Roscof on the other side of the English Channel, with me still oblivious as to where and what we were singing. No sooner had we set foot in Brittany than we were whisked away to a reception in Gouesnou, the small town which was twinned with Brecon. Afterwards, a short journey took us to the outskirts of Brest, where we moved into a Youth Hostel close to the sea. What a place! My idea of a Youth Hostel had always been so different to this institution: a beautiful, palatial modern building set in spacious grounds; gorgeous food and plenty of it, indeed when the main course was wheeled in at the principal meals the assembled company would break into applause; house wine in an unending supply; table tennis and pool tables plus a football game; no wonder the six cathedral choirboys who had come along with us were soon as 'happy as sandboys', as were the Cathedral Singers. 150 yards away stood an extraordinarily hospitable café/bar where always each visitor was greeted warmly with a personal handshake. 100 yards further on was a sandy beach where various members of the party sunbathed or swam, drank or fished; one boy caught a crab which wandered off while he busied himself trying to catch another. Even rehearsals seemed leisurely as the Singers quickly picked up from where they had left off two years before in Paris.

The first concert was given in Gouesnou and here the Singers learned something about the French: beginning to sing at 8.30 pm before a respectable though not very numerous audience, by 9.00 pm they were singing to some two hundred and fifty people. They also learned that at the end of a concert, when loud applause turned to rhythmic, insistent clapping, more was required. Next evening found the Singers some thirty miles north of Gouesnou, at Guisseny on the Britanny coast. There first they sang at a Mass conducted in Breton, then they shared a concert with a specialist Breton choir; as this was followed by a reception, they did not arrive back at the Youth Hostel until 2.30 am which caused someone to remark: 'as bad as an Eisteddfod'. On Sunday morning they sang Mass at the church in Gouesnou and during the sermon learned that no-one in the diocese had offered himself for ordination to the priesthood that year, seemingly because celibacy was a stumbling block for young clergy in the Roman Catholic Church. As Gouesnou church had been heavily restored after damage sustained during severe fighting around Brest in the Second World War, Singers discovered in the churchyard some British Commonwealth war graves still immaculately maintained after more than forty-five years. So, too, at Lannilis, around twenty miles north of Brest, where another concert was given a few days later; here also could be seen more immaculate British Commonwealth graves. Inevitably these concerts all adopted the same unplanned ending because with the Bretons sharing not only some of their language with the Welsh language but also the tune of their National Anthem with that of Wales, so each event concluded with some Welsh hymns along with 'Maen Hen Wlad fy Nhadau'. The final concert was given in the main Roman Catholic Church in Brest which was a vast warehouse-like structure with such resonance that there was a glorious ten-second echo. However, before this took place there was a strange 'happening' back at the Youth Hostel. One evening two German girls had been refused admission because they had arrived too late to sign-in. Later that night, while everyone was sleeping, someone broke into Hazel's and my bedroom through the open window from the roof, muttered something unintelligible in a foreign language, then disappeared into the hostel. Naturally we raised the alarm and eventually the fellow was accosted and questioned by Wynn Davies the language-teacher bass singer. So we discovered that the intruder had taken pity on the two German students and had broken into the Youth Hostel hoping to find some spare beds where they could rest their weary heads but to no avail as the caretaker unceremoniously evicted him from the building. At around this time one other crisis was narrowly averted: in the dining room, on the last day of the tour, the Cathedral Singers discovered that they had drunk dry the Youth Hostel of its House Wine!

However, Brecon beckoned and when back home the Singers soon started work on the music for the third and final concert of their twenty-fifth anniversary year. Having underestimated the complexities of Mozart's great 'Mass in C minor' – I was left with a lot of work to do at the Tuesday evening rehearsals and many a harsh word was uttered in desperation. First, however, there was a Cathedral Singers Twenty-Fifth Anniversary Dinner at The Castle of Brecon Hotel on Friday, November 1st, which was a great occasion as so many dear friends had made the effort to be there. During the proceedings I was presented with a beautiful tapestry created by soprano Annie Watkins, on which she had woven my name along with a picture of the Cathedral, the flag of every country that the Singers had visited along with the date of the visit, also a list of works performed during this special year, 1991. On the next night came the concert itself with its extraordinary programme. Specially for counter-tenor William Purefoy there was J S Bach's magical solo Cantata 170. Specially for pianist Chris Knott, now the husband of Frances one of the 'cellists in the Gwent Chamber Orchestra, there was Benjamin Britten's unique Canticle 'Abraham and Isaac', sung by Rogers Covey Crump who by now had achieved an international reputation as a tenor. Afterwards the two singers joined sopranos Eldrydd Cynan Jones and Suzanne Flowers, also my son (bass) Nick, and the Cathedral Singers in the performance of Mozart's stunning 'Mass in C minor' that ended the first half of the programme. The second half began with Rogers singing Benjamin Britten's haunting 'Serenade' for tenor, horn and strings, a favourite of mine. The demanding solo horn part was magically played by Angus West, Principal Horn of the Welsh National Opera Orchestra; not long before he had married violinist Jane Tunley who, when a pupil at Ebbw Vale Comprehensive School, had helped start the Gwent Chamber Orchestra. The final work was Samuel Sebastian Wesley's anthem 'Ascribe unto the Lord', which I had long wanted to perform in its full orchestral version. S S Wesley had always numbered among my idols because during the middle years of the nineteenth century he had campaigned tirelessly to improve the working conditions of cathedral musicians at a time when they had been treated like second-class servants of the Established Church. I doubt if he would ever have heard a performance like this one, with a full orchestra and a large chorus that had been properly rehearsed. It was a rare treat and a wonderful ending to a special weekend.

Meanwhile, some more interesting Cathedral Singers statistics emerged from Annabelle Mills' 'A' Level project in the latest concert programme. For example, as far as the Cathedral Singers were concerned, thirty-seven of them liked to sing the music of J S Bach most of all, while eighteen preferred that of Mozart, with only seven opting for Handel and six for William Byrd; surprisingly, just two Singers enjoyed singing Claudio Monteverdi's or Edward Elgar's music most of all. As for listening to music, twenty-eight revelled in that of Mozart while sixteen preferred that of J S Bach, six championed Beethoven's music with only four preferring that of Elgar, Haydn or Mendelssohn and three opted for the music of Brahms or Schubert. When it came to listing actual musical works 'sung and enjoyed most of all', here were some surprises because while twelve Singers listed J S Bach's 'St Matthew Passion' or Monteverdi's 'Vespers', eleven listed Elgar's 'Dream of Gerontius' or Bach's 'Mass in B minor'. Only nine Singers liked singing Mozart's 'Requiem' best while eight preferred Handel's 'Dettingen Te Deum'. Surprisingly, only five Singers enjoyed singing Handel's 'Messiah' most of all which was as few as had enjoyed Anton Bruckner's fascinating 'Mass in D minor'. The same number of Cathedral Singers admitted liking everything that had been sung while three opted for the two Palestrina Masses – 'Aeterna Christi Munera' and 'Papae Marcelli', also three for the unaccompanied motets by C V Stanford. At the bottom of this list came the Brahms 'Requiem' which attracted the devotion of only two Singers. Music 'sung but least enjoyed' produced from sixteen Singers the philosophical observation that while they often at first disliked the music they were learning, eventually they usually grew to like it. Surprisingly twelve Singers failed to enjoy singing Elgar's 'Dream of Gerontius' while eight did not get any fun out of singing Constant Lambert's exuberant 'Rio Grande'; nor did five Singers enjoy singing J S Bach's 'Mass in B minor', the same number that grumbled about Handel's 'Dettingen Te Deum' indeed in rehearsals of this 'A' level set work, the altos constantly were complaining about the number of times they sang the note D! Three Singers complained about singing Christmas Carols, as many as were disenchanted with Joseph Haydn's 'Creation'. Only two Cathedral Singers failed to enjoy singing either Bach's 'St Matthew Passion' and 'St John Passion', or Monteverdi's 'Vespers' and Bruckner's 'Mass in D Minor' , while only one got nothing out of singing William Byrd's 'Mass for four voices' and another disliked singing Mendelssohn's 'Hear my Prayer' with its popular 'O for the wings of a dove'. Devotion to the Cathedral Singers threw up the information that eighteen singers travelled forty or more miles to attend rehearsals, indeed two travelled as many as eighty-six miles while two more travelled ninety miles every Tuesday evening. Finally two reasons were provided for attending Cathedral Singers activities: one person admitted that he came to rehearsals for pleasure while another complained that he was dragged there by his wife!

The two Singers who had made the round trip of eighty-six miles were Ivor and Dorothy Phillips; they used to travel up to Brecon from Killay on the other side of Swansea and on the way would stop at Abercraf to collect dear Annie Watkins, the lady who had made my tapestry. All three were not only the 'life and soul' of rehearsals but also of the drinking session afterwards at the Conservative Club, indeed many is the time that they failed to leave for home until well after 'chuck-out time', 11.00 pm. Even then, such was Annie's hospitality that whenever Ivor and Dorothy went to drop her off at her home they were usually enticed inside for more refreshments, no matter how late the hour! Annie was greatly revered wherever she went, particularly in Women's Institute circles, indeed she it was who featured on the WI postcard entitled 'Welsh Lady', complete in Welsh costume and wearing the black stovepipe hat. She even persuaded me to conduct the Brecknock WI choir for a year to prepare it for a WI competition and although unplaced, the choir acquitted itself honourably. It was not long after this that Annie organised a trip for the Abercraf WI; being in charge, she sat in front, on the Courier's seat, close to the driver. Coming to a bend in the road where an approaching car had been parked stupidly, in such a way that it was impossible to see what was coming in the opposite direction the driver slowed down to crawl gingerly around the bend only to crash head-on into a lorry. Annie was injured sufficiently as to be taken to a nearby hospital where she was kept under observation for a few days until sadly, unexpectedly and quite unnecessarily, she suffered a heart attack and died. The many Cathedral Singers who swelled the already large congregation at Annie's funeral in the little Non-Conformist Chapel in Penycae, sang Mozart's 'Ave Verum' for her, a parting tribute to a very special lady. As for me, I now treasure all the more my twenty-fifth anniversary tapestry because it has turned out to be her last creation.

Strange to relate at around the same time a similar sad fate awaited one of the Cathedral Singers basses. Paul Jones was only thirty-nine years old and a much respected teacher at Crickhowell County Primary School, also a Non-Conformist with strict enough religious principles as to prefer giving a donation rather than purchase a raffle ticket when supporting a good cause. He was killed when the car he was driving was involved in a head-on collision with another car on the infamous 'Heads of the Valleys' road, near Brynmawr. At the ensuing trial at Merthyr Crown Court, it was explained that the driver of the other vehicle had been seen overtaking at speed in the middle lane of this road, the A465, just before the accident occurred whereupon his car had been seen to suddenly veer from the nearside lane right across into the path of Paul's car. While the judge agreed with jailing drivers who caused death by reckless driving, he suggested that in this case the other driver's reckless driving, serious as it was, only involved overtaking before the accident. So he went on to suggest that the actual accident was caused by the front tyres of this man's car which were fitted wrongly while one of his rear tyres had become deflated because it had a faulty valve. So it was that the driver of the car which had caused the accident was sentenced only to four months in prison suspended for twelve months, and banned from driving for the same period of time, in addition he paid £250 costs and a contribution to his legal aid. Sadly, however, Cathedral Singers bass Paul Jones had paid with his life, having done nothing wrong.

LIII

Helping to organise Brecon and Christ College Music Society, also organising concerts and organ recitals at the Cathedral resulted in my receiving a considerable amount of correspondence from potential recitalists or from their Agents. So it was that one day I received a circular from an organisation entitled 'The Stephen Sherwin Music Management' which was based in Nottinghamshire. In this I was offered the services of an Organ Recitalist who advertised himself as Assistant Director of Music at Christ College, Brecon, and Assistant Organist at, believe it or not, Brecon Cathedral. I knew that he was not my Assistant Organist and a telephone call to my friend Jonathan Leonard, Director of music at Christ College, confirmed what I had thought, that he was not Jonathan's Assistant there, rather he was only the College Organist. A few more telephone calls on the part of Jonathan Leonard, produced the information that he had not obtained all the qualifications that he claimed, which were: BA(Hons), MusB(Cantab), ARCO, LRAM, LTCL, FNSCM, FSCM; indeed the Royal Academy of Music threatened the young man with legal action, while neither Jonathan Leonard, nor Hazel or myself had ever heard of the final two qualifications. Subsequently in a brochure giving details of a 'Welsh Choral Project' sponsored by the Welsh Amateur Music Federation, the same young Organist described himself as 'an examiner to a number of examination boards', but failed to name any of them. What a fraud! Not surprisingly, after this his stay at Christ College was short-lived; soon he returned to England from whence he had come.

Yet at around the same time a still more interesting example of this sort of dishonesty and deception emerged from nearby Merthyr Tydfil. One Saturday afternoon when the Cathedral Choir had sung a special service, a young man named Mark, came to talk with me. He explained how he had been Assistant Organist at Winchester Cathedral but had given that up to become a sheep famer at Cefn Coed, on the outskirts of Merthyr Tydfil. He went on to ask me if he could do some practice on the Cathedral Organ to which I agreed providing that this was done early in the morning, before most visitors were wandering around the Cathedral. All went well for a while until Mark began to abuse his privilege by staying for too long and by playing the organ too loudly. Eventually he became a nuisance in that he began to destroy the peace and tranquillity of the Cathedral and I was forced to take action. I asked him to make a little less noise also to play for less time earlier in the day, but to no avail. Then I asked him to do something for the Cathedral in return for all this free practice to sing tenor occasionally in the Cathedral Choir, yet still I got nowhere with him. Meanwhile, the owner of a music shop in Brecon was also experiencing problems with Mark; the young man would purchase organ music from the shop then would take a long time in paying for it. Initially he asked for a discount on the grounds that he was a professional musician, then he would ask for time to pay as Sheep Farmers were experiencing difficulties. This only served to exasperate the shopkeeper who eventually asked him to make up his mind: either Mark was a professional musician in which case he could have a discount but would he mind paying up now, or he was a sheep farmer in which case he must pay in full when money became available. I must confess that by now I was puzzled. Winchester Cathedral had long enjoyed a fine reputation for its music and musicians yet in no way could Mark have held down the position of Assistant Organist there. So I telephoned Martin Neary who had recently become Organist of Westminster Abbey but who had previously been Organist of Winchester Cathedral at a time when this young man claimed to have been Assistant Organist there. However, Martin Neary had never heard of Mark, indeed he knew nothing about him. The crunch came when I received a telephone call from the present Assistant Organist of Winchester Cathedral. Apparently Mark was visiting Winchester and had presented himself at the Cathedral Organ Loft claiming to be the Assistant Organist of Brecon Cathedral, but the Winchester Cathedral Assistant Organist was not convinced and was checking out the claim. For me this was the end, I had had enough. I wrote to Mark and asked him not to use the Cathedral Organ any more and to stay away. Not long afterwards he appeared at St Mary's Church in Builth Wells where he tried to oust the Organist, my friend Anne Jones who had long been a member of the Cathedral Singers. The Vicar was a Canon of Brecon Cathedral who I knew well, so I was able to put a stop to this.

The summer of 1992, was marked by the first of an annual series of concerts given in British Cathedrals by The London Festival Orchestra, sponsored by British Gas. Ross Pople always directed the musical proceedings, sometimes from his 'cello, except for one item which featured the resident Cathedral Choir accompanied by the orchestra which was conducted by the resident Cathedral Organist. In this, the first year of such an enterprising venture, the orchestra visited as many as twenty-three cathedrals ranging from Edinburgh and Glasgow in Scotland to Newcastle and Durham in the North of England, to Lincoln and Peterborough in the East of England, to Canterbury and Portsmouth in the South of England, to Salisbury and Wells in the West of England and to Brecon and St Asaph in Wales. The programme at Brecon Cathedral, on Saturday June 13th, opened with some of Handel's 'Water Music' and continued with Elgar's 'Serenade for Strings'. The first half ended with the Cathedral Choir singing Mozart's 'Missa Brevis in Bflat, K275', which should have been accompanied by string instruments without the violas but for some reason an edition was used which included parts for violas which had nothing to do with the great composer. After an interval came Malcolm Arnold's 'Oboe Concerto' and Joseph Haydn's 'Farewell Symphony', no.45 in Fsharp minor, which ended as the composer intended, with players leaving the orchestra as their part finished, so that all that remained as the music drew to a gentle conclusion were two violinists. This was highly effective but not new to Brecon Cathedral because a few years before, the Gwent Chamber Orchestra had ended a concert by performing this symphony in exactly the same way. However, this earlier performance was still remembered simply because as the young horn player, Peter Francomb, (then of Albion Ensemble fame, now Principal Horn in the Northern Sinfonia Orchestra), finished playing and stood up preparing to depart quietly, so he succeeded in demolishing his music stand with great aplomb much to the amusement of the orchestra!

Two weeks after this London Festival Orchestra concert, the Gwent Chamber Orchestra had its own prestigious concert. A large barren part of Ebbw Vale had been transformed into a magnificent Garden Festival as the result of a national plan which had set out to bring beauty to certain areas of industrial desolation. Included in this project was the provision of a theatre with open-air seating for an audience. Here on Saturday afternoon, June 27th, the Gwent Chamber Orchestra accompanied violinist Miranda Dale in a performance of Vivaldi's 'Seasons', complete with an electronic harpsichord supplying a continuo part to add authenticity to the proceedings.

Just over three weeks later the Cathedral Choir was on its way to Swabia, just outside Bavaria, to Blaubeuren, Brecon's twin town in Southern Germany, where the choristers stayed in a Youth Hostel; for almost a fortnight. The joy of rising every morning to the accompaniment of a rising sun, and gazing down upon the little town nestling in a hollow surrounded on three sides by rocky tree-clad hills, was just one part of the magic. The town itself was like a dream with its beautiful, picturesque half-timbered houses and its magical Abbey Church with its own complex of gorgeous, mediaeval, monastic buildings dating back to 1085. On a more mundane level there was also an ice cream parlour with forty-seven ice cream combinations on the menu, where initially the choristers made known their requests in what little German they knew coupled with pigeon English, only to discover that the delightful young waitress was a Maori girl from New Zealand who spoke perfect English. There were also some lovely playing fields where the choristers were able to while away many a happy hour playing soccer, cricket and rounders, much to the amusement of local youngsters who occasionally joined in. A large open-air swimming pool with its own café, completed the amenities, and was most welcome as in the afternoons temperatures could soar into the 80sF; small wonder just occasionally there could be amazing storms with thunder, lightning and huge hailstones. On Sunday morning the Cathedral Choir sang at the town church service where the congregation of more than one hundred souls really did sing lustily the hymns to traditional tunes which were always introduced by an organ chorale prelude and for which they sat down, standing only to pray. There, that evening, the choir gave a concert to a large, appreciative audience; afterwards the choristers enjoyed a reception in the fine parish rooms. On the next day the choir sang an Anglican unaccompanied Evensong in the monastery church which attracted and held the attention of such a large congregation that there was standing room only. The next day another Evensong was sung there, again in front of the High Altar of this lovely, cool, resonant church; this time the congregation was even larger. One day the Choir visited Lake Constance and experienced more magic, then on another day there was a trip to Munich where the Blaubeuren Town Council paid for everyone to go to the top of the Olympic Stadium Tower to see breath-taking views of the city. Afterwards the choristers invaded the city centre, some to sample an amazing beer parlour, all at 5.00 pm, gathering outside the Town Hall to watch its carillon take ten minutes to chime the hour. The climax of the tour, in some ways, was the visit to Ulm Cathedral which was more than twice as long as Brecon Cathedral and 135 ft. high, boasting the tallest spire in the world at 528 ft. high, containing four pipe organs and having a six seconds echo. The choir gave a concert there on the evening of Saturday, August 1st, and were rewarded with one of those newspaper reviews which makes all the hard work so very worthwhile:

> '.... In cardinal red cassocks the group took up position in the choir to demonstrate even with its very first performance 'Hosanna to the Son of David' by Thomas Weelkes, its high standard in choral singing. Clear boys voices, tenors soaring effortlessly to the highest notes and strong basses brought about a sound which in its tenderness and harmony spread its own magic. They achieved everything, so it appeared to the eye and to the ear, so effortlessly, whether-without audible strain-precise entries or the equally seamless weaving of the lines of music into a flawlessly beautiful choral structure .....'

What more could we ask for? The next day, the Choir set off for Asch, a small village a few miles outside Blaubeuren. Here in the Evangelischen Kirche, Welsh and Germans joined together in a service of Holy Eucharist; so many people attended that the proceedings lasted for an hour and a half, the distribution of the bread and wine itself taking forty-five minutes. The lovely atmosphere created at this services was exceeded that evening at the final concert given by the choir which was followed by an amazing party in the garden of the Pastor's house, with lovely food in plenty, beer and wine flowing freely. Towards the end of the proceedings there was an amazing candlelit soccer match in which Wales defeated Germany 4 – 1, the final goal being scored by the oldest player – me, a fitting end to a wonderful tour that had been set up by Walter Boehringer of Asch, and Wynn Davies of the Cathedral Choir.

The Cathedral Choir returned to Brecon in time for the Jazz Festival, which by now had become the best of its kind in Britain, and the younger choristers picked litter at a furious rate around the town and at the outdoor jazz venues, so to earn more money for the next tour. One gentleman who was on his second visit to the Festival, took umbrage at the fact that he arrived at the Cathedral to attend a morning service which had been advertised at one time but took place at another. So he wrote rather crossly in a letter to the Dean:

> 'Another splendid weekend was spoiled for me by the discrepancies between the services in the Cathedral as advertised on the board outside, and those that actually took place.

I arrived at the Cathedral at (I believe) about five to eight on the Saturday morning for mass, only to find the building locked. It was only later, and from the Organist, that I was able to discover that, contrary to the information on the board, the service was not until much later in the morning on Saturdays.

Fortunately, Mr Gedge was thoughtful enough to warn me that the arrangement on ordinary weekdays was also not as shown (matins at 7.30, mass at 8.00), but in fact one combined service, the Eucharistic section commencing at about 7.45, fifteen minutes before the advertised time.'

As so it was. Back in Alwyn Our Dean's day and that of Dean Ungoed Jacob, the Holy Eucharist had always been said in full in one of the three chapels in the Cathedral which were used in rotation so that each one was utilised twice every week; afterwards all the clergy would move into the choir stalls and say Matins together, in full, at 8 am. Now the clergy complained of a cold cathedral and devised this hybrid service which combined parts of Matins with parts of the Holy Eucharist into one single service lasting little over half an hour; this became known as 'The Meucharist' in Garth Cottage. Sadly the three chapels were no longer used as all the services were said in the St Lawrence Chapel with rumours abounding that it was soon to be encased in glass screens to enable it to be heated separately from the Cathedral, solely for the comfort of those attending this daily ritual. Evensong also was said in the St Lawrence Chapel which left the ancient monastic choir used only for the three weekly choral services. To me this was sad as I always felt it right for a visitor who walked into the Cathedral during either Matins or Evensong to find it being said in the body of the church rather than surreptitiously in a tiny corner. However, these were not the only changes being implemented in the Cathedral at this time. Recently the Cathedral authorities had come to the conclusion that if there were inadequate financial resources to heat the building properly, why not make it look warmer; so the whitewashed walls of the Chancel were painted magnolia. Next, the Chancel floor was partially covered with a new carpet donated by Mrs Hilda Lloyd in memory of her late husband. Mrs Lloyd was persuaded to choose a red colour to impart a feeling of warmth but unfortunately this clashed with the colours of all but one of the High Altar frontals, also it destroyed the serenity of the Chancel which had benefited from the old gentle grey carpet, furthermore it distracted the eye of the beholder from the altar itself which should have been the focus of attention. To me, however, the saddest change of all, despite only being a small matter, occurred in the St Lawrence Chapel. As old as this chapel may look, it was in fact the creation of the Cathedral Architect, W D Caroe, in the 1920s, and was beautiful in its simplicity and understatement; the perfect venue for private prayer in its peace and tranquillity. Now the faded blue velvet curtains that hung from the wooden reredos behind the altar, were deemed to be shabby and unworthy of their situation, so were taken down to be replaced by strident orange curtains in order to brighten up the chapel. I was devastated. On the wall of my music room at Garth Cottage, I still hang a photograph of this chapel as it used to be. Yet more change was in the air because it was now that the idea of a glass screen in the fine mediaeval porch suddenly reared its ugly head and set in motion a controversy that raged on for some time until it died a natural death with its architect, the former Planning Officer for Breconshire, Phil Holborne. His idea had been to create a heat barrier in the porch so to eliminate draughts in the Cathedral, although there was no guarantee that this would work. At the same time it was rumoured that some of the magnificent hedges in the Cathedral grounds were to be razed to the ground to create 'vistas'; and so they were much to the consternation of many locals who, like me, had no idea of the monumental developments that were beginning to be planned for the future. However, D Huw Jones' time as Dean was coming to an end. Alwyn Our Dean, who had become Bishop of St Asaph now had been elected Archbishop of Wales and needed an Assistant Bishop to help him with his diocesan work. I, laughingly, in a telephone conversation with Alwyn, recommended our Dean, and to my amazement he was appointed. We had endured a turbulent ten years working together in Brecon, but, to be fair, everything musical that he had taken from us at the start of his time here, he had now returned to us, except for the venue of the Holy Saturday concert which still remained at St Mary's Church. Furthermore, there was no denying the fine, intellectual quality of his sermons although just occasionally, it did seem as if he was lecturing us. Now Hazel and I awaited with trepidation the appointment of our fifth Dean.

LIV

Meanwhile, the new buildings at Builth Wells High School were reaping their reward as in the 'A' level examination league tables for 1992, Builth Wells High School was placed fifth in Wales and fifty-first in England and Wales. This indeed was a colossal achievement when is remembered the lack of academic prowess in the school when I first taught there. I had now been teaching there for twenty-seven years, organising the music department, doing all the 'O' level and 'A' level teaching, directing the music at shows, concerts, school eisteddfodau and other similar activities, yet only now did I succeed in obtaining a Responsibility Allowance. Initially I had been refused one along with pension rights on the grounds that I was a part-time teacher, yet I could never understand why I could not have at least the relevant proportion of these allowances. Then when finally I had become full-time and gained my pension rights, it had taken a further ten years to obtain what I considered to be my just reward, this extra cash. I felt this all the more at this time because another crop of seven instrumental pupils had passed the much coveted grade 8 Music Examination which also was an amazing achievement for so rural a school, indeed at this time one pupil had even been accepted into the National Youth Orchestra of Wales while another had made it to the National Youth Brass Band. The Music Room nowadays was a hive of activity with perpetual chamber music during breaks, lunch hours and after school which was how it should be, giving pupils a chance to experience good classical music. It was not that I had turned my back on Pop Music because the Senior School Pop Group had commandeered, then wrecked my new Drum Kit after which they never bothered me again, but my philosophy was that these pupils would make their own music with or without my encouragement whereas they would not touch classical music unless led along the way.

It was now that TV Presenter and Personality Mavis Nicholson and John Tagholm of Pineapple Productions took an interest in me and my work. They were planning a series of television programmes about six personalities in mid-Wales entitled 'Local Hero' and I was to be one of them! For five days early 1993, they shadowed me at school and in the Cathedral, with the Cathedral Choir and Singers, not forgetting the Gwent Chamber Orchestra. Hazel was interviewed, I was interviewed; Headmaster, Mr Brown was interviewed – he unwisely stated that I was the only member of staff he would hate to see go; Deputy Head Jeff Bale was interviewed and laughingly labelled me 'eccentric'; Harriet was interviewed and looked stunning. The resulting film appeared on BBC(Wales) TV on Maundy Thursday and created quite a stir locally and among our friends and colleagues. New to the Cathedral Choir at this time were twins David and Simon Harris; they had come to Brecon from Swansea where they had had as many as ten foster parents in the previous nine years, now they had been given to a lovely Brecon couple, Bill and Di, who looked after them for the next six years. So David and Simon found their way into the Cathedral Choir just in time to appear on the film of the choirboys playing snooker in the Choir Room; indeed one of them was caught by the camera slying helping a ball into a pocket with a hand.

One bonus from this film was a most welcome fee of £250. At this time I was embroiled in a dispute with the Chapter over my salary as Cathedral Organist. I hadn't helped the situation by stating on the film that I was the lowest paid Cathedral Organist in England and Wales; the Canons were not amused. I was paid £4,902 per annum and lived in a Cathedral house rate and rent free, but the best paid Cathedral Organist in Wales, that of Llandaff Cathedral, received £10,573 per annum. Over in England only the Organists of Derby and Leicester Cathedrals received less than £11,700, indeed the majority were being paid £13,000 - £15,000, and a few as much as £17,000 - £18,000, furthermore, most of them had 'tied' houses, pensions and considerable expenses. Laughable was Hazel's salary as Assistant Organist: £150 per annum, which was a disgrace when is considered what was paid to other Assistant Organists whose annual salaries ranged from £1,790 to £17,469, although £8,000 - £9,000 seemed to be the norm. The Canons insisted on arguing that I should include the value of Garth Cottage in my salary. To me this was all very well for them because when they retired and left their Vicarages, they were given help with purchasing a house in which to live whereas when I retired I would simply be put out of Garth Cottage and left to fend for myself! Undoubtedly, some of the Canons never lost sight of the fact that I added to my Cathedral Organist salary the salary of a teacher. While that was all very well, what was never considered was the need for Hazel and me to run two cars, one to take me to and from Builth Wells High School which amounted to around ten-thousand miles annually for which I received no financial assistance, the other to take Hazel to Christ College where she had some piano pupils but needed to be able to return home at regular intervals to check on her mother who was now well and truly in the grip of the dreaded Alzheimer's Disease. Nor did the Canons ever consider the expenses involved in my work as Cathedral Organist, indeed all that they contributed was my telephone rent. I had a heavy weekly drinks bill because the Cathedral Choirmen/Lay Clerks were a very sociable group and the thrice-weekly visits to The Bulls Head were important social occasions. Thus after a heavy two-hour practice on a Thursday evening most of the Lay Clerks would retire to The Bull's Head to put the world to rights while Friday Evensong would be followed by a few beers and supper before returning home, furthermore on these occasions sometimes members of the congregation or, occasionally, a clergyman joined us; finally, Sunday morning service also was followed by a sociable drinking session during which some Lay Clerks enjoyed what I considered to be the cheapest Sunday lunch in Brecon. These occasions were important for the morale and well-being of the choir, allowing time to sort out amicably any problems that arose, but such was the good spirit among the Lay Clerks that this happened but rarely and my only regret was the frequent lack of clergy involvement.

However, the socialising did not end here because on Tuesday evenings there were the Cathedral Singers rehearsals which brought me into contact with a completely different set of singers; some of these also were partial to a drink after their weekly rehearsals, then on Wednesday the Gwent Chamber Orchestra players inevitably had a quick drink at The Bridgend, Brynmawr, before wending their various ways homeward, and here was a completely different set of lovely people who did much for the Cathedral with little but more often no payment. As for the Cathedral Concerts and Organ Recitals, many of these were financially subsidised by me. True: the Dean and Chapter gave me £500 per annum towards the Summer music and the Advent Cantatas while Nigel Emery of the South East Wales Arts Association saw that I got £800 towards the Easter and Summer concerts, yet the quality of the music-making at these events was such that there was always a financial shortfall. This July, for example, when the Cathedral Singers sang Brahm's 'German Requiem', the programme also included the Brahms 'Double', the famous concerto for violin, 'cello and orchestra, with sisters Miranda and Caroline Dale as soloists. On the next night, Caroline, a 'BBC Young Musician of the Year' winner, returned to play Elgar's wonderful 'cello concerto which I always found was a nightmare to conduct! Such concerts did not come cheaply especially as so large an orchestra was required, nor was I paid for any of this work with the Cathedral Singers and Gwent Chamber Orchestra, indeed even the weekly forty mile round trip to Ebbw Vale to take Gwent Chamber Orchestra rehearsals was always at my own expense. Yet I suppose the Dean and Chapter could argue that no-one asked me to do all this extra work but I considered that it did much to raise the profile of Brecon Cathedral. As for the important work that I did with choirs in the diocese that also was unpaid although the Bishop did at least give me £75 per quarter towards my petrol costs.

An unexpected 'sweetener' came at this time to make me partially but not entirely forget the disputes: an award of the MBE for services to music in Wales. For the first time ever the presentation ceremony was made outside of Buckingham Palace with the result that I was presented with my MBE by HM Queen Elizabeth II at Cardiff Castle towards the end of August. Also for the first time ever I was attired in a morning suit much against my will, as was Nick, while Hazel and Harriet were dressed most elegantly. I didn't exactly excel myself. Instructions were given as to how to receive the award including the advice never to turn your back towards the Queen. Needless to say, I got into a hopeless muddle. Having felt I had to say something, I started to tell Her Majesty how I had sung in the choir at her Coronation but became so unusually tongue-tied and confused that I ended up turning my back on her as I moved on. It was a performance best forgotten but it did leave me the proud possessor of the MBE. At this time also there was a magnificent Flower

Festival at the Cathedral and the Choristers had been given the irksome job of manning the Car Park. So I exchanged the grandeur of rubbing shoulders with the high and mighty in Cardiff Castle with the menial job of Car Park Attendant at Brecon Cathedral later that same day.

Yet 1993 was a special year in other ways. Not only was it the nine-hundredth anniversary of the founding of the Priory Church of St John the Evangelist, Brecon, but it was also the seventieth anniversary of the founding of the Diocese of Swansea and Brecon with the Priory Church as its Cathedral, in addition it was the nine-hundredth anniversary of the founding of the town of Brecon. Small wonder there were special services galore in the Cathedral which made for some interesting occasions. September, for example, began with the customary Choral Evensong on the first Sunday afternoon attended by the Breconshire Guild of Weavers and Spinners, a service which always ended with everyone singing the hymn 'Joyful, joyful we adore thee' to Beethoven's famous 'Ode to joy' melody, a marriage of words and music which I and the Cathedral Choir have never found convincing. Anyhow the Lay Clerks had livened up the proceedings somewhat by adding a touch of realism to the Guild's pastoral model of sheep grazing in a field, which adorned the floor at the back of the nave. Sweeping up some bat droppings from the Cathedral floor they deposited them beneath the model sheep but no-one seemed to notice! A week later a Civic Service attended by the Chairman of Powys County Council gave a perfect example of the liturgical mess that the Anglican Church appeared to be encouraging. This adaptation of Choral Evensong began with the hymn 'O worship the King All-glorious above' and continued with the opening Responses as set to music by William Byrd. Then for no apparent reason, The Lord's Prayer was sung but not by the Cathedral Choir, instead the choir of nearby Llangorse Primary School performed it. Now in the place of the customary Psalm the Chairman of Powys Council read the First Lesson in Welsh with no translation provided. At this point, instead of The Magnificat the Cathedral Choir sang Psalm 121 to Walford Davies' lovely chant. The Second Lesson followed, read in English by the Canon in Residence, after which one of the County Councillors, who obviously fancied herself as a singer, rendered a solo. Then came the sermon delivered by the Bishop of Swansea and Brecon after which a hymn was sung in Welsh, again with no translation provided. Intercessions followed, led by another Residentiary Canon, and when these were finished Crickhowell High School Choir sang as an anthem Gabriel Fauré's lovely 'Cantique de Jean Racine'. Finally, the hymn, 'Mine eyes have seen the glory of the coming of the Lord' was sung whereupon the Bishop gave a Blessing and the charade was over. My son, Nick, had the good fortune to avoid this travesty of a service by accepting the invitation of PC Richard Williams, a long-time and much-loved member of the Cathedral Choir, to take part in an Identification Parade at Brecon Police Station for which he received £5!. After the Service, a letter from the Chairman of Powys County Council commented on the excellence of the proceedings and how favourably it had been received by all present; however, no-one had asked the choristers what they had thought about it, least of all Hazel and me. Another week later, on Saturday, September 18th, there was a Service of Thanksgiving for the 900th Anniversary of the Cathedral and the 70th Anniversary of the Diocese, at which the preacher was Alwyn Our Dean who was now the Archbishop of Wales. On this occasion, to my sorrow, during the Holy Eucharist the Creed was said despite my twenty-seven years of ensuring that on all diocesan occasions the Gloria and Creed could be sung congregationally to the ancient music of John Merbecke. Here in the space of a week, was a second example of how some of the great traditions of Anglican Cathedral Worship were being eroded. That was sad!

Sad as that may have been to me, worse was to follow a few weeks later in St Peter's, Rome of all places! The Cathedral Singers spent a hot, scintillating few days in Rome and on Sunday, October 24th, sang Mass in this great Cathedral. However, they were not allowed to sing any of the Mass itself but were restricted to providing a few unaccompanied motets and some Welsh hymns with organ accompaniment, to grace the proceedings. Yet there were compensations. A reception at the British Embassy to the Holy See brought us face-to-face with Monsignor David Lewis, a striking Welshman from Bridgend, who smoked incessantly and had an endless repertoire of naughty stories. What a character! Initially he had worked in theatre but suddenly, at the age of forty-nine years, he had unexpectedly changed direction and become a Roman Catholic priest. Posted to Gatwick Airport as Chaplain he had attracted the attention of the Pope when he was about to tour Great Britain, and was sent to work at the Basilica of Santa Maria Maggiore in the Vatican with the instruction to raise £8,000,000, to restore it. This he promptly did and to stunning effect. So the Singers sang Mass in this wonderful church with the command ringing in their ears: 'Sing what you like but don't make the service last more than an hour otherwise I shall have to pay the Caretaker overtime'. When it came to the service itself, the Monsignor suddenly realised that his congregation consisted mainly of a tour group from Manchester and the Cathedral Singers. So he substituted English for Latin explaining to everyone that this made far more sense and we, as we had been bidden, completed the service in less than an hour. The Cathedral Singers also gave a concert in the Basilica di Santa Croce which was a moving occasion not just because the church was still administered by some Cistercian monks but also because the building was so peaceful and had a wonderfully warm and generous acoustic. Another concert found us in the ornate English church of St Paul Within The Walls which I found fascinating as it was the creation of the eminent Victorian architect George Edmund Street, also it contained wall tiles by William Morris and mosaics by Edward Burne-Jones. What pleased me especially about this trip was that two of my 'A' level pupils from Builth Wells High School, Bethan Jones and Jenny Grain, were able to be with us to enjoy the visit of a lifetime which took in the magnificent Vatican not forgetting the fantastic Colliseum and the famous fountains. What an experience!

Back at Brecon Cathedral a new Dean had been settling in, Canon John Harris, formerly Vicar of Maindee in the diocese of Monmouth. His gentle demeanour hid a determined personality but he and I seemed to 'click', aided perhaps by the fact that we shared a birthday – March 12th, which, incidentally, was also my son Nick's birthday. He was ably supported by his wife Beryl who was a lively character; as we got to know each other better I began to caller her 'Beryl the Peril' much to her amusement and mock horror. At last something was stirring in the Cathedral Close and while the previous Dean, D Huw Jones, must have signed the relevant contracts, I am sure that a lot of what was being proposed was due to the dynamic Vicar of Swansea, Canon Don Lewis, who had the foresight to bring his architect friend, Dr Geoff Worsley, onto the scene. Projects I had long dreamed of in the past suddenly were becoming a reality and if all went according to plan, many of the ruinous buildings in the Close would soon be enjoying a new lease of useful life. So it was proposed to restore the Cathedral Tower at a cost of £155,000, then to do work to the Bell Chamber and Bells at a cost of £40,000 which would leave the Cathedral with a peal of eight bells that could actually be rung. Much to my delight, plans were afoot to restore the dilapidated Tithe Barn, to turn it into a multi-purpose hall with video, TV and sound systems, also to create a Refreshment area with an outside terrace for use in the summer months; all this at a cost of £290,000. £32,000 was to be spent on routine maintenance and repairs to the organ, also to complete the scheme begun in 1973, when the instrument was last rebuilt on a 'shoestring' budget. With all this amounting to a cost of £568,000 an appeal was launched in what to Brecon was a most unconventional way: a drinks party in the very Cathedral itself with background classical music supplied by my Builth Wells High School musicians. At last something exciting was happening.

LV

1994 started off well with the Cathedral Singers and Gwent Chamber Orchestra back in the Cathedral on Holy Saturday performing JS Bach's 'St Matthew Passion'; after a ten year absence it felt good. St Mary's Church had been rather cramped for such large-scale music, also the acoustic was not helpful, yet it was kind of the people there to put up with us as they prepared the building for Easter Day. In the Cathedral, however, there was ample room for the choir and orchestra, also the acoustic was helpful, then, of course, there was the sublime atmosphere of the ancient monastic building itself.

At this time there was a very interesting Minor Canon at the Cathedral, Morgan Llewellyn by name, and thereby hangs a fascinating tale which was told in The Church Times of 16 July 1993:

> *'One lunch hour in 1986, a major and a brigadier sat side by side on a bench on the Victoria Embankment. A nosy passer-by would have noticed that the major was energetically talking and the brigadier was silent and troubled.*

Christianity was the topic. The troubled brigadier was Morgan Llewellyn, and that hour on the bench turned out to be a turning-point in his life. The talking major, who worked under him at the Ministry of Defence, was doing a spot of lunch-hour evangelism, and it worked. The two men went back to the MOD chapel and prayed. Morgan Llewellyn returned to his office feeling that a burden he had been unaware of had been lifted. He couldn't concentrate and slipped out to buy a Bible in Victoria Street. He could only find a Good News one. From that day on, he changed from a vague Christian 'with a small c' to a fully committed Christian, with a rage for learning about the gospel and an urge to lift burdens from others'

This rage eventually took hold of his life forcing him to exchange his role as Major –General Morgan Llewellyn, Chief of Staff at Headquarters United Kingdon Land Forces, also Colonel of the Royal Welch Fusiliers and of the Queen's Own Gurka Transport Regiment, for that of a humble ordinand at Salisbury and Wells Theological College. Here his training turned him into a priest who was not against Evangelicals, Anglo-Catholics or Liberals, nor the Ordination of Women, but one who wished that the Anglican Church would stop going on about what the Cathedral Lay Clerks called irreverently 'Priestesses', and get on with making its presence felt in the war zones of the world. His coming to Brecon Cathedral was ideal as his home was barely fifteen miles away at Llangattock Court, where his wife, Polly, ran a nursery school. Morgan arrived hoping that his army experience would eventually help him bring something useful to the Anglican Church, initially however, as the Church Times put it, he was happy 'to baptise babies in Brecon, wholeheartedly relishing parish and cathedral life, until the way ahead emerged.'

It was not long before Morgan's diplomatic skills were put severely to the test. When HRH Prince Charles attended Morning Prayer in Brecon Cathedral on Sunday, July 3rd, 1994, and the choir was lining-up downstairs in the Vestry, a fracas unexpectedly occurred. Two newspaper reporters rushed in from the Close and made for the door into the Cathedral but their way was barred by Morgan Llewellyn who refused them admission because they did not have the necessary passes. So they were escorted out whereupon the choir processed into the Cathedral to start the service and there the matter should have ended but for the fact that one of the reporters was Michael Boon of The Western Mail. In Wales newspaper reporters tend to be held in awe and reverence and unfortunately Michael Boon was one who was accustomed to having his own way. His report on the incident, published in The Western Mail, was sufficiently detrimental as to make me write to the Editor:

> 'I was sad to read The Western Mail report of the visit made by the Prince of Wales to Brecon Cathedral. The disgruntled reporter who complained about being refused admission, did not have an invitation with his name written upon it. Surely an experienced reporter would have realised that the named invitation card was simply a security measure. Suppose he had been admitted and had turned out to be an anonymous terrorist posing as a reporter who had gone on to murder the Prince, then The Western Mail would have ridiculed both the security arrangements and the clergyman involved. Even my choristers from the youngest to the oldest, had to have named invitation cards so that they could be checked by security personnel before being admitted to the Cathedral. As for there being plenty of available space for a larger congregation, the only part of the building that was empty was the Regimental Chapel and Transept which the Prince was to tour after the Service.'

The Editor's reply was dismissive, claiming that having made his own enquiries, he believed that my letter was 'wrong in almost every aspect,' claiming also that Michael Boon, 'and all his colleagues had checked with the Prince's staff before the visit to Brecon and had been assured that all accredited reporters would be admitted to the service.'

Unbeknown to me, Morgan Llewellyn himself had written a letter of protest to the Editor of The Western Mail. He pointed out that 'The Palace had made the prior decision that, as the Prince was not participating in the service and was there as a worshipper, this was to be regarded as a private part of the visit. No press were, therefore, given access to the Cathedral except for a documentary team from the BBC by express prior arrangement with the Prince of Wales's Press Secretary'. Still, however, the Editor was dismissive; Michael Boon had told a different story and that was the one he was believing. So Morgan Llewellyn had to endure being called 'One Grumpy Cleric' by Michael Boon in The Western Mail while the BBC, on the other hand, wrote to him to say, you and your colleagues were most helpful, even when we were asking the impossible.' Who was right will never be known but still I have in my mind, a vivid picture of the Cathedral Choir on the verge of processing into this service whereupon two reporters barge into the vestry trying to force their way into the Cathedral. If I had been Morgan I am quite sure that I would have reacted in exactly the way that he did.

It was at around this time that Minor Canon Morgan Llewellyn suffered another set-back in his new life. At the meeting of the Governing Body of The Church in Wales the chief issue for debate was the vexing question of the Ordination of Women to the Priesthood. After a long and lively debate it was obvious that the majority of delegates were in favour of the motion but would the number of 'YES' votes reach the magic figure of two-thirds? However, before delegates could vote the Archbishop led them in prayer, in the course of which he invoked the guidance of the Holy Spirit. Afterwards everyone voted and this was the result:

The House of Bishops:	5 - 1	a majority of 83%
The House of Clergy:	75 - 47	a majority of 62%
The House of Laity:	148 - 51	a majority of 74%

So while 70% of the total votes cast were in favour of the motion, the motion was actually lost because the House of Clergy failed to get the two-third majority. Had seven clergy voted the other way, the motion would have been carried. Many delegates were moved to tears at this outcome but others were angry and dismayed; they looked for ways of bringing back the Bill at the earliest opportunity. The Bishops, for example, wanted the matter brought back to the Governing Body within twelve months instead of the customary three years which was normal for the re-appearance of a Bill. This led to one letter-writer in The Times newspaper asking: 'Are we now to suggest that because the vote did not go the way that the Bishops wanted, the Holy Spirit was absent from the proceedings?' After all, having prayed for the guidance of the Holy Spirit, who was to say that the Holy Spirit had not been at work. It was indeed an unhappy episode in the history of The Church in Wales.

An unhappy incident in the history of the Diocese of Swansea and Brecon also came to fruition at this time. At the annual gathering of The Friends of Brecon Cathedral in the previous year, Hazel and I had chatted with a clergyman friend who had been a popular and hard-working Minor Canon at the Cathedral some ten years before and who had gone on to enjoy a meteoric rise in the diocesan career stakes, becoming Vicar of Sketty while in his early thirties – this parish being acknowledged as second only to St Mary's Swansea. 'You'll be seeing a lot more of me soon', he had said, while enjoying tea in The Chapter House. 'Will we?' I had replied, adding 'Why is that?'; 'I am to be made a Canon on Monday', he had announced with a smile, 'the youngest ever in the history of the diocese'. When Monday arrived, however, it was not the Canonry that was announced in newspapers, but his arrest by the Swansea police over the week-end for a number of serious sex offences involving young boys. It is said that for the next month or so no-one could be seen wearing a dog-collar in Swansea, such was the reflected shame felt by the local clergy at the seriousness of the charges. All this came to a head in the spring of 1994, when the clergyman appeared at Swansea Crown Court on nineteen charges of sex offences which landed him with a four year jail sentence. Yet this was exceedingly tragic because he was undeniably a priest with both a vision and charisma, who could get things done; what was so sad was that he had been let down by an uncontrollable personal weakness.

Meanwhile at the Cathedral the Appeal was gathering momentum largely because of the driving force of the Appeal Chairman, Michael Jepson. In his determination to succeed he could be impulsive and this led him to cross my path twice although on neither occasion do I think it was ever intentional, he just had not thought hard enough about the consequences of his actions. Ever mindful of the value of good publicity he gave a report on the progress of the appeal on BBC/TV; later Hazel and I watched the programme at home and to our horror heard the organ being played as background music, but not by us. We were furious because if there had to be organ music to accompany references to the use of appeal money on the instrument, then we should have been consulted to ensure that the music truly reflected the musical standards that we were striving to maintain at the Cathedral and not be provided by any pupil who happened to be at hand. Not long after this Michael Jepson organised a concert at St Mary's Church, Swansea and asked me if I would bring the Cathedral Singers to perform as he had approached two professional choirs and they had declined. I consoled myself with the thought that J S Bach was the third choice for his final position as Cantor of St Thomas's School, Leipzig. However, when I discovered that the two 'professional' choirs were, in fact, Male Choirs from Morriston and Pontardulais, I was not amused. Those choirs were no more professional than the Cathedral Singers themselves, indeed I was firmly of the opinion that in Wales, Male Voice Choirs always had been placed on a pedestal which gave most of them far more 'kudos' than they deserved. Few, if any, could be as musical as John Cynan Jones' Treorchy Male Choir, or as adventurous as Glynne Jones' Pendyrus Male Choir, or as perfectly in tune as Martin Hodson's Risca Male Voice Choir. So I swallowed my pride and let the Singers line up with The Band and Drums of the 1st Battalion, the Royal Regiment of Wales and the concert was a resounding success. Twice more the Cathedral Singers sang for the Appeal Fund, each time at the invitation of the High Sheriff, Susan Ballance, who had made this the main beneficiary of her charitable activities while in office. A special performance of Handel's 'Messiah' raised £4,500, while a Carol Concert later, early in December, raised additional funds and created a lot of seasonal good will.

Susan Ballance is of more than passing interest because she had long been a good friend to the Cathedral Singers. She lived in Abercamlais, a lovely country house five miles from Brecon along the A40 road towards Carmarthen which she had inherited from her parents Captain Neville Garnons Williams, a former Lord Lieutenant of Breconshire, and his wife Violet, a niece of musician Basil Harwood, who played the organ at nearby

Penpont Church. Every year she generously donated to the Cathedral Singers a Christmas Tree for their annual fund-raising event – 'Christmas Cheer'. Every year also, she and her husband, Christopher, entertained tenor soloist Rogers Covey-Crump at Easter, as they had done for this performance of 'Messiah'. Finally, she kindly gave to St Mary's, Brecon, the elegant Henry Russell Chamber Organ of 1825, which formerly had stood in the Hall at Abercamlais and which had been so useful as a continuo instrument when the Cathedral Singers had been banished to this church for their annual J S Bach performances on Holy Saturday.

Despite such diversity of activities the highlight of the year, as far as the Cathedral Choir was concerned, was its trip to Cork. Not all that many years before the diocese of Swansea and Brecon had been twinned with the diocese of Cork, Cloyne and Ross but the union had lasted only three years and now was no more. Nevertheless, if a little late to benefit from such a special relationship, Brecon Cathedral Choir was going to Cork with three mini-buses, taking enough choristers, music and baggage to fill them. There was, however, another special relationship which I wanted to verify during our time in Cork. Our accommodation was at Brookfield Holiday Village where there were rows of attractive, new, landscaped houses which provided University College, Cork students with accommodation during term time and tourist accommodation during holiday time. Some of these houses accommodated seven people in five single rooms and one double room, with a shower on each of the two floors, a fitted kitchen/living room and a sitting room with arm chairs and a colour TV, which for our youngsters was bliss. The 'icing on the cake' was the free membership of the University Sports Club which gave everyone the use of a swimming pool, sauna, an exercise room and more. Of course the idea was that you cooked your own meals but if anyone did not feel like doing this there was an excellent café on site, which is where I often went to enjoy an 'English Breakfast'! All this was overlooked by a large, gaunt Georgian house named by coincidence – or was it(?), Brookfield.

In my younger days I had known a Bernard Gedge who had divided his time between being a stockbroker in London and a gentleman of leisure in Cork, whose wife was related, so tradtion had it, to a former Archbishop of Armagh. They had lived in a house called 'Brookfield' and they had given land to the University, therefore was this house by any chance 'Brookfield'? Bernard had been one of the 'York Gedges', sons of the Revd Sidney Gedge who had been a Vicar Choral (Minor Canon) of York Minster, who were distantly related to my branch of the Gedge family, but my clergyman father had little to do with him because he and his first wife had been divorced. Bernard and his second wife had called on Hazel and me in Brecon many, many years ago while on their way to Swansea where they were to board the Cork ferry, but I could remember little about her and he had recently died.

One afternoon that week, I plucked up courage, walked round to this house and knocked at the front door which, after a short while, opened a few inches to reveal a frail old lady who in reply to my question, said that she was indeed Mrs Gedge, but would I mind going round to the back door as she could not open the front door any wider. So I renewed acquaintance with Muirne, Bernard's widow, who showed me around the few rooms that she lived in and explained how every Sunday morning at 10.45, a taxi arrived to take her to the Anglican Cathedral for Morning Service. Originally this service had been Choral Morning Prayer, commonly called Matins, because the Anglican Church in Ireland tended to be Low Church to counter the Roman Catholic High Church traditions which centred around the Mass. In more recent years the Anglican Church in Ireland had become less sensitive about this issue so that in many cathedrals and churches now, Holy Eucharist had become the main Sunday service. So it was at St Finbarre's Cathedral, Cork where Brecon Cathedral Choir sang the services in the morning and evening on Sunday and on Wednesday evening, although we were asked to try to avoid singing anything using Latin words.

The Cathedral itself was an astonishing building, created by the Victorian architect William Burges, who is famous in South Wales for his colourful restoration of Cardiff Castle and for his creation of magical Castell Coch, a stunning minute castle that he had built high up on a cliff above what is now the A470 road from Brecon and Merthyr to Cardiff. His Cathedral had twelve hundred pieces of sculpture, a considerable number of fine brass fittings including a magnificent lectern, an enormous quantity of colourful Victorian tiles, its great height helping create the impression of a cavernous building that defied its short length, while topping it all were three magnificent tall spires and an impressive West Front. It was a further example of a great Victorian architect creating a finer Gothic cathedral than many a great mediaeval architect himself. Strangely and uniquely, its fine four manual pipe organ was sunk twelve-feet into the floor of the North Transept although its console-keyboard was placed conveniently alongside the Choir Stalls.

St Finbarre's Cathedral, Cork was not the only cathedral in the diocese but it was the chief one; however, there were two more, hence the name of the diocese which was Cork, Cloyne and Ross. Cloyne consisted of one main street and a few houses, shops and pubs, yet it housed a magnificent mediaeval cathedral which was slightly longer than Brecon Cathedral. Its nave, empty of chairs, was most impressive; its long narrow chancel which had choir and clergy stalls at the West End, culminated in an imposing bishop's throne at the East End, to the right of the altar, that contained not a wooden seat of great antiquity but a modern armchair in which many of the Brecon choristers sat to have their photograph taken. The decrepit Magahy two-manual organ which was sited near the choirstalls, included one stop knob which when drawn came out to a length of two feet or more. This intriguing pile was ruled over by lively Dean Hilliard who had arranged for Brecon Cathedral Choir to take part in a concert along with a local ladies choir and a soloist. During the half-time interval, performers and audience alike decamped to the nave where trestle tables had been set up laden with wine, biscuits and cheese, all of which were most welcome not the least to the young choirboys. It was a fun evening which everyone enjoyed enormously as Welsh and Irish mingled happily, swopping music and stories.

The third Cathedral was at magical Rosscarbery, forty miles west of Cork, a town of around four hundred inhabitants with eleven pubs for the adults and lovely pedal-boats for the youngsters although they also managed to sneak into the pub that the Lay Clerks adopted. The Cathedral itself was extraordinary with its tall, narrow tower outside and inside a nave that was uncluttered by any chairs and served as ante-chapel to the Choir and Sanctuary from which it was separated by a solid stone wall. Pride of place in the Choir was given to some magnificent clergy stalls paid for around one hundred years ago, by a Dean who seriously believed that the diocese of Ross was about to be revived and separated from Cork and Cloyne, even though it would only have contained four parishes; perhaps he had visions of being promoted to Bishop. The choir stalls were less grandiose but here the Brecon choristers sang Evensong with accompaniments being played on yet another Magahy of Cork organ. As Jonathan Leonard had played the organ at Cloyne Cathedral, so Kelvin Redford played the organ at Rosscarbery Cathedral. This lesser pile was ruled over by Dean Townley, a fascinating man who kept a flat in the West End of London where he had been a curate, and who had his Georgian Deanery at Rosscarbery stuffed full of antiques. Being a great traditionalist, he presided over a 1662 Book of Common Prayer Evensong and then afterwards, entertained everyone, choir and congregation, right royally in the Cathedral Hall. Driving mini-buses back to Cork after such an evening was an exhausting experience; at one small town I found myself driving up a one way street in the wrong direction, but no-one seemed to mind. So the diocese of Cork, Cloyne and Ross had three Cathedrals, one Bishop, three Deans and around thirty clergymen; interestingly the Deans of Cloyne and Rosscarbery were also ex-officio members of the Chapter, (Canons), at St Finbarre's Cathedral, Cork.

While there may have been three Cathedrals to become acquainted with, pride of place actually went to 'The Enterprise Lounge' below St Finbarre's Cathedral, by the South Gate in Cork City, close to the Beamish Brewery. Only in Ireland could such a successful Bar have been named after a famous sea disaster of the 1950s. What a Bar! The doors opened at 10.00 am, not closing again until 12.00 midnight; the food and drink, be it coffee, Guiness, Murphy's, Beamish, Robin Redbreast Irish Whisky and much more were magical, always served graciously by Finbarre O'Shea or by his wife Dolly, by their son Dennis or, in the evening, by Patrick, and by their marvellous team of helpers, none of whom really expected you to go to the bar to place your order – they came to you. Nothing was too much trouble, while the comfortable surroundings were unbelievable; it was all so civilised. Unbelievable also was the Champagne Party that they gave us as a farewell gesture which I would never have believed actually happened had I not been there. We knew we would be coming back.

LVI

A curious anomaly occurred early in 1995, when for the first time in all my twenty-nine years in Wales, Ash Wednesday fell on March 1st and, according to The Church in Wales Calendar, knocked St David's Day off its pedestal and led to it being celebrated that year on March 2nd. I wondered how ardent Welshmen would accept this, St David being usurped by Ash Wednesday, especially when, according to Bass Lay Clerk, Wynn Davies, in the Non-Conformist Chapel that he had attended in his childhood days in Ammanford, Easter Day always had been given over to rehearsing the hymns that were to be sung at the Easter Monday Gymanfa Ganu – Singing Festival. That, it appears, was of far more importance than commemorating the resurrection of Jesus Christ from the dead. Doubtless this clash of dates would have amused dear old Bishop 'Jack' Thomas had he not peacefully passed from this world to the next on February 27th at the age of eighty-six years. Obviously, he had not been unused to such controversies because his obituary in The Church Times mentioned how as an English-speaking Bishop in Wales, he had been exposed to critical comment from two other bishops 'who were enthusiasts for the cause of the Welsh language', a crisis which he had ridden with courage and dignity. His funeral on Tuesday, March 7th at 12.00 noon, was a moving occasion, a Requiem Mass with, as he would have liked, no announcements, and with the Kyrie, Sanctus, Benedictus and Agnus Dei sung to the ancient music of John Merbecke. The hymns included his beloved 'O what their joy and their glory must be', 'Blest are the pure in heart', the Easter hymn 'Loves redeeming work is done', and, during the Communion, the plainchant 'Thee we adore, O hidden Saviour, thee', along with 'Jesu, the very thought of thee', sung to Gordon Slater's magical tune 'St Botolph' which he had loved so much, ending with 'O thou who camest from above'. For me, all that was missing was the catafalque created by standing six tall candlesticks around the coffin over which should have been draped the lovely crimson pall. This was how Bishop Thomas had set out the coffin of his friend and my first Dean, Gwynno James, back in early 1967, to create a setting for a funeral that was so dignified and moving, and this I wanted for the Bishop himself, but to no avail. Sadly, never again had these great candles and the pall been used in this way. The Bishop's son, David, formerly Principal of St Stephen's House, Oxford, now Vicar of Newton in Swansea and a Canon of Brecon Cathedral, was very appreciative of everything, especially of Hazel's playing on the organ before the service J S Bach's Chorale Prelude 'Wenn wir in höchsten Nösten sein' – 'When in the deepest hour of need', and of her playing afterwards the Sinfonia from J S Bach's Funeral Cantata, 106, 'Gottes Zeit ist die allerbeste Zeit', - 'God's time is best'. These to him were the cream on what he described as an already very lovely cake. In a letter that arrived at Garth Cottage a few days later, David reminisced about his father:

'He and my mum thought the world of you both. I still remember him coming in all excited one day early in 1966 because he and Gwynno were sure they'd found just the right people for the cathedral choir and organ – a young couple called Gedge, whom he was having round to sherry that night! (I remember, too, that having 'oiled' you with sherry, he suddenly made for the piano and very gently and subtly established that you really did know more about music than he did and – much more important to him – that you cared as much as he did about music and liturgy.)'

When Hazel and I had come to Brecon all those years ago, Gwynno James, as well as being Dean of Brecon Cathedral, had also been Vicar of St Mary's,Brecon, while I was Organist at both places and therefore in charge of both choirs. Gwynno's vision was that both congregations should work in harmony with each other and he begged me to do all that I could to assist him in this; one result had been The Cathedral Singers. So it now came as a shock to find the Churchwardens and PCC at this time asking the Bishop if St Mary's could have its own priest-in-charge. The local 'Brecon and Radnor Express' got it wrong with the result that on June 1st 1995, the main headline on the front page read: 'Split in Brecon Churches'! So in a letter to the Editor published later, the Bishop refuted this and outlined his plans and hopes for the future. Firstly he explained that there was no split in Brecon churches but simply that he had invited Canon Elwyn John to be a full-time Residentiary Canon and also to be Priest-in-Charge of St Mary's, Brecon while continuing to exercise his diocesan responsibilities as Bishop's Advisor for Rural Life and Ministry. It all sounded very grand but what it hid was the fact that John, our kindly Dean, had recently had a heart attack and therefore, not being in the best of health, wanted less to do. Nominally he would remain Vicar of St Mary's, but Canon Elwyn John would do the work. Hazel and I were unhappy about it all as to our way of thinking if left two rival establishments where we had been trying to help establish one happy unit. Meanwhile, Canon John now proceeded to use the room beyond the Choir Room as an office. Unfortunately, I had been using the room beyond the Choir Room as a Store Room for the past thirteen years and now it was housing a lot of music. Canon John asked me to empty the room immediately as he wanted to move in; I asked if he could possibly wait for a month until the end of term when I would have time to clear the room. My words fell on deaf ears. The next day when I entered the Choir Room for my choir practice I discovered that he with the help of his sons, had emptied the room of its contents and piled them high on the Choir Room floor. I was furious as were the Cathedral Singers when they arrived to attend their weekly Tuesday evening practice, although those Singers who came from Builth Wells, where the Canon had previously been Vicar, were not the least bit surprised. That mess remained for a month until the Dean and Chapter had extra shelving installed in the Choir Room at a cost of £1,000. Worse was to follow. Anxious to move into the Almonry, the Canon had told Minor Canon Morgan Llewellyn to remove his belongings by a certain date. Unfortunately, Morgan was unable to comply because he was moving on to become Chaplain at Christ College where his predecessor had died unexpectedly from meningitis and the shocked widow still had not been able to complete her move out of the College house to make way for him.

On Saturday, September 16th, Nicholas Gedge married his beloved Kate Robinson at Painswick Church in Gloucestershire, the next day the Grafton Singers sang the Sunday services in the Cathedral while Kelvin Redford played the organ for the services at St Mary's Church. When Hazel and I arrived home that night we received a telephone call from Kelvin asking us if we knew that from next Sunday onwards, Evensong at St Mary's was not to be at 6.15 pm but at 3.00pm. This was the first we had heard about this and by coincidence Canon John had chosen to make the announcement on one of those rare occasions when we were absent from a service. We were not amused! Over recent years we had built up a tradition in St Mary's where Evensong was conducted in the small chapel sung by a quartet of singers standing around the historic Henry Russell Chamber Organ. The Responses were sung to the Ferial Setting, the psalm and canticles were sung to Anglican chants, also a short anthem was usually sung. Unfortunately, this was to be swept away because at 3.00 pm Hazel and I were busy at the Cathedral dealing with Choral Evensong. How tragic! Kelvin kindly saw to it that the Church authorities did not cut our salary which amounted to only £15 per Sunday, because the problem was of their making. This was not all. A few months later when the Easter Vestry – the Church's Annual General Meeting, was called, it was arranged for 3.00pm on a Sunday afternoon rather than on an evening. This excluded anyone who attended Choral Evensong at the Cathedral which was wrong because Hazel, me and anyone who chose to be, could be on the Electoral Roll of what was, after all, our Parish Church, and therefore eligible to attend this important meeting. I duly sent a letter of apology for non-attendance to the PCC Secretary, who, quite properly, read it out at the meeting. Not long afterwards I was summoned to appear before Canon John and his Church-warden to explain my position! They both felt that I shouldn't have done that – why, I do not know!

However, this was not my only brush with clerical authority at this time. At Priory Church in Wales Primary School next to the Cathedral, the Headmistress was about to go into hospital to have an operation; this necessitated appointing a temporary Head Teacher. Now it so happened that Bass Lay Clerk Wynn Davies, who had exchanged his German teaching job at Gwernyfed High School for the more lucrative job of an Advisory Teacher in Information Technology for Powys Local Education Authorty, recently had spent a considerable amount of time in that school helping to sort out some problems involving computers and the like. Having endeared himself to staff and pupils alike he was encouraged to send in an application for this job by the Head and Deputy Head. Wynn was only too happy to do this because he had become the victim of Powys LEA financial cuts and had lost his permanent job on the basis of the 'last-in-first-out' policy, with the result that he had to depend upon whatever work he could obtain. So Audrey Bayliss, Deputy Head of Llanfaes County Primary School, Brecon, and Wynn Davies were invited to attend interviews for the position of Acting Headteacher at Priory C in W (Aided) School. However, what was not told to Wynn was that on the recommendation of Mike Barker, the County Director of Education, and Andy Hawkins, the School's Education advisor, only Audrey Bayliss was to be interviewed. If at that meeting she was not thought by the School Governors to be suitable for the temporary post, only then would anyone else be interviewed. So two hours before Wynn thought that he was going to be interviewed, he was visited by the Chairman of the Governors, who told him not to attend but gave no reasons. Audrey Bayliss duly was appointed to the job, leaving a devastated Wynn. To me what was sad and wrong was that no-one, just no-one had bothered to explain to Wynn why this had happened, indeed he was left to put up with the situation. I was furious and wrote a circular letter which I sent to the Director of Education for Powys LEA, the Diocesan Director of Education, the Bishop, the Dean, the Chairman of the Governors, the Headteacher and Deputy Headteacher of Priory School. It read:

> *'I am deeply disquieted by what I have heard today about the appointment of a temporary Head Teacher of Priory Churchin Wales Primary School yesterday.*
>
> *I gather that Wynn Davies was asked to put his name forward for this appointment by various members of Priory School staff. For the past few years Wynn Davies has been an Advisory Teacher for Information Technology for Powys Education Authority and before that he taught both German and French at Llandrindod Wells High School, then at Bryngwyn Comprehensive School, Llanelli, and finally at Gwenyfed High School where he was Head of Department, therefore there can be no doubts about his teaching credentials. However, further to that, Wynn is a loyal churchman being a regular communicant at Brecon Cathedral, a member of the Cathedral Choir and Cathedral Singers, also he organises the Cathedral Servers. Considering that Priory Church in Wales School is supposed to be attached to the Cathedral I think it appalling that having been asked by the Chairman of theGovernors to present himself for an interview at 7.30 on the evening of Wednesday 7th June, Wynn Davies should arrive home two hours before this time to be informed by this very Chairman of the Governors not to attend this interview. This denied Wynn Davies the opportunity of presenting the interview panel with his CV as well as the opportunity to put forward his reasons for his suitability for the position. The Chairman of the Governors laid the blame for this at the hands of the Diocesan Director of Education, the Revd. Canon Anthony Pierce. Incidentally, Wynn Davies is the one member of the IT department who has to be made redundant because of the financial climate.*
>
> *The sad fact of the matter is that the Diocesan Director of Education is a member of the Cathedral Chapter; the Chairman of the Governors is Treasurer of St Mary's Church, Brecon; the County Personnel Officer is a Lay Reader*

attached to the diocese of Swansea and Brecon, also the Dean of Brecon is an ex-officio Governor of the School, yet Wynn Davies, a loyal member of the Cathedral congregation, who was asked to apply both by the Head and Deputy Head of the school, was treated in a disgraceful manner.

These facts have been conveyed to me by Wynn Davies therefore, if any are incorrect, I would be delighted to know because at the moment I am very unhappy about the way in which my church seems to have conducted itself.'

I was cut down by both the Bishop and the Director of Education for the Diocese of Swansea and Brecon, indeed the Bishop's reply was such that I wrote again to Canon Pierce whom I had long admired and whom I had regarded as a friend among the clergy having known him since his days as a Curate at St Mary's Church, Swansea:

'The Bishop tells me that I have made a personal attack on you. If that is the impression my letter gave then I am exceedingly sorry. I had three people take the letter apart (two you do not know, the third was Kelvin) because I was anxious not to cause offence for which reason I made the first part of the letter as factual as possible.

I really am sorry if you have interpreted it in that way because I have so much respect for you and always have done. It is a shame that the Head and Deputy Head persuaded Wynn to put his name forward because he had never intended applying for the job, indeed the thought had never crossed his mind. If you had known how excited he was at the prospect of a light at the end of the redundancy tunnel you would have understood his bewilderment at the outcome.

I cannot grovel any more but hope that this sheds light upon what you must feel rather odd.'

I sometimes wonder if the Bishop had second thoughts about what I had written, realising perhaps that maybe I had been motivated by compassion for Wynn's situation. Who knows? However, life had to go on and later that same month there were not one but two ordination services on successive days in the Cathedral. On Saturday, June 24th, when the Anglican Church celebrates the Nativity of John the Baptist, eight ordinands were made Deacons. That this was a large number was due to the fact that a 'Wind of Change' was blowing through the Church because of these eight, no less than six became NSM's – Non Stipendiary Ministers which meant that they gave their services to the Church without payment while continuing with their own full-time employment or careers. These six therefore included a Senior Police Officer, a teacher, two clergy wives and an Accountant. On the next day, Sunday, June 26th, five Deacons were priested, all having served for a year as Curates in the dioceses, and of these one was a teacher while another was a headteacher. What impressed me particularly about these two services was the number of Swansea choristers who came to both services. On Saturday they led the singing of The Brecon Mass which Philip Moore, Organist of York Minster, had composed recently for the diocese, and helped me teach the music to the vast congregation so that everyone could join in. On Sunday when the Mass for two choirs and two organs by C. M. Widor (of Toccata fame) was sung, they provided one choir while the Cathedral Choir provided the other. At both services the Gloria and Creed were sung to music by John Merbeke, with the litany being sung to plainsong, and the entire congregation was encouraged to join in. Presumably none of this was lost on Bishop Dewi Bridges because on the very next day he sent me a card thanking me for my 'excellent support this weekend' and added 'a little extra' to the quarterly cheque that I always received towards the cost of the travelling that I did in the diocese when attending rehearsals of the Swansea choristers for occasions such as these.

A few days later, when I wrote to him complaining about what Canon Elwyn John had done to my belongings in the room beyond the Choir Room, he not only wrote a very understanding reply but went further and shared with me some of his visions for the future. He was excited that the transformation of the derelict Tithe Barn into a Heritage Centre and Shop was nearing completion and was hoping that the complex would be completed with the addition of a café and the transformation of the Victorian garages into new, plush toilets. He also looked forward to the time when the Canonry might become the Deanery, although his dearest wish was to turn the Deanery Centre – the Old Deanery, into Diocesan offices complete with meeting rooms, so that the entire Diocese of Swansea and Brecon could actually be run from the Cathedral Close. It was indeed an exciting prospect but would it all come to fruition? By now the estimated cost of all this work had gone sky high, way past the original Appeal Target but what saved the day was Lottery Money – monies from the National Lottery that were 'earmarked' for charitable purposes. The first bite at this 'cherry' brought £70,000 towards the restoration of the Cathedral Organ; the second brought as much as £107,250 towards the cost of turning the tithe barn into a Heritage Centre. At this point the Archbishop of Wales, who for some years before had been 'Alwyn Our Dean', unfortunately, chose to speak out against the use of Lottery Money in this way by the Church. He went further and was critical of the whole idea of a National Lottery complaining that it encouraged the hopes and dreams of unlikely riches among those who could least afford to purchase scratch cards and the like. Unfortunately, his stance on this issue was very much weakened by the Dean and Chapter of his own St Asaph Cathedral applying for some of this Lottery money, furthermore Bishop Dewi Bridges made a point of reminding the Archbishop that at a meeting of the Bench of Bishops earlier that year it had been resolved that it was acceptable for parishes to make application for grants from the various National Lottery Funds. So while the Bench of Bishops appeared to be in disarray over the use and abuse of Lottery money, the Brecon Cathedral Appeal Committee had no hesitation in using it to achieve its aims.

LVII

A crisis was looming on the horizon as the number of boys in the Cathedral Choir had dwindled to seven, although to be fair, these few were doing a marvellous job. Indeed, not many months before the choir had made a CD entitled 'Mainly 19th Century'. This had included four anthems by my idol Dr Joseph Pring, the Organist of Bangor Cathedral who had sued his Dean and Chapter for misappropriating monies from the Tithes of Llandinam which should have been used in part for the Cathedral Music. The choir had recorded these with reluctance, knowing that it would give the CD an individuality which it might otherwise not have had, and therefore could help sell the finished product. Also on the CD was a complete performance of 'Praise the Lord, O my soul', by Sir John Goss; all of S S Wesley's magnificent 'Let us lift up our heart'; an unknown double-choir anthem 'Great is the Lord', which the Revd. Sir Frederick Ouseley Bt. had composed for the re-dedication of the rebuilt organ at St Michael's College, Tenbury; and an unknown but beautiful anthem by 'Daddy' Mann of King's College, Cambridge fame, 'I will lay me down in peace and take my rest', which I am sure is modelled on 'Ye that know sorrow' in the Brahms 'Requiem'. Opening and closing the CD were the Magnificat and Nunc Dimittis known as 'The Third Service', by my friend Christopher Knott, which I admired very much. However, to be absolutely sure of my top line for this recording I had drafted in three sopranos to bolster up the few boys and all had gone well. For me the CD struck another blow for the preservation of nineteenth-century Cathedral Music, a cause which was dear to my heart.

I suppose the crisis over the lack of boys in the choir was partly brought on by the fact that boys were not bringing along more boys as had happened in the past, so the task of recruiting choristers had become the lot of the Minor Canons because I was at Builth Wells High School all day and therefore unable to visit schools. Increasingly Minor Canons had been suggesting choirgirls but I had resisted this as long as I could until in the end, I was forced to let girls into the choir and I have never regretted it. Among the first intake were Nikki Taylor and Olivia Williams who, as I write this six years later, are still in the choir having developed into excellent leaders. They joined Tim Morgan who turned out to be easily the most successful musician the choir ever produced, also Rhodri Morgan (no relative), Michael Keddle and the infamous Harris twins, Simon and David, most of whom, incidentally, came with me to Builth Wells High School. Such was the reputation of this school that pupils were going there from a wide area which included Brecon, with the result that in addition to running the Music Department, I now also drove a minibus there and back every school-day, which took up to seventeen additional pupils to the school and, incidentally, conveniently provided me with a means of taking choristers home after after choir practices.

Almost by coincidence, the collapse of the all-male choir at Brecon Cathedral was accompanied by the death of Eileen Carden whose husband, Humphrey, had been the first Cathedral Organist, the one who had done so much to establish this tradition back in 1923. She was of a great age, being 96, and for most of her seventy-three years in Brecon had played her violin whenever it had been needed, be it in the town, the country or in the Cathedral, also she had made the most wonderful, artistic, natural flower arrangements in the Cathedral at all hours of the day or night. She had been such a lovely person for so long that latterly it had been sad to witness how her decline in health had cruelly, and unconsciously to her, changed her personality. Strangely, two days later, dear Mel White also died. He had been one of Humphrey Carden's choirboys in the early days of the Cathedral Choir and had sung throughout his long life until ill health as he fought cancer, stopped him near the end. A lovely man, he was a rock to the choir, always there, always encouraging, always an impeccable Treasurer of the Choir tour fund, such a support that it was difficult to imagine that he would be no more seen. Thankfully his widow, Iris, is still with us, looking after the choir cassocks and surplices, also helping to organise the monthly Coffee Mornings in aid of the Choir tour fund. On the right of the door leading into the Choir Room is a photograph of some cottages at the side of the road up Priory Hill, which now, sadly are no longer there although the outline of some front doors still can be made out in the wall. Mel had lived in one of these and loved to recount how on Sunday mornings he would lie in bed until the Cathedral bell began tolling to announce the 11.00 am Service. Only then would he leap up, dress with all speed, run across the road to the Choir Room, don his cassock and surplice and join the Choir procession into the Cathedral. A third death at this time took away another Cathedral stalwart: Jasper Selwyn a descendant of George Augustus Selwyn, first Bishop of New Zealand, in whose memory Selwyn College, Cambridge, was founded in 1881. A regular worshipper at Brecon Cathedral, Jasper Selwyn was also a member of the Governing Body of the Church in Wales and at the time of his death was serving as Mayor of Brecon. A fourth death at this time took away the Cathedral Chapter Clerk, Ken Anthony, a former Chairman of Brecon Magistrates Bench. He actually died while watching an international rugby match between Wales and England at Twickenham.

Meanwhile the Cathedral Organ was being given a new lease of life at a cost of £110,000. Compared to the sums of money being spent at this time on the organs at St Woolos Cathedral, Newport, and at Christchurch Priory, Dorset, this was a bargain. At this time the Cathedral Appeal Organisers had been fortunate in obtaining a further £25,000 from the Foundation for Sports and the Arts to add to the £70,000 from the Lottery making total grants of £95,000, leaving the Appeal Fund to contribute only £15,000. The firm of Percy Daniel & Co. Ltd. Of Clevedon, Avon, again did the work, hence the reasonable price. The opportunity was taken now to complete the scheme started back in 1973, not that I had ever imagined having a second chance to modify this lovely instrument. So room was found on the Swell Organ for an Oboe 8' and a Flute 4', also the pitch of the mixture stop was lowered to improve the blend of sound. On the Great Manual a new, complete Clarion 4' and a Trumpet extension down to 16' completed the lively reed chorus. On the Positive Manual a clarinet stop was provided but with the pipes housed in the Swell Box to put the stop under expression. The crowning glory was the Fanfare Trumpet 8', placed on the Positive Manual. Having long admired this stop on the organ at St John's College, Cambridge, I had asked Chris Manners of Percy Daniel's, to provide one on the Brecon organ which was louder than Full Organ and he did just that; nor was I alone in thinking it to be better than its Cambridge counterpart, it was superb! I also made sure that the Fanfare Trumpet could not be coupled through to the Great Organ as I had visions of organists noisily adding it to Full Organ for final chords of rowdy, showy music. 'Musicianship by force' someone said. The organ was re-dedicated at a special Evensong on Saturday, February 17th, 1996 at 4.30 pm, sung by the Cathedral Choir augmented by a large number of friends. The Canticles sung to C V Stanford in A were magnificent, especially at the words in the Nunc Dimittis, 'And to be the glory of thy people Israel', when the Fanfare Trumpet stop was used to solo out the organ melody just as I had heard it done many times at St John's College, Cambridge. In the words of Chris Manners of Percy Daniel's, 'it was spine-tingling'. So, too, in Sidney Campbell's anthem, 'Sing we merrily', when at the words, 'blow up the trumpet in the new moon', the stop came into its own yet again. Canon Arthur Howells, Vicar of St James's Church, Swansea wrote later

> 'Saturday's Choral Evensong at the Cathedral was superb! The choice of music, the singing and the organ all combined gave us a magnificent sound. I couldn't get over what a remarkable difference the improvements to the organ have made to its effect.'

After Evensong, some ninety people sat down to dinner at the Castle of Brecon Hotel to celebrate Hazel's and David's thirty years at Brecon Cathedral. Among the guests was the publisher Basil Ramsey who was also Editor of the magazine 'Choir and Organ'. This was his first visit to Brecon and he was bowled over by it all. Yet there was more to come. Next morning at 11.00 am, the augmented choir sang Louis Vierne's 'Messe Solennelle' with great aplomb. On returning home Basil Ramsey penned an article for The Church of England Newspaper comminting on these Festivities, saying that:

> 'Those who came were therefore paying homage to David and Hazel Gedge. In most cases they had moved heaven and earth to clear the weekend of other engagements. They crowded the choirstalls for Festival Evensong on Saturday afternoon after an intensive two-hour rehearsal. There were no gimmicks. Mainstream cathedral music filled the air and touched the hearts of everybody. Yet again, a tradition pronounced dead and buried by some was seen as alive

and vibrant in a small Welsh cathedral as it is in, say, Westminster Abbey. To use BBC Radio 3 phraseology, the canticles were sung to Stanford in A and the anthem was Sidney Campbell's 'Sing we merrily unto God our strength'. The organ was heard in its new glory and was as merry as the rest of us.

I can hear the populists lamenting the musicians who persist in clinging to 'artificial' music. If only the most forceful of them had been in Brecon witnessing the events and talking with a lively bunch of young people! This radiant response to music affirms the sensitivity of those who find it an essential life-giving force. Why is it fashionable to overlook or simply smother evidence that music of this quality continues in cathedrals and often in churches and chapels where slender resources are miraculously transformed by talented choir directors?

As further evidence of a distorted view, a recent article in 'The Observer' droned in the usual monotome: 'the hymns are unsung, the cathedrals lie empty and silent'. Well, try Brecon for a start.

Sung Eucharist on this particular Sunday morning balanced two musical elements. The Creed was sung to Merbecke – music that will never wear out – and then blossomed the wondrously colourful 'Messe Solennelle' for choir and two organs by Louis Vierne. (Brecon also has a chamber organ). This is a far cry from the flashy little numbers that do for parish communion these days. When a real composer puts his soul as well as his craft into his music an act of worship takes on a new dimension. Few of us were aware of the wind and rain sweeping over Brecon that morning'.

The next Musical Extravaganza in the Cathedral occurred at the Easter weekend which was not long in arriving and when it did it was full of special interest. On Good Friday, for example, the evening concert included an unusual work for solo violin entitled 'The Cresset Stone'. This had recently been composed by an up-and-coming Welsh composer, Hilary Tann, who hailed from the Rhondda Valley but who now taught in an American University. While visiting Brecon Cathedral three years earlier she had discovered the ancient Cresset Stone at the west end of the Cathedral and had been moved to describe it through the medium of music. This particular Cresset Stone is renowned for being the largest one in Britain having thirty-six hollowed out stone cups which would have been filled with oil and lighted wicks; it had been discovered buried in a garden close to the Cathedral. In mediaeval days it would have been placed at the foot of a pillar to help light the Priory Church at night; now it was a little piece of history. Hilary Tann had set out to create a meditation on stone and light, indeed in part of the work she used phrases from an eleventh century 'Kyrie' to add a touch of authentic antiquity, and this had resulted in some fascinating and highly original music. The next day, Holy Saturday, the evening concert featured Mozart's 'Requiem', which I had put on for the benefit of my 'A' level pupils at Builth Wells High School as it was a set work, furthermore, one of these pupils, Laura Jones, supplied the programme note for me. Coupled with the

'Requiem', however, was a 'Miserere' for choir, soloists and string orchestra of extraordinary power, by Francesco Scarlatti, who came from a famous Italian family of musicians but who had settled in Dublin presumably to get away from his more illustrious relatives. Yet hereby hangs a typical Brecon story! For the previous two years, 'The Bull's Head' had been run by a baroque violinist Chris Hair who was making a special study of Francesco Scarlatti and his music. Indeed as these studies developed so he had ceased to open The Bull's Head at lunchtime leaving himself more time to concentrate on producing an article about his hero for the next edition of Grove's 'Dictionary of Music and Musicians'. One Thursday evening after a choir practice, Chris had told me about this 'Miserere' which he had given to the Oxford University Press some five years before but which still had not been published. So I offered to put on a performance for him from manuscript copies and this we did on Good Friday last year. Now on Holy Saturday 1996, we were giving what I believe to be the first performance from the printed copies. When I opened a printed copy for the first time, I found there the following, kindly introduction:

> 'Gratefully dedicated to David Gedge, the Lay Clerks, and all involved in the first performance at Brecon Cathedral on 14 April 1995, Diolch yn fawr.'

Finally, on Sunday evening, the evening of Easter Day, there was another rare performance, this time of Beethoven's 'Triple Concerto', leaving me to wonder just how many Breconians ever realised what fascinating music was continually being churned out at their cathedral. The soloists were violinist Miranda Dale who had played 'The Cresset Stone' on the previous Friday, Chris Knott our pianist and composer friend, along with the young 'cellist Paul Watkins. Paul had turned out to be a phenomenon. The son of John Watkins who had helped me start the Gwent Chamber Orchestra and who still led the viola section, he had been a finalist in the BBC/TV 'Young Musician of The Year' competition and at the age of twenty years, had been appointed Principal 'Cellist in the BBC Symphony Orchestra; he played like a dream with the result that Easter 1996 ended on the highest note possible. Down at The Bull's Head that night, Paul Watkins signed himself in the Cathedral Choir Visitors Book as 'No. 1 'cellist BBCSO, No. 3 Gwent Chamber Orchestra', behind his first teacher Stephen David and Frances Knott wife of pianist Christopher, the two regular 'cellists in The Gwent Chamber Orchestra.

That summer holiday found nearly sixty singers from the Cathedral choir and Singers in London at St Paul's Cathedral singing services for a week in celebration of David's and Hazel's thirty years at Brecon. Everyone stayed in the Cathedral Choir School close by to enjoy a very 'laid-back' week since mornings and evenings were free and only the afternoon was taken up with singing. Constant fun was provided by bass Lay Clerk Richard Williams who had been with the Cathedral Choir since my first days at Brecon. Now a

Detective Constable based at Brecon Police Station he was known affectionately as 'PC Plod' or 'Pilchard'. Anyway he and a young bass nicknamed 'Chunk' kept everyone amused with their constant banter. Said Richard in fun to Chunk, while they were both surveying the City from the top of The Monument that had been built to mark the spot where the Fire of London had begun in 1666: 'Chunk, how is it if the Fire of London started here, this tower is still here?', Grunted Chunk to Richard after a long pause, during which he had looked most puzzled: 'How should I know'. One afternoon as the choir rehearsed for Evensong in the Cathedral, the basses were joined by Mark Wildman who, fortunately, was well aware of Richard's sense of fun. As Mark found a place to sing, Richard leaned over to Chunk and whispered wickedly in his ear: 'I think you'd better go and stand by him, he doesn't really know what he is doing'. So Chunk dutifully stood by Mark to guide him through the music at both the practice and the service, not realising that he was in fact standing next to an ex-chorister of Gloucester Cathedral who now was in charge of the Singing Department at London's Royal Academy of Music. The next day another friend arrived to join the basses and again Chunk was despatched to help him. This time the visitor was Bruce Grindlay who had been Organist at Christ College, Brecon, and now was Director of Chapel Music at Bedford School. There was never a dull moment. One morning someone from The Times Newspaper arrived to photograph Hazel and me with some of our young choristers in the organ loft at St Paul's, because I was the longest serving Cathedral Organist in England and Wales. Unfortunately, when published in the illustrious newspaper, the caption read:

> 'Mr and Mrs Gedge, who with the choir will be playing and singing at services in St Paul's all this week, are the longest serving organists in England and Wales and the only husband and wife team of organists.'

As a result I received a few disgruntled letters from various organists who had been playing in churches for far longer than I had in the Cathedral. Not long afterwards Hazel and I took delivery of a bottle of Laurent-Perrier Champagne; the accompanying card read:

> 'Every week day during his morning programme on Classic FM, Henry Kelly selects from the national newspapers a person whose actions have most identified their 'Joie de Vivre'.
> It is our pleasure to present the Winners with a bottle of the excellent Laurent-Perrier Rose Champagne which we sincerely hope you will enjoy.'

Welcome as this champagne was, the best musical 'wine' was yet to come, having been left to last. At the final Evensong on Saturday the anthem was to be Hubert Parry's magnificent 'Blest Pair of Sirens' with St Paul's Cathedral Organist, John Scott himself, playing the organ. What an exciting prospect. That morning everyone had packed their bags so that they could load them onto the two Williams (Cwmdu) buses that had arrived early in the afternoon; onto the bus also went all the music that had been sung earlier in the week and therefore was surplus to requirements. As the choir lined up in the South Choir Aisle in preparation for Choral Evensong, the Cathedral Organ was strangely silent. Minutes later we found out why when John Scott descended from the Organ Loft complaining that he could not start it, whereupon he disappeared. As we waited for progress reports so five minutes became ten and ten minutes became fifteen by which time the choir should have been singing Evensong, but still the organ remained silent and John Scott was nowhere to be seen. The Canon in Residence suggested that perhaps the choir could sing an unaccompanied Evensong as it had done on the day before but unfortunately all the music had been packed away on the bus. Half an hour had elapsed before John Schott reappeared, bringing with him one of the Organ Builders who soon brought the great instrument back to life whereupon, forty-five minutes late, the Cathedral Choir and Cathedral Singers processed into the great Cathedral to begin their final Choral Evensong.

Back in Brecon I began to look forward to the first celebrity recital on the newly restored Cathedral Organ which was due to be given on Friday October 11th, by the same John Scott. In making this part of the annual programme of the Brecon and Christ College Music Society, it became possible to pay John Scott the sort of fee that he deserved. To my amazement around one hundred and twenty people came to Brecon to hear him play. He opened with Edwin Lemare's arrangement of Richard Wagner's 'Overture to the Mastersingers', which I thought was a strange choice. However, it was extraordinarily effective, so much so that when towards the end John played the Mastersinger's March on the Fanfare Trumpet against the remainder of this stunning music on 'full organ', I unashamedly wept at the magnificence of the sound.

LVIII

Hazel's mother had now been living at Garth Cottage for around eight years, gradually losing touch with us as Altzheimer's Disease took hold of her; it was especially hard for Hazel to see her mum slowly become enclosed in a world of her own. Morgan Llewellyn used to visit her regularly not only when he had been a Minor Canon at the Cathedral but also when he had moved on to become Chaplain of Christ College, Brecon. While praying with her one day he had begun to recite the traditional version of The Lord's Prayer whereupon she had suddenly started moving her lips to the familiar pattern of the words. One evening she had become unconscious so that Hazel had to call out the doctor but unfortunately, just as he walked through the front door, she regained consciousness and acted as though nothing untoward had happened. By now Hazel was regularly sitting up with her until late into the night to keep her company but one night in particular, she sensed that something was not right. When mum once more became unconscious she had an idea that the end was near and continued to sit with her, but being very tired eventually she fell asleep. When she awoke an hour or so later, her mum had gone. Hazel then roused me and I telephoned the doctor to explain that mum was dead and to ask him to come and provide a Death Certificate. He arrived quickly, did what he had to do, asked if we were alright, then left. Hazel telephoned our good friend Beth Wainwright to chat, then we telephoned Colin Griffiths the Undertaker who had taken care of Dad's funeral so well. Finally, by 9.00 am Beth was round at Garth Cottage removing all traces of mum's bedroom from what had originally been our sitting room; within an hour our sitting room once more was as we used to know it; an era had come to an end. The funeral was just like Dad's although Mum's was in the Cathedral so that the friends she had acquired in her eight years at Brecon could join us there. Then after lunch at Garth Cottage the coffin was taken down to the lovely crematorium at Narberth where the final goodbyes were said. Later mum's ashes were placed with dad's in the churchyard at St Mary's, Kidwelly, the church in which they had been married and where they had spent so much time together in happier times.

At the Cathedral itself, these also were difficult days. Yet despite the elation at the success of the new Heritage Centre and 'Pilgrims' the Café', along with the successful restoration of the bells and organ, not forgetting Hazel's and my thirtieth anniversary celebrations, all was not well. One of the problems of running a cathedral like Brecon was that while the twelve canons individually could be pleasant and charming during their one month in residence in the new Canon's flat which had been constructed in the Deanery Centre, when they were altogether at their quarterly Chapter Meetings they could become so different. At this time new Fire Regulations had decreed that there should never be more than fifty people in the Choir Room at any one time with the result that the Dean and Chapter instructed me to move the Cathedral Singers rehearsals to the Refectory, next door to Garth Cottage. When I pointed out to them that there was no piano in the Refectory and asked if they would be prepared to supply one, the new Chapter Clerk sent this reply, dated 23 September 1996:

> 'Dear Mr Gedge,
>
> In reply to your letter of the 27th August 1996, I regret to inform you that the Dean and Chapter are in no financial position to provide you with a piano. However, they are prepared to let you have the piano from St Mary's on a permanent loan arrangement. They are also prepared to pay for the transfer of this piano, and for tuning it .....
>
> ...They have also asked me to inform you that the Choir Room will have to be vacated by the 30th September, and in no circumstances should this room be used after that date.'

At the same time I received a second letter from the Dean and Chapter which read:

> 'Dear Mr Gedge,
>
> I have been asked by the Dean and Chapter to write to you concerning the period between 3.30 pm and 5.00 pm on Choir rehearsal evenings. Apparently members of the choir who are under the age of 14 arrive at 3.30 pm and are unsupervised until 5.00 pm when the rehearsal commences. This is a contravention of the Children's Act, and these children, therefore, must be supervised at all times. Some parents of these children may be prepared to supervise them during this period. If you have any problems with this matter, the Dean and Chapter are prepared to discuss them with you.
>
> Yours sincerely
> G F Thomas
> GLANVILLE THOMAS
> CHAPTER CLERK '

In response to these letters, I wrote:

> 'Dear Glanville,
>
> Thank you for your letters. Both of them I find sad. Firstly, I realise that the Singers have to move out of their home for the past thirty years but a piano has to be found. The one at St Mary's, sadly, is no good because it is a semi-tone flat and cannot be tuned at concert pitch. The Dean is putting a request in 'The Beacon' next month. Could not the Dean and Chapter extend the time by one month, after all, I can think of three funerals this year alone which have benefited from the presence of thirty or more Cathedral Singers, including that of your predecessor? (Incidentally, to date the number of Singers at a rehearsal this month has not exceeded fifty and the attendance records can be checked at

any time in the Choir Room – third cupboard along). Furthermore, the Cathedral Choir could not have sung at St Paul's Cathedral this summer without the support of the Cathedral Singers and that was a good publicity trip for Brecon Cathedral.

As for the other matter, the contravention of the Children's Act. I hardly think it likely that any parents will come and supervise the choristers as we cannot even get any of them, with one exception, to any services to hear their own children sing. The young ones have been brought up to love and use that room. It would be tragic if this was stopped. If you force the youngsters to go home you may not get them back again. I cannot do anything about my time of arrival because I do not leave school (Builth Wells) until 3.30 pm (Monday & Friday) and 4.30 pm (Wednesday). Could not the Verger keep an eye on them, or the Minor Canon, or even the Residentiary Canon? I would be grateful for support and understanding as running a choir these days is not easy and although we have a Cathedral School, sadly, until six months ago, very little support for the choir came from there (along with the five girls). At St Asaph Cathedral, I believe you will find that the boys are given tea before weekday practices, by an organised band of ladies – Hazel has to teach after school to earn a living of some sorts and this is the time that suits most of her pupils who are still at school.

What I find really sad is that in a community like ours, where so many of us have known each other for so long and have worked together for many years, we are reduced to communicating by letter to each other. At least the Dean was good enough to tell me all this before your letters arrived. At some Cathedrals the Organist is invited to attend Chapter Meetings to discuss such matters as these.

With good wishes
Yours sincerely
DAVID '

Canonries at Brecon Cathedral were highly prized among the clergy of the diocese and the duties were not onerous: one month each year spent at Brecon Cathedral attending the daily services, preaching on Sunday morning twice, and attending the quarterly Chapter Meetings. Such appointments in Wales are the gift of the Bishop. To me, Canonries in the diocese of Swansea and Brecon had become Long Service Medals as usually they were given to clergy who had served in the diocese for many years. Only once in my thirty years at Brecon did a Bishop of Swansea and Brecon have the courage to appoint a Canon purely on the grounds of intellectual ability. That was quite early on when Bishop Jack Thomas gave a Canonry to David Walker who was Senior Lecturer in History and Dean of the Faculty of Arts at University College, Swansea, and who was attached to St Mary's Church, Swansea as a Non-Stipendiary Minister. Bishop Thomas was firmly of the opinion that the Chapter would benefit from the presence of this intelligent and caring priest and he was quite right. Why twenty-five years later the same could not have been done for Morgan Llewellyn I shall never understand, because a man who can rise to be a General in the British Army and a Colonel to two regiments, must surely have had something to offer the Church in an executive capacity, yet he remained ignored. When Hazel suggested this to a clergy wife, the reaction was one of horror as the lady in question replied: 'But he hasn't served as a Curate yet.' How pathetic and small minded!

It was extraordinary how some canons could be so devout and caring while others could be so pompous and unsympathetic. One in particular impressed me because he always arrived early for the daily Eucharist which in those days was at 7.30 am, genuflected then knelt in prayer for some considerable time, while another appalled me by insisting on singing Evensong with the choir one Friday evening whereupon he ruined the Responses, laughed it off afterwards and told me that I fussed too much about the music. Many Canons counted it a privilege to attend choral services while in Residence, but one in particular avoided choral services as often as he could. It was at this time that Ted Hunt was installed into an Honorary Canonry at Brecon Cathedral and I should have been thrilled. Ted Hunt had enthusiastically supported my musical activities in the diocese from the moment I had arrived, furthermore for many years he had not only been a much-loved Vicar of Christchurch, Swansea, but he had also been a highly effective Chaplain of Swansea Prison which was next door to his church. Why therefore should this well-earned preferment have come to Ted just as he was preparing to retire, it seemed so unjust?

It was at this time that the question of Women being ordained as Priests arose again. I must confess that I could sympathise with both sides of the argument and often I wondered what my father would have said. So it came to pass that in the autumn of 1996, the Governing Body of the Church in Wales met to debate again the issue concerning the Ordination of Women Priests. This time, all six Bishops voted for the motion, there being a new Bishop of Llandaff, while the Laity, once again voted convincingly in favour of Women Priests, 136-47, the clergy, however, were defiant to the end but while they voted 'for', 85-40, they carried the motion with just one vote to spare. There was much jubilation and weeping for joy among the delegates who had voted for this historic motion while there was much weeping and gnashing of teeth among its opponents. The 'Western Mail' adopted a sensationalist approach to the outcome of this vote and predicted that:

> 'The exodus from the Church in Wales over the ordination of women priests will start with a mass resignation in January.'

but common sense prevailed. Betty Saunders in 'The Church Times' quoted one potential woman priest as saying:

> 'I'm impressed by people who voted against who are talking about the importance of unity because we're a small Church, and unity is all. I'm glad and relieved.'

So the Church in Wales joined the other Anglican Churches in Britain in accepting women as priests. The Church in Ireland had been the first to take the step back in 1992, while the Church of England and the Scottish Episcopal Church had followed two years later in 1994. Provisions were made for providing financial assistance in case of hardship for anyone resigning from the ministry on conscientious grounds, furthermore, a bishop was to be appointed to undertake the pastoral oversight of those people who could not accept women priests, who would also represent their views in the councils of the Church in Wales.

The mass ordination of the first women priests was scheduled to take place at Epiphany-tide; The Church Times headline announcing this, put it quaintly: 'Women priests arrive with wise men.' Seventy-seven of the seventy-eight women deacons were to be priested on either Saturday, January 11th or Sunday, January 12th, depending on arrangements made within each diocese. Interestingly, the one woman deacon not to be ordained priest was herself an opponent of the Ordination of Women Priests and has remained so to this day. Meanwhile, on Saturday, December 21st, at 1.00 pm, our good friend David Thomas, formerly Principal of St Stephen's House, Oxford but now Vicar of Newton on the outskirts of Swansea, and a Canon of Brecon Cathedral, himself also an opponent of women priests, was consecrated Assistant Bishop of the Province of Wales in St Asaph Cathedral. The only son of Bishop Jack Thomas, this was the first time since disestablishment that a bishop's son had been consecrated Bishop and for that occasion he wore his father's ring and cross. So the Church in Wales now had its own 'flying bishop' to administer to the 'rebel' parishes, and although he was based in the diocese of Monmouth he was licensed by the other five bishops to work in their dioceses as required. He made his home in Abergavenny and went on to do the obvious, which was what some people said the Diocese of Monmouth should have done when it came into being in 1921: he used the magnificent ancient Priory Church of St Mary, Abergavenny as his base for ordination services and the like.

On the afternoon of Sunday, January 12th, 1997, history was made in a packed Brecon Cathedral when Bishop Dewi Bridges ordained eight women priests. He also licenced three others to work in the diocese; they had 'jumped the gun' by hopping off to England some time before to be ordained Priests there. There were no protests, just joy and happiness and as usual, the Swansea choristers came along to enable the Cathedral Choir to make the most of the Mass for two choirs and two organs by C M Widor. It was a splendid occasion. A few days later the Diocesan Warden of Ordinands wrote to me:

'Dear David,

The Ordination of the eight women deacons to the Priesthood on Sunday was a truly momentous occasion for the candidates, their families and for all of us who shared their joy. I have already received many calls and comments of appreciation from people around the Diocese who attended the service in Brecon.

May I therefore take this opportunity to express my personal thanks for your kindness and support with the arrangements for that Ordination Service last weekend.

I was thrilled that everything went so well and I felt this was only due to the fact that so many people played their part on the day. Thank you once again. I look forward to your continuing support in the future.

Yours sincerely
Canon ROBERT J WILLIAMS
Vicar of Sketty

Sadly, so epoch-making an event was swept out of the local Brecon and Radnor Express a few days later by a sensational report concerning the sexual habits of Welsh youngsters. This announced that:

'Young people in mid-Wales are having sex more often than in other parts of Wales, according to a television survey to be revealed next week. They have sex every day of the week, have more sexual partners and have more one-night stands than in any other county in Wales, a London-based company will claim in a programme, which begins on Thursday of next week'.

So the headline, 'Builth's youngsters top Wales sex league' replaced 'Historic Occasion at Brecon Cathedral', and a claim was made that 'many youngsters from Builth Wells see themselves as Casanovas.' Next morning I looked at the happy, cheerful faces of my senior school musicians at Builth Wells High School with disbelief ….!

LIX

If the year 1997 had begun in an upbeat way it certainly continued with what had by now become the regular programme of ten choral services and four concerts during Holy Week and the Easter weekend. Starting with the Good Friday morning service when the Passion story was always movingly sung to plainsong it continued with an evening concert that once again held the audience in awe.

There was another airing of Francesco Scarlatti's 'Miserere' along with an Albinoni oboe concerto, a Handel concerto grosso, motets by Byrd, Lotti and Mozart, and two J.S. Bach organ chorale preludes. Holy Saturday's J.S. Bach's 'St John Passion' was praised by Aldon Rees in The Western Mail for its 'Blessedly Smooth Performance', so much so that 'Even the unflappable David Gedge, the Cathedral maestro with the legendary standards, must have been pleased with the flow not to mention emotional impact' of the music. On Easter Sunday evening, Miranda Dale played the Brahms Violin Concerto; after the interval Huw Watkins, brother of 'cellist Paul Watkins, played the Schumann Piano Concerto. The Gwent Chamber Orchestra was suitably augmented for this concert and did sufficiently well for Huw to comment to his father afterwards that our players had done 'a much better job than the King's College orchestra", which was a reference to a performance which he had given in the previous term at Cambridge where he was studying for a music degree at that time. Truth to tell, the Gwent Chamber Orchestra had found the finale a nightmare to prepare because of the complex, syncopated rhythms that occurred from time to time. In the end I cheated and having found a way round the problem, conducted accordingly. Principal horn player that night, Angus West, who was married to violinist Jane Tunley, a founder member of the orchestra, and who himself was Principal Horn in the Welsh National Opera Orchestra, having previously led the horns in The Hallé Orchestra, admitted afterwards that it was the first time he had ever felt comfortable in that movement. Some time later, when I told this story to the Associated Board of the Royal Schools of Music Examiner at Garth Cottage, a lady who actually taught conducting at one of the London music colleges, she was horrified and proceeded to show me how it should have been done. However, I am convinced that neither the orchestra nor I could have coped with the music in this way however technically correct it may have been. In any case we shall not be playing that concerto again as we were so relieved to get through it without experiencing any problems. All that was left after this was Bank Holiday Monday evening when Adrian Lucas, whom I had first encountered when he had been Organ Scholar at St John's College, Cambridge but who now had been appointed Organist of Worcester Cathedral, gave an organ recital. So the Easter weekend drew to a close and despite the initial problems it had been a great success both musically and socially, with eighteen barrels of beer being consumed at the Bull's Head.

It was now that Kho Kho entered our lives. Since our six and a half stone boxer dog wedding present, Hannibal, had departed this life, Hazel had gone in for smaller dogs and had fallen in love with pugs. So we had given a home to dozey Pompey and his adorable one-eyed sister Chloe, who had quickly carved out a niche for themselves in Garth Cottage. Next came Bella who became so much a part of the family that when she died of natural causes in Hazel's arms we could not think of replacing her. Unfortunately, we were invited to take on a black pug, one year old, who had endured four owners; we gave in. Yet before Kho Kho, for that was her name, could arrive, Hazel spotted in The Brecon and Radnor Express, in the Hay-on-Wye News, the following request:

> 'FREE-LOVE a very small Chihuahua with a silky fur is looking for someone to love, details from The Seven Stars!'

Promptly, she reached for the telephone directory, then for the 'phone; within an hour she was picking up another rejected dog who immediately transferred to her any devotion that remained, because she had changed homes so many times. 'Maisy' was her name but we changed that to 'Daisy', added to it 'Mary', the name of our next door neighbour who was fascinated by her, and finally, because of her posh walk, arrived at 'Lady Daisy Mary'. Before Kho Kho could arrive there was the small matter of a Cathedral Singers trip to Brittany to deal with; so, towards the end of July, the Singers set out on what turned out to be a magical, Musical, mystery tour. At Pont L'Abbé they sang a Mass on Sunday morning called a 'Pardon' because it began with a statue of the Blessed Virgin Mary being carried in procession into the church. As the most solemn moment in the service approached, so the congregation, which included one lady wearing a traditional tall Breton hat, launched into a French song to a melody that resembled the English folk song 'Old Macdonald had a farm'; many of the Singers were reduced to silent hysterics so funny did it sound. Afterwards, while drinking wine in the Square, they discovered that the congregation had been singing 'The Lord's Prayer'! There followed some lovely outings: to Quimper where the Singers sang some gentle sixteenth century music at a concert inside the glorious Cathedral while outside a Folk Festival raged in full swing; to Saint Brieuc where they sang in the fascinating old Cathédrale Saint Etienne and enjoyed a standing ovation; to Guehenno where they saw a stunning stone 'Calvary'; to Vannes where the Cathedral almost rubbed shoulders with mediaeval half-timbered houses and where they endured temperatures of around 93°F as they walked around the walled city; to Josselin where they saw a fantastic castle perched on rocks high above a river; to Locronan, an incredible mediaeval village where time appeared to have stood still for hundreds of years – no wonder it had been used on countless occasions as a backcloth for countless historical television and film dramas. Back home it was difficult to pick up the threads of life again but on this occasion Hazel and I had a distraction as we took delivery of Kho Kho. When Hazel collected her, then sat her on the back seat of the car and drove her to Brecon, there was just one, solitary little whimper. After that there was no looking back as Kho Kho immediately took over us, and Garth Cottage, quickly learning how to live with Lady Daisy Mary who could be a little crusty on odd occasions.

Meanwhile at Builth Wells High School, one of the third year (now called Year 9) pupils had managed to be accepted at Chetham's, the music specialist school in Manchester. This was a fantastic achievement on the part of Susan Pryce the Brecon flute teacher who had taught the lad in question from his first day at the school. Barry Griffiths indeed had come from a musical family with his grandfather, Dr Griffiths, having been Head of Music at Llandrindod Wells High School and Conductor of the Radnorshire Youth Orchestra when first I had arrived at Builth, and his father having played violin in a radio orchestra in Ireland until illness had brought about early retirement. A quiet, hard-working lad, incredibly well mannered and a pleasure to teach, Barry fully deserved his success. So, too, did Joanna Williams, a senior school flute pupil of Susan Pryce, who not long afterwards was accepted as a pupil at illustrious Kneller Hall, on the way to attracting national media attention by becoming the first female member of the Welsh Guards Band. Such successes, while attracting attention to the Music Department also deprived the school of its best musicians but it was great to see such youngsters being plucked out of obscurity and given the chance to develop their musical talents far further than would have been the case had they remained in as rural an environment as Builth Wells, lovely a place as it may have been.

Early in the autumn Richard Marlow, a friend from my Southwark Cathedral days had brought his chapel choir from Trinity College, Cambridge to show Brecon why it numbered among the finest of British choirs; for two hours he guided it through an amazingly difficult and varied programme of unaccompanied music. This proved to be a successful opening concert for what turned out to be one of the last of the Brecon and Christ College Music Society seasons as it was becoming more and more difficult to find audiences in and around the town to support a regular series of small scale professional concerts. Indeed, before long, the affairs of the Society sadly were wound up for lack of interest because audiences rarely numbered more than thirty people which just did not generate enough money to fund the concerts, even with additional financial help from the Welsh Arts Council.

The Cathedral Singers, however, always had been more fortunate because apart from each member paying an annual subscription, their concerts were supported by a substantial number of patrons, almost one hundred. These had been gathered together and looked after by the choir's remarkable secretary, Mary Kneen, and this represented a valuable injection of welcome cash. More help came from the Welsh Amateur Music Federation and still more from the National Federation of Music Societies; then when all was added together it was possible for The Cathedral Singers to give two full-scale concerts with orchestral accompaniment every year for some considerable time. Later this autumn, for the first time, the Cathedral Singers hosted the Annual Wales Meeting of The National Federation of Music Societies which was masterminded by Mary Kneen and which in one particular way, must have been unique. To end the proceedings, all the delegates from the other choirs who had attended the day's events, found themselves singing Evensong in the Cathedral, alongside the Cathedral Singers and Cathedral Choir. For many of them, this was a new experience as, to their credit, they chanted a psalm, sang the Responses, also the unaccompanied 'Short Service' by Orlando Gibbons, along with the great Samuel Sebastian Wesley anthem 'Ascribe unto the Lord'.

Towards the end of the year, on Saturday 22nd November, Hazel and I were awarded the distinction of being the first recipients of the newly created 'Archbishop of Wales Award for Church Music'. In a ceremony at the Chapel of St David's College, Lampeter, our old friend Dr George Guest, the former Organist of St John's College, Cambridge, read out the two Citations whereupon the Archbishop of Wales, who many years before had been 'Alwyn our Dean' at Brecon Cathedral, presented us with our awards. It was a lovely occasion made all the more memorable by the well nigh perfect weather and the presence of so many old friends. Bliss!

LX

The new year, 1998, had not progressed very far before the town of Brecon was thrust onto the National limelight when two local men blew-up both themselves and the house they had been sitting in while making a bomb with explosives that had been stolen from the local army camp-an event which even attracted the attention of none other than *Private Eye*.

It was while all this was going on that Fr Timms chose to depart from this world at the great age of eighty-seven years. He had been such an important influence on my life, firstly as a Minor Canon at Southwark Cathedral when I was an unruly choirboy; then as Vicar of St Mary the Virgin, Primrose Hill where I began as an undisciplined Organist and Choirmaster, and became mesmerised by worshipping in so much beauty. Next as Archdeacon of Hackney when he lived in an imposing vicarage in Holborn and, if asked, allowed Hazel and me to enjoy free accommodation in the very centre of London; and when finally, in retirement at Minster-in-Thanet, where he let us enjoy many a holiday in Kent, we watched him and occasionally helped him edit the New English Hymnal With his passing we had lost more than a friend and it was sad that his last days had to be spent in so uncongenial a nursing home, especially when at his great age, so few of his friends were left to help him pass his last days. His funeral service at Birchington Church was a mess, completely lacking in the detail and style to which he had always been accustomed. When the Bearers brought his coffin into the church, they laid it to rest the wrong way round in relation to the altar. As for the candles on the altar, these were near to the end of their lives, while the only flowers visible were to be seen around the last few inches of the pascal candle. There were no candles around the bier, no appropriate altar frontal, furthermore, his chosen hymns had been ignored with the excuse that their complexity required a choir which had not been provided. Finally, the address was short because, in the words of the Vicar, there was 'not much time', presumably because the crematorium was waiting! It was a shoddy affair. Worse was to follow: on the day when the ashes were to be laid to rest in the churchyard at Minster-in-Thanet, the undertaker had forgotten to have the hole dug so that mourners were forced to wait while this was done before they could make their final fond farewells to this wonderful priest. It was a sad end for someone who had served the Church so royally. Fortunately, Fr Timm's successor as Archdeacon of Hackney decided to remedy the situation; he set about organising a great memorial service at St Andrew's Holborn, and he invited Hazel and me to organise the music. It was a glorious service. Some of Fr Timms's hymns were sung by a large congregation, also parts of his congregational Mass from the New English Hymnal. An eloquent sermon in his honour was preached by his old friend the Bishop of Bath and Wells. His old favourite, the Thomas Tallis motet 'If ye love me' was sung from the organ gallery by a well-nigh perfect choir consisting of Helen and William Purefoy, John Bowley (tenor) and our Nick (bass) during the Communion. Hazel played the organ while I directed the musical proceedings; indeed there was only one musical hiccup and that was beyond our control. Dear 'John' Warrell, who had been Fr Timms's Organist at St Mary the Virgin, Primrose Hill before me, and who had been a good friend of his and had helped him produce The New English Hymnal, was due to play the organ before the service but did not appear much to Hazel's and my bewilderment. After the service however, he rushed up to the organ full of apologies, to explain that while he had been at his local Eltham station, as a train arrived so a lady had thrown herself in front of it and had been killed, leaving him in no state of mind to play the organ at the service. Some days later Hazel and I received a note from the Archdeacon of Hackney:

'Dear David & Hazel,
    I know it was all 'for George' but I just wanted to thank you for your encouragement before the service, arrangement for the splendid singers, and help with the service. I and many others are glad we did it.
Thank you
As ever
Clive

There was something else that reared its head at this time. Ever since I had arrived at Brecon back in 1966, I had voluntarily organised diocesan choral events starting with an annual Festival in the Cathedral in May which most times was a fully choral Evensong but sometimes was a choral Eucharist. I had followed this by having Archdeaconry festivals to make the congregational musical setting of the Communion Service by John Merbecke known to more people. Next to be introduced had been the Advent/Christmas Carol Service which was taken to a different church in Swansea each year. Last came participation in the annual ordination service in the Cathedral to make it a truly diocesan event. Four hundred singers came to the first Diocesan Choral Festival, but over the years numbers dwindled to below one hundred, while around forty choristers usually sang in the carol service and thirty singers joined in the Ordination. One possible reason for this drop in numbers was my insisting on those singers who attended the Choral Festival and Carol Service coming to at least three rehearsals; those attending the Ordination always came to one rehearsal in Swansea. In this way high performing standards were achieved and to me this was important. There was no charge for taking part, nor did I insist on choirs belonging to the Royal School of Church Music because this was expensive and I realised that most churches had enough trouble paying their annual financial quota to the diocese of Swansea and Brecon. Just occasionally, with the help of Eileen Jones, Organist at Christchurch, Swansea, who acted as Secretary, and Ted Hunt who had recently retired from being Vicar of Christchurch and Chaplain at Swansea Prison, who acted as Chairman of a so-called RSCM committee, tuition events were organised for example an evening to help organists, or an evening to introduce simple choir music, but, sadly, support usually was lukewarm. Suddenly, however, the RSCM decided to muscle in on these activities but charging for attendance because it needed to generate more cash to keep in business. So having appointed Dr Ian Graham, Organist of St Paul's Church, Sketty, as Education Officer, and having appointed Christopher Barton, Organist of St Woolos Cathedral, Newport, as a deputy Area Commissioner, the RSCM began to organise events in Swansea. Particularly popular were the Half-Day Choral Events which consisted of an afternoon's practice, tea, then a short service, because it was all over and done with inside a few hours without the chore of attending regular rehearsals. Perhaps I over-reacted but I felt 'miffed' at what was happening, especially when attending the concluding service at one such event in St Mary's Church, Kidwelly, I found many choristers from a Swansea church who had never appeared at my events, lapping up all that was given out. This course had been directed by a Cathedral Organist from England and the specially-put-together service consisted of hymns, readings, prayers and four musical numbers three of which were of very dubious quality being the sort of flashy items that I tried to avoid. In the congregation also was Llywela Harris who after five years as Warden of the RSCM had retired to St David's where her father had once been a Canon at the Cathedral. Afterwards I took her to Hazel's family home, Bridgend House, for tea and purposely said nothing about the service. Suddenly, while we were eating she blurted out: 'what did you think of THAT?' and immediately we all fell about lamenting at what was happening to Anglican Church Music, and at what had happened in that service.

It was while taking a rehearsal for my Diocesan Choral Festival in a church in Swansea that I discovered a leaflet announcing a day of events at Llanelwedd to celebrate the 75th Anniversary of the Diocese of Swansea and Brecon. The date was Saturday 2nd May, the very Saturday which for years had been the day of the Diocesan Choral Festival. I was not amused and gave vent to my wrath which brought forth from the Bishop a letter which began thus:

> 'Dear David
>   I believe the Dean spoke to you following the meeting of the Rural Deans in December about the Diocesan Day at Llanelwedd on 2nd May 1998. We had no choice about the date but had to accept what we were offered. No one realised that the date conflicted with the annual Choral Festival at the Cathedral ....'

This only brought home to me how little genuine interest there really was in the diocese, for the efforts to keep alive the tradition of Cathedral music, a point which was emphasised by the lack of clergy involvement. Forgotten was the idea that such music can 'bring all heaven before our eyes'. So many people seemed to have surrendered the desire to worship through the beauty of word, beauty of sound, also beauty of surroundings. I went to this Diocesan day at The Royal Welsh Agricultural Showground at Llanelwedd on the outskirts of Builth Wells. It began with various displays and workshops and culminated in a celebration of the Modern Alternative Eucharist of the Church in Wales with music provided by a Youth Orchestra along with a Folk Mass setting which was used by some of the Swansea parishes. Apparently, copies of the music for the Eucharist along with the words and music for the modern hymns, were supposed to have been circulated to all the churches in the dioceses yet none seemed to have reached Brecon. My experience of organising the music for the Province of Wales 'Celebration 80' event in Cardiff Arms Park, had taught me that events like this needed adequate preparation and this included area practices, but I was not called upon to help with this service in any way. The service itself was a great success if you like worship of that sort: mediocre music, arm-waving in hymns, up-to-date English which had no ring about it, little if any meaningful ceremonial. I drove home to Brecon, across Mynydd Eppynt, with a heavy heart, thinking back to what Bishop Jack Thomas and Canon Harry Williams, Vicar of Swansea, had put together back in 1973, to mark the 50th Anniversary of the diocese of Swansea and Brecon.

Nor was I particularly happy to receive the following letter from the Cathedral Minor Canon not many days later:

> *'Dear David*
> *I felt that I ought to put pen to paper following the incident with the junior choir in the music practice room in the Cathedral on Monday 18th May. Whilst I appreciate the position that you find yourself in, with concern to supervising the practices for the junior choir, I feel that this particular incident highlights the dangers within the current system. The fact that some of the children are travelling straight to the choir room as soon as they leave school means that they can be unsupervised for a considerable period of time. The behaviour that I witnessed, both in terms of physical activities and the verbal abuse I received from a seven year old when I tried to control the behaviour occurring is I believe testament to the current inadequate situation…..'*

Actually, this letter highlighted deficiencies in the Cathedral ministry. I had to augment my meagre Cathedral Organist stipend by teaching, consequently, all my musical activities had to be done after school and in the evening which left me with little or no time to do pastoral work with the choristers. However, what was stopping the Cathedral Clergy from visiting choir homes and establishing closer links between their families and the Cathedral community. Had the Minor Canon in question done this he would have discovered that the seven-year old boy who had told him to f…. off, not only had a bigamist for a father but also had for a step-father a man who beat up his mother to the extent that she had to be lodged in a 'safe' house. However, rather than become involved in such pastoral work, the Minor Canon chose to send copies of his letter to the Dean and Chapter (Canons). They in turn were forced to react in a way that was not helpful to me, insisting that until I retired from school teaching the choristers would have to stay away from the Choir Room unless supervised – this is where the Minor Canon could have been helpful. Again, I had a heavy heart because while I understood the reaction of the Dean and Canons, I also understood how for some of these youngsters, the choir room had become a refuge, a second home, a haven of fun, but now this privilege was being taken away from them.

LXI

At the turn of the year, the Dean, John Harris, had announced his retirement. For me this was a moment of sadness because I had grown very fond of him and his wife, Beryl, and had enjoyed working with them. Although he could have gone on for longer as Dean, truth to tell he was not in good health as he had suffered a heart attack a year or so ago. Always he had given the impression of being easy-going but in reality he had much determination; once his mind was made up he was immovable. During his five years at Brecon he had watched over the transformation of the Cathedral Close, indeed when doubt had been cast over the financial wisdom of building Pilgrims, the Cathedral's café, he had pushed on with great resolve and was eventually proved right when the café, once completed, was an immediate success and received favourable mention in The Times Newspaper, no less. Another important part of the development was accomplished when he and Beryl had moved from Blackstone to The Canonry which, after seventy-five years, now became the Deanery. As for the ancient Tithe Barn, this now was such a superbly designed Heritage Centre that it was mentioned for a national award and even though this didn't materialise it was still a magnificent transformation from the wreck of a building that I had known for so long. The Old Deanery also had received attention, more than £300,000 worth of it. Now as The Deanery Centre it housed a kitchen, meeting rooms and the Chapter House on the ground floor; Diocesan Offices and Cathedral Offices on the first floor; also a flat for the Residentiary Canons on the second floor. Throughout the building there was an adequate supply of toilets which was a change! Up in the Cathedral tower the ten bells were in place and being rung, while in the Cathedral itself the organ had been magnificently finished, the new Fanfare Trumpet pipes its crowning glory.

However, it was all going too well, so much so that perhaps I should have been alerted by a decision taken by the Dean and Chapter which resulted in the Holy Eucharist on the first Sunday of every month being sung congregatonally to a setting that Philip Moore, Organist of York Minster, had composed recently for the Diocese of Swansea and Brecon Choral Festival. This was far from traditional Cathedral worship but John Harris as Dean, had gone along with it. Then there was the letter he had written to me after the incident concerning the Minor Canon and the young choirboy, banning the choristers from the Choir Room if I was not there, that also seemed out of character.

Early in the summer Bishop Dewi Bridges announced his own retirement which was to take place in November. He had ensured that he would go out in a blaze of glory by making two spectacular appointments: he appointed the first ever Lady Canon in the diocese when he made the Revd. Sybil Coleman, Vicar of Hafod, an Honorary Canon, then he appointed Canon Geraint

Hughes, Vicar of Llandrindod Wells, Dean, the first time for fifty years that a Dean of Brecon Cathedral had been promoted from within the diocese. These appointments were greeted with great enthusiasm, especially that of Geraint Hughes, although I commented to the Lay Clerks 'Wait and see'. I remembered the new Dean's father, Hubert Hughes, Archdeacon of Gower, who had been a very strong character, one who had always gone his own sweet way.

During the week of July 18th – 25th, the Cathedral Choir paid another visit to Cork for a singing holiday and had a tremendous time which, as usual, did wonders for morale. At the time I didn't realise how important this was to be until the next month when, during a few days at Bridgend House, Kidwelly, I received a telephone call telling me that on Friday September 4th, when there was to be an installation of Canons during Choral Evensong at the Cathedral, the Canticles – Magnificat and Nunc Dimittis, were to be sung not to the usual musical settings but to Anglican Chants. I was devastated. I telephoned the new Dean to ask if this was really necessary but all he would say was: 'You're a strong man, you can take it'. Well I couldn't; to me this was the deliberate destruction of the great Cathedral Music tradition which, as far as I was concerned, mattered a great deal. A letter of protest to the Bishop merely produced this reply:

> '... As far as the Collation and Installation of the new Canons on 4th September is concerned, I believe it would be good to sing the Canticles to well-known Anglican Chants. As someone who served in parishes for 30 years where it was the normal practice to have Choral Evensong Sunday by Sunday, I regret the fact that this is no longer the case in many places.'

I, too, for thirty years had been responsible for Evensongs like this at St Mary's, Brecon; to me these were Parish Evensongs, very different to what I had been responsible for during those same thirty years at Brecon Cathedral which to me were the true Choral Evensongs. However, all became clear to me at the service itself on Friday, September 4th. At the end of the First Lesson but before the choir and congregation could begin to chant the Magnificat, the Bishop's wife leapt to her feet and said loudly to all the Canons' wives who were seated around her: 'Come on girls, sing up, we've been waiting years for this'. So what should have been a great Cathedral service adorned with music intended to bring 'all heaven before our eyes', was reduced sadly to a parochial bawl, where those who sang loudest carried the day. I suppose I shouldn't have been surprised at this because there had been a famous occasion when Hazel had been teaching her organ pupils in the Cathedral on two successive afternoons and the Bishop's wife had happened to be wandering around on each occasion watching some flower arrangers at work. On the second afternoon the Bishop's wife had muttered loudly enough for all to hear: 'She must be doing alright, she was here yesterday'. One of the flower arrangers happened to be a good friend of Hazel and duly reported back all that was said. In actual fact Hazel had only two organ pupils, much to her sorrow, as it was her first instrument and she would have loved to have passed on her skills to more people. So Hazel actually was doing far from well financially, bearing in mind also that her annual salary as Assistant Organist was an appalling £350 per annum!

Ten days after that infamous Installation of Canons, there was a meeting of the Cathedral Chapter. At this, Chancellor Elwyn John, to give him his correct title as Senior Canon, who by virtue of this exalted position had been looking after Cathedral matters during the interregnum, reported that:

> 'there had been some difficulty over the form of the last service for the Collation of Canons.'

He went on to state that the Service 'was not Choral Evensong but a service held for a specific purpose'! Strangely, however, the service had followed exactly the form of Evensong as set out in the Book of Common Prayer, furthermore, at the foot of the cover of the special Service Sheet was the statement that the Collation and Installation of the Canons was to take place 'During Evensong'. Finally, 'He, therefore, proposed that at the next Collation Service, as in the previous Service of Collation, the canticles should be sung to Anglican Chant'. Obviously, it had never occurred to Chancellor John that year in and year out the Lay Clerks had come voluntarily to the Cathedral to sing Evensong on a Friday, to enhance the beauty of the worship, and now he and the other Canons were preparing to hijack that offering. However, I suppose the choir should not have been surprised at this as whenever Chancellor John came into residence at the Cathedral, he made a point of avoiding choral services as often as possible. Of the twelve Canons only one, Nigel Hall, who had succeeded Elwyn John as Vicar of Builth Wells, spoke up for the choir but was ignored, with the result that Chancellor John's motion was carried, presumably by eleven votes to one.

Five days later, on Saturday, Septemeber 19th, Canon Geraint Hughes was Collated and Installed as Dean in a splendid fully Choral Evensong which months before, the Bishop had decreed should replace the Diocesan Choral Festival that should have taken place on the first Saturday in May but which had to make way for a diocesan gathering at the Royal Welsh Showground. So Evensong was sung with great aplomb by a large number of choristers from Swansea who joined with the Cathedral Choir to make a joyful noise in C V Stanford in B flat and Sidney Campbell's anthem 'Sing we merrily'. Unfortunately, despite the jubilation, one of the hymns chosen by the new Dean, rang alarm bells: 'I, the Lord of Sea and Sky'. Afterwards Dean Geraint wrote in a letter to Hazel and me:

> 'Although I have spoken to you a number of times since Saturday I thought I would like to put on paper my appreciation of the music that you provided for the Choral Festival and in which I was honoured to share. Please convey to the Cathedral Choir in particular and all others who worked with you.

It was a joyful occasion and I will never forget the music that you provided which could not have been bettered. I would not have wished to have changed a single note or item in it.

Thank you for your great kindness and I look forward to working with you over these next few years.

Yours sincerely
GERAINT '

The next Collation and Installation of Canons occurred on a Friday Evening at the end of October at 7.00 pm; this meant that within two months five new Residentiary Canons and two Honorary Canons had been installed. Again the service was parochial with the Canticles sung to chants, but this time the Lay Clerks decided to lodge a subtle protest. As the Installation Service was not until 7.00 pm they decided to sing a Men's Voices Cathedral Evensong at 5.45 pm. This they did but with the complete absence of clergy, the only one coming anywhere near being the Dean, who shuffled around at the back of the nave for part of the time. Members of the choir read the Lessons, I sang the Service and we all read the final prayer together.

The Bishop's Farewell Service took place on Advent Sunday morning at 11.00 am, when the Holy Eucharist was sung to music by Herbert Sumsion, except for the Gloria and Creed which were sung as usual to the music of John Merbecke. Afterwards the Bishop sent me a card:

'*Dear Hazel and David*
Thank you both (and the choir too) for the lovely service at the Cathedral last Sunday morning. We were deeply moved by it all and enjoyed it thoroughly ....'

Often he had sent to me little messages of appreciation like this after divine services in which he had been involved; it was very thoughtful of him and was one of his endearing qualities even if he and I hadn't always seen eye-to-eye over Cathedral or Diocesan matters. During this service the Bishop had lit the first of the five large Advent Candles, while on the remaining three Sundays in Advent and on Christmas morning Dean Geraint lit the other four candles. In doing this the Dean made it appear as if he really had no interest in meaningful ceremonial; often he would forget to involve the servers, leaving them marooned at the High Altar while he wandered down to the Candles which stood in front of the pulpit. Indeed when asked what he thought was the role of a Cathedral he had replied: 'to reflect the work of the parishes'. There was some light relief: notably a wedding in the Cathedral which involved the full choir; the bride was an air hostess who opted to pay the Lay Clerks with bottles of duty-free whisky! Then there was the writer in The Times newspaper, who chose to describe Long-Haired Chihuahuas like our Lady Daisy Mary as 'Stick Insects with fur'! However, there was the joy of singing the J S Bach Advent Cantatas at Evensongs on the four Sundays in

Advent – such wonderful music which sounded all the better from being sung with orchestral accompaniment and in a liturgical context.

Our first Christmas with Dean Geraint certainly was different. At the Blessing of the Crib service, apart from the copious printing errors on the service sheet, he put down as the final hymn: 'O come all ye faithful', including the final verse which begins:

'Yea, Lord we greet thee, born this happy morning'.

Well it was not even 4.15 pm on Christmas Eve so the choir lodged a practical protest by singing:

'Yea, Lord we greet thee, born tomorrow morning',

while also Lay Clerk, Dudley Palmer, refused to sing any of the hymn and sat down! Worse was to follow. Dean Geraint steadfastly refused to acknowledge that the Lay Clerks sang Evensong on Christmas Day at 5.45 pm; not only did he refuse to include it on any specially printed lists but furthermore he did not attend it himself. It seemed that as far as he was concerned, Christmas ended with 'Christmas Dinner', consequently when the traditional service of Nine Lessons with Carols came around, as it always did on the Sunday after Christmas Day, December 27th this year, he was nowhere to be seen having gone off to Llandrindod Wells for the day. As for Sunday, January 3rd, which according to the Church Lectionary is designated 'The Second Sunday in Christmas', he did not include a single Christmas hymn at that morning's service of Choral Eucharist. The three hymns listed were:

1. 'On this day, the first of days, God the Father's name we praise'
2. 'O Christ the same through all our story's pages' a New Year hymn sung to the 'Londonderry Air', and
3. 'Lord Jesus Christ, You have come to us', one of my pet hates!

So much for Christmas yet so many lovely Christmas hymns had not been sung. It was sad!.

Brecon Cathedral from the air photographed by Nicholas Taylor.

The Venerable G.B. Timms, Archdeacon of Hackney and Editor of the New English Hymnal.

Left to Right: Kelvin Redford, Tom Redford, Hazel Gedge, Doris Gulvin, Florence Redford and Walter Gulvin having tea outside Garth Cottage around 1987.

Archbishop Alwyn Rice-Jones with David and Hazel Gedge having presented them with AWACM Medals (Archbishop of Wales Awards for Church Music).

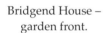

Bridgend House – garden front.

David and Hazel at the organ in Brecon Cathedral.

Rehearsing Beethoven's Triple Concerto with Paul Watkins (cello), Huw Watkins (piano), Miranda Dale (violin) and the Gwent Chamber Orchestra.

Nutmeg – our fifth Pug.

Back Row (L to R): Matthew Morris, Bethan Moses, William James, Amy Morris, Nia Chapman, Kate Robinson, Charlotte Hacche, Natalie Brown.
Front Row: David Gedge, Hazel Gedge, at our Farewell Dinner.

LXII

This new year was special as it heralded the final year of the twentieth century. In Brecon it was doubly significant because it opened with the election of the eighth Bishop of Swansea and Brecon, an affair which went into the second day of voting. It resulted in the Venerable Anthony Pierce, Archdeacon of Gower, being elected, the first clergyman from within the diocese of Swansea and Brecon to be accorded such preferment since my friend Jack Thomas had been elevated to the episcopate back in 1956. For me this was interesting because much as I admired the new Bishop as a priest, I had upset him over the appointment of the new Head Teacher at Priory Church in Wales Primary School, with the result that relations between us were somewhat cool. It had not been the best time of year to lock the forty-seven electors into Brecon Cathedral for a day and a half. On the previous Friday for example, the choir had sung Evensong there in a temperature of 47oF; by Sunday this had risen to 52oF, but the sudden injection of heat, as usual, had created such downdraughts as to leave some people thinking that perhaps a cold Cathedral without the downdraughts was preferable to a warm Cathedral with them. Always this dilemma left the choir wishing that the powers-to-be would be sensible and switch on the heat permanently towards the end of September when the summer sun had warmed the stone walls to around 60oF, because so many people had commented that if the heat was left on all the time, but regulated by a thermostat, the cost would be no greater and the building would never get sufficiently cold for the downdraughts to be created. However, commonsense never prevailed!

Come the month of March, new floodlighting had been installed in the Cathedral grounds, furthermore it had won a Swalec and Wales Tourist Board 'Lighting up Wales' award worth £7,000 of the total £8,000 cost of installation, the remaining £1000 being provided by an anonymous benefactor. The idea behind the award was to encourage lighting projects which would enhance the night time enjoyment of some of Wales's finest architectural features. Dean Geraint intended for it to be possible to illuminate the Cathedral over the coming Millenium but his efforts resulted in the following letter from bass Lay Clerk Trevor Benwell, appearing in the columns of the Brecon and Radnor Express:

> 'Sir – Whilst one was very pleased to read that Brecon Cathedral has been selected as one of the two places in Wales to have extra floodlighting for the Millenium, it is with some trepidation one reads further that the running costs must be met by the Cathedral.
>
> This present winter, the Cathedral has been miserably cold on many occasions and this has been a mild winter. Now, it seems, money is planned to be spent from the Cathedral budget on running this extra floodlighting, thus reducing the inadequate amount available for heating.

Catering for the flamboyant, with apparent disregard for basic necessities, it seems to me, is neatly summed up when Glaswegians say of the people in Edinburgh 'Fur coats but no knickers'.

The Easter week-end at the beginning of April found some spectacular music being performed in the Cathedral, including JS Bach's 'Mass in B minor' on Holy Saturday, along with Prokofiev's Second Violin Concerto in G minor played by Miranda Dale, and Grieg's famous Piano Concerto played by Huw Watkins, on Easter Sunday night. Furthermore, at this time, former Choirboy Oliver Galletta, now a pupil at Wells Cathedral School, but who was still based in Brecon, became the Texaco Young Musician of the Year – a great achievement. Down at The Bull's Head at this time also, the Easter weekend musicians also achieved distinction by consuming twenty-two barrels of beer during their stay, a record yet to be broken.

Meanwhile, on the first Sunday of the month the Dean had decreed that the Alternative Rite of the Holy Eucharist, according to The Church in Wales, be used. So was introduced a modern English version of the service which was far from popular with the choir. The new book contained three versions of the Prayer of Consecration which meant that the service was continually being prompted by announcements of page numbers which helped to disturb any flow that could be created in the service. When this service had been introduced into St Mary's Church, Brecon, by Canon John, music had been needed to clothe the new words. Hazel and I, therefore, had consulted as many as sixteen modern, 'trendy' settings and liked none of them, most of them coming unstuck over the question of satisfactory verbal accentuation. So Hazel composed her own setting which was modelled on Fr. Timms's congregational 'Folk' Mass in his New English Hymnal. To this I added an adaptation of John Merbecke's Creed and a harmonised version of the Agnus Dei for the choir to sing. This service now became a regular feature on the first Sunday morning every month in Brecon Cathedral; on the monthly service sheet the musical setting was described as 'Missa de Sancta Maria (Anon)' as it had been composed initially for St Mary's down the road!

By now the Archdeacon of Gower, Tony Pierce, had been consecrated Bishop of Swansea and Brecon, so there remained his enthronement which was to take place in the Cathedral on the afternoon of May 1st, St Philip and St James' Day. For the second time, I decided to open up the choir for this service to Swansea choristers, provided that they attended three rehearsals; some of the Cathedral Singers also joined in. The choral statistics make interesting reading:

56 sopranos, of whom 25 attended all four rehearsals; 8 others failed to qualify.
15 altos, of whom 5 attended all four rehearsals; 1 other failed to qualify.
14 tenors, of whom 5 attended all four rehearsals; 2 others failed to qualify.
10 basses, of whom 5 attended all four rehearsals; 3 others failed to qualify.

That 95 singers took the trouble to support this occasion bears out the regard that the people of Swansea had for their new Bishop who, after all, had been born, educated and served all his ministry in their city. The service was a triumph, the music was wonderful. Here is how Dr Ian Graham described it in his Archdeaconry of Gower Newsletter:

'It was a full house on Saturday the 1st of May, the Feast Day of SS Philip and James, when the combined choirs of the Diocese joined an invited congregation on the occasion of the enthronement of Anthony Pierce as the 8th Bishop of Swansea and Brecon. Preparation for the music had already been underway for some time beforehand with a series of Monday evening rehearsals at Christchurch. For this event David Gedge had insisted on all choristers attending a minimum of three of these practices, together with the final rehearsal in the Cathedral on Saturday morning. All agreed that this was an essential precondition in view of the complexity of the music. There were even those who, having missed a practice at Christchurch, travelled to Brecon for an extra qualifying rehearsal with the Cathedral Singers.

The music chosen for the massed choirs was a mixture of the old and new. Stanford's Te Deum in Bb, as well as Parry's 'I was glad' had both been sung fairly recently: the latter at the installation of the new Dean. The work that was new to most of us from the parishes had been written by Basil Harwood (1859-1949), himself a former parish church musician (at St Barnabas, Pimlico) before becoming successively Organist at Ely Cathedral and Christchurch, Oxford). O HOW GLORIOUS IS THE KINGDOM, which many regard as Harwood's master-piece for the church, at first sight seemed an over-ambitious anthem to tackle for such an important occasion. Nevertheless, as David Gedge explained, it is sung regularly by the Cathedral Choir and therefore he knows those sections where potential troubles lie. Accordingly, difficulties were pre-empted and the whole work came together remarkably quickly. There is also a virtuoso organ accompaniment that was tossed off with aplomb by the inimitable Hazel. The day itself was remarkable for a number of reasons. During the morning rehearsing the finishing touches were put to the music, part of which was the introduction of a brass trio led by Tony Small. To be a part of massed choirs singing the Parry and the Stanford accompanied by the might of the cathedral organ and fanfare trumpets is an experience that is both unforgettable and rarely repeatable. The disposition of the singers was arranged remarkably smoothly although there were moments of unstable trepidation for those on the podiums. The real musical triumph was the final result of about a hundred singers, some from choirs with large repertoires and some from churches with small, all able to contribute to a glorious sound in a venerable building on a rarely to be experienced occasion.

And what of the installation? It was all a service of this nature should be. The sense of reverence, dignity and timelessness, which seemingly only the church at its best can produce, was there in abundance. The procession of the new Bishop along the length of the Cathedral to the strains of I WAS GLAD

WHEN THEY SAID UNTO ME showed how the power of music can deeply move as it lifts the worshipper to new heights.

It is timely to say yet again that in other dioceses, on such occasions, it is customary for the cathedral choir alone to provide the music: to show what they can do – as one former precentor put it. In Swansea and Brecon, probably uniquely, we are all given the chance to participate in the major events of the diocese'.

Dr Ian Graham concluded kindly:

'At the end of the rehearsal David thanked us for taking part. No David – it is for us to thank you.'

Nineteen churches were represented in this choir: Swansea – St James, St Jude and St Mary; then from around the city: Clydach, Cockett, Cwmbwrla, Glantawe, Gowerton, Killay, Llangyfelach, Loughor, Manselton, Morriston, Newton, Penllergaer, Reynoldston, Sketty, Townhill and Waunarlwydd, not forgetting Christchurch itself, where the rehearsals had been held. In addition it must not be forgotten that those of the Cathedral Singers who sang, were representing churches from the Archdeaconry of Brecon at the northern end of the diocese. At the end of the next month, several of these choristers returned to sing with the Cathedral Choir at the annual Ordination Service, the first one taken by Bishop Anthony. This gave them the chance to sing the Kyrie, Sanctus, Benedictus and Agnus Dei from Louis Vierne's great 'Messe Solennelle' along with three unaccompanied sixteenth-century motets, yet another fascinating musical experience for these lovely and enthusiastic singers.

Sometime now the Cathedral Choir gave the first performance of a fascinating Te Deum which had been specially composed for it by an equally fascinating young man who had been singing among the tenors for the past year. Hugh Houghton had studied classics at Cambridge University but then had opted for ordination to the Priesthood. First, however, he wanted greater experience of life and to that end had come to Brecon to work in a L'Arche Community house and soon was spending much of his spare time making music with the Cathedral Choir. At the end of his year in Brecon he had paid the Choir the compliment of calling it the most Christian organisation that he had found in the town. Before he moved on he duly handed me this weird and wonderful 'Te Deum' which the choir took a lot of trouble to learn and now sing regularly at the monthly service of Matins. Hugh's next port of call was a church in Bradford where he ran a bar before he finally moved on to Mirfield to train for the sacred ministry. Coming originally from Birmingham he may return there to serve his title but he keeps in touch with our choir and how I wish he would come back here to work as a Minor Canon. For now, however, the choir perpetuates his memory by singing his strikingly original 'Te Deum'.

Most importantly, while here Hugh had helped the Lay Clerks come to terms with what was going on at the Cathedral liturgically, spiritually and otherwise because many of the Lay Clerks were unhappy with developments. Indeed Sub Organist Kelvin Redford had made various attempts to discuss matters with Dean Geraint. On one occasion he had asked why a psalm had been 'sung' by the congregation at a funeral when there was no choir to lead the singing and when the service sheet had been so full of misprints. He also asked why the hymn 'Living Lord' had to be sung so often when really it is little more than a Pop tune and, after all, there are 499 other hymns in the hymn book. Similarly he asked why a greater variety of psalms could not be sung so that the younger choristers could get to know the Psalter better. Then Kelvin asked if it was really necessary for the Cathedral to ape a Parish Church and provide no 'quality' experience at, for example, an Installation of Canons. Also he asked why the Cathedral should continually go for the lowest common factor instead of taking pride in doing things properly, with the highest possible standard of worship in music, language and ceremonial. Kelvin went on to explain how at a weekday evensong he had attended recently in Ripon Cathedral there had been a congregation of forty-five people (Ripon being a town little bigger than Brecon) and he had asked him why this should be? Kelvin reminded the Dean of how Trevor Beeson, a Canon of Westminster Abbey, had said recently of cathedrals in general, that they 'should inspire a sense of awe, reverence and permanence; representing the unchanging in the face of a changing world.' Kelvin also suggested that if the youngsters in the choir could actually enjoy singing Thomas Weelkes's 'Hosanna to the Son of David', and learn through it to recognise 'class', why should adults not be encouraged to do the same.

However Kelvin was fighting a losing battle and I was constantly reminding him and the Lay Clerks of what I had said when Geraint had been appointed Dean: 'Wait and See.' So, I suppose, it should have come as no surprise when, as I was leaving the Cathedral by the north door one Monday evening at the end of July, just about to go on holiday to Kidwelly, I spotted a small, unassuming sheet of paper pinned onto the notice board which hangs in a dingy corner of the porch. I went across to find out what this was and discovered to my horror, a notice of an application for a Faculty to move the High Altar forward. Not only had nothing about this been announced at the services on the previous day but furthermore, the notice was being displayed for the statutory month at a time when many of the regular members of the congregation would be away from the Cathedral on holiday. This just seemed sad especially when it concerned such an emotive issue, therefore I notified as many people as I could in the time available, before setting off for Kidwelly in the hope that some protests would be made.

The main points at issue included the fear that in moving the High Altar forward, the unified design of High Altar and Reredos, which contributes so much to the beauty of the Sanctuary and is a masterpiece of architect W D Caröe, would be destroyed. There was also the desire that Holy Communion should continue to be celebrated by a priest facing East rather than using the more trendy Westward position which would impose a face and human personality between God and his congregation. Among other points aired was the suggestion that if the Lightning Conductor was not re-instated soon on the tower and a thunderstorm led to the Cathedral being struck by lightning, there might be no High Altar to move forward. Then there was also the pressing need to put right the leaking roof above the sanctuary, not forgetting the completion of the tower pointing which had been badly done not long before so that rain was still working its way into the Cathedral there; would it not be more useful to spend any available money sorting out these problems? Finally, uppermost in many people's minds was the installation of a sensible and efficient heating system which would render the Cathedral 'User-Friendly' in the depths of winter.

Kelvin Redford, in his letter of protest, pointed to expensive mistakes in the past made by Deans and Chapters. He recalled the heating system before the present one, which could not be run at low temperatures to provide background heat during the week; also he gave a reminder that the chancel had been painted with magnolia emulsion paint in the mistaken belief that this would make the building look warmer when in fact, because the paint is oil-based, it can only be removed at great expense – this whole operation had in any case, been ludicrous because the Chancel previously had been correctly coloured with whitewash as is usual for all mediaeval chancels.

Come the end of August, when the statutory four weeks had ended, the Faculty application business was swept under the carpet while attention was focused onto Tuesday September 14th, Holy Cross Day. On this day 906 years ago, the Priory Church had come into being, on this day 76 years ago, the Diocese of Swansea & Brecon was founded. This day in 1999 opened with a celebration of the Holy Eucharist by the Bishop, with the Dean and Chapter in attendance along with many other people connected with the Cathedral. Early that evening the Cathedral Choir sang an Evensong during which two Canons were Collated and Installed, also Gerard Elias QC was installed as Chancellor of the Diocese. For some reason, on this occasion, the choir was allowed to sing a musical setting to the Canticles, maybe because it was such a special day, who knows? However, this really was fortuitous because by chance Gerard Elias was a great supporter of the Lawyers' Temple Church in London, and its celebrated choir, therefore it seemed right that a good dose of Cathedral Music should accompany his installation. So the Cathedral choir sang T A Walmisley's inimitable setting of the Evening Canticles in D minor, along with the anthem 'Salvator Mundi' – O Saviour of the world, who by thy cross and precious blood hath redeemed us', by John Blow, which was so appropriate on Holy Cross Day. That was not all. At 8.15 pm The Gwent Chamber Orchestra gave a concert in the Cathedral at which there were three young soloists: the flautist, Barry Griffiths who had recently moved from Builth Wells High School to Chethams Music Specialist School in Manchester; bassoon player and former Cathedral Chorister Oliver Galletta, who was

Texaco Young Musician of Wales; and Flora York Skinner the soprano. Afterwards everyone moved out from the Cathedral into the grounds around for the switching on of the new floodlights; it was a magical evening.

Thirteen days later, one of Hazel's former piano pupils, Stephanie Openshaw, died at the age of thirty-four years after a courageous battle against cancer. So it seemed appropriate that The Cathedral Singers and Gwent Chamber Orchestra should give a performance of Handel's 'Messiah' early in December which raised £3,200 for Brecon War Memorial Hospital's Millenium Appeal. This gave rise to a wonderful notice in the inimitable Brecon and Radnor Express which found its way into The Daily Telegraph:

> 'The Messiah will come to Brecon Cathedral next Saturday, in a final bid to raise money for the town's hospital.'

A few days later, at Dean Geraint's invitation, the Mid and West Wales Fire Brigade also came to Brecon Cathedral but for its annual Christmas Carol Service. The Cathedral Singers contributed two Basque Noels: 'I saw a maiden' and 'Sing Lullaby'; The Brecon Town Concert Band contributed 'Wings of Freedom', 'In the bleak Midwinter', 'Lion King', and 'Abba Gold'; The Aberhonddu and District Male Voice Choir contributed: 'Bryn Myrddin', 'Steal Away', 'Rachie', 'Take me home', 'Amen (this little light)', and 'An American Trilogy'. Fortunately, there were six congregational Christmas Carols and some Christmas readings, because apart from the Cathedral Singers minute input most of the musical items had nothing to do with Christmas in any way. I left the Cathedral after one and three-quarter hours of this charade which had been delivered in a temperature of 50oF, feeling thoroughly depressed. These feelings continued over Christmas as the Dean banned the Christmas Day procession, 'to save time', although rather ludicrously in that case, the choristers stood still in their Stalls to sing all six verses of 'O Come All Ye Faithful'. Already he had spent five minutes telling the assembled congregation about his two forthcoming Millenium Services, failing to mention the Lay Clerk's Evensong by Candlelight later that day, and the Service of Nine Lessons and Carols the next afternoon, neither of which services he, the Dean, attended. It was thoroughly depressing. Once again in The January Beacon – the Cathedral magazine, he gave a lengthy resumé of all that had happened in the Cathedral during the run-in to Christmas carefully avoiding to make any mention of the vast contribution made by The Cathedral Choir and The Cathedral Singers. So we moved on to the Millenium Services although I was full of foreboding as I could discover nothing about them other than the choir was not required. On New Years Eve, the last day of the Twentieth Century, I arrived at the Cathedral for the 'New Millenium Prayers' but found myself surplus to requirements. There in the pulpit was the Dean armed with a microphone through which during the course of the service he sang two Taizé chants unaccompanied, therefore minus their atmospheric supporting harmonies; at the end of this one-man-show he led the congregation in singing: 'One more step along the world I go, From the old things to the new, keep me travelling along with you.' The next day I entered the Cathedral shortly before 12 noon for the Celebration 2000 service to be greeted by strains of Vaughan Williams's 'Lark Ascending' being blasted out over the loud speaker system. I went up to the Dean and asked: 'The same as yesterday?'. 'Yes', he replied. 'Then you'll not be needing me', I replied and promptly left the building, and went to the service at St Mary's Church.

The next day, Sunday, January 2nd, 2000, at 3.00 pm in the Cathedral, there was a Brecon Community Service to mark the start of the new Millenium. Sadly it was little better than what had gone before. For me, while the appearance of the hymn 'Lord for the years your love has kept and guided', with its uncomfortable rhythm on the word 'guided', and the re-appearance of 'One more step along the world I go', were a disappointment, the version of Psalm 139 read out was a disgrace:

> 'Lord, you have examined me and you know me;
> You know everthing I do.
> You see me when I am working or resting;
> You know all my actions.'

When compared to the 1662 version, much is wanting:

> 'O Lord, thou hast searched me out and known me: though knowest my down-
> sitting and mine uprising, thou understandest my thoughts long before.
> Thou art about my path and about my bed:
> And spiest out all my ways'.

Lay Clerk Bernard Adams summed up the reaction of many people, in a letter to The Western Mail:

> 'Sir- Permit me to express my dismay at the general quality of the material that made up the special Millenium Service held in Brecon Cathedral on the afternoon of Sunday last, January 2.
>
> When one considers that for centuries countless famous artists, architects, painters, musicians, writers, have contributed their very best efforts (in the words of Francis Bacon) to the glory of God and the relief of man's estate, it was sadly disappointing that in almost an hour we heard not a word from such glories of the English language as the Authorised or Revised Versions of the Bible; modern versions, the authors of which strain every nerve merely to be ingeniously different, took their place.
>
> There was not a single piece of serious devotional music despite the participation of an augmented Cathedral Choir, musically the high point was Parry's hymn-tune Repton, rising like a rock above a sea of mediocrity and worse. Scholarship too was in short supply: the work of Wesley, Newman or

other great hymnodists was not represented, while banality was rife. And not a word in Welsh except the Bishop's final blessing.

In short, what could and should have been an inspiring and memorable occasion turned out to be a cultural desert. Is this sort of thing really symbolic of what people want or need? Is this what Christianity has really sunk to in our day and age? Is culture in fact the pariah that an ignorant clergy wish to make of it? Or am I and laymen like me merely dinosaurs awaiting final extinction along with the values that we cherish? Is the Church of the 21st Century, dumbing-down rather than uplifting, no longer the place for the man or woman of education and taste?'

This said it all; rather well too!

LXIII

At this time, my son, Nicholas, had decided to forsake London and work in Wales. He had come to this momentous decision while holidaying with his family at Bridgend House, Kidwelly, with Hazel and me. I had taken him to meet Judge Michael Evans who lived in Reynoldston Old Vicarage, and who used to sing in the Diocesan Choral Festival; soon he was convinced that his future as a barrister lay in Cardiff. Before long he was ensconced in Chambers, in 33 Park Place, right in the centre of the city, as happy as a 'sandboy', commuting daily from Bwlch, near to Brecon, where he and Kate had purchased a lovely old farm house with four acres of land, looking towards glorious Llangynidr Mountain. As for daughter Harriet, she was now Sales Manager for Music Sales, in the Far East, having a marvellous time working in Hong Kong, Singapore, Thailand, Kuala Lumpa; in Japan she met up with a Kidwelly schoolfriend of Hazel, who had married a Japanese businessman!

Meanwhile the Cathedral Lay Clerks had found the perfect distraction from what was going on at the Cathedral. They had become involved in a production of a new opera by Welsh composer Alun Hoddinott – known to them as 'Whodunnit', called 'The Tower'. This was yet another product of enterprising 'Opera Box', the brainchild of Londoners Brendan Wheatley and Bridgett Gill who liked to bring aspiring young opera singers to Brecon each year to put together a series of opera performances. Where possible local singers were involved, indeed some years before young Ben McCalmont, when a treble in the Cathedral Choir, had sung solo in Benjamin Britten's opera 'Albert Herring'. More recently the full choir sang the chorus parts in a performance of Purcell's 'Dido and Aeneas' and thoroughly enjoyed themselves. 'The Tower' was different. Terry Heath wrote in The Guardian:

> 'Turning a true story of industrious struggle into an opera is an artistic challenge. However, the drama played out at Tower Colliery in South Wales which climaxed in 1994 when 239 miners chipped in with £8,000 apiece to rescue 'their pit' and turn it into a successful workers' cooperative, is the stuff of theatre. It prompted the Brecon-based company 'Opera Box' to set to work a couple of years ago with the aid of a £290,000 lottery award from the Arts Council of Wales. The result is a decidedly unstuffy production which director Brendan Wheatley says reinforces his belief that opera is not simply for posh people ....
>
> ....Tower the opera mirrors Tower the colliery, once deemed by British Coal to be uneconomic but now turning in healthy profits and paying good wages. The opera also reflects the social history of Wales. Two male-voice choirs add volume to the production and local schoolchildren invade the stage in crowd scenes that recreate the community spirit of mining villages ....'

The Lay Clerks did their best to learn Alun Hoddinott's music but apart from Joseph Parry's song 'Myfanwy', it was not easy nor much fun, yet they persevered. When the company's Music Director, Fraser Goulding, came to rehearsals in the Choir Room, he was pleased with the outcome, especially when the Lay Clerks stayed in tune while singing 'Myfanwy'; apparently they were the first singers to succeed in doing this, indeed one male voice choir had sunk down as much as a minor-third when on stage. The two performances at Theatr Brycheiniog on February 18th and 19th were fun; especially when on the second night an elderly couple stormed out of the theatre after ten minutes because, in an effort to give the performance an extra touch of realism, the opening scene in the pit showers found the miners standing naked in the gloom. Afterwards Fraser Goulding wrote to me:

> *'I am writing to thank you and the choir for taking part in the recent performances of 'Tower'. Your participation contributed greatly to the success of the venture.*
>
> *I do congratulate you on the way you and the choir members tackled and learned the music. I really appreciated the musicality and secure intonation.*
>
> *For myself, rehearsing, performing and talking with you all was one of the most important and enjoyable parts of the whole project. I hope that you enjoyed working with us as much as we did working with you ....*

At this time also the subject of my low pay as Organist of Brecon Cathedral had reared its head yet again. Now that I had retired from teaching at Builth Wells High School in the previous year I had less money to live on and with which to support my work. A year or so before, in preparation for this moment, I had asked the then Dean, John Harris, if he thought that the Dean and Chapter could possibly pay me £10,000 a year and he had not dismissed the possibility. My financial problems were exacerbated by the fact that as I had been teaching full-time for only seventeen years, my actual pension amounted to only 17/80 of my final salary. My lump sum, paid to me when I retired, had been swallowed up in putting my financial affairs into order and in having Hazel's dream kitchen installed at Bridgend House, Kidwelly. Now I needed to consider the future.

It had been while on our last trip to St Asaph to stay with the Archbishop of Wales, formerly Alwyn our Dean, shortly before he retired, that I had learned about the Pilling Trust Fund from the Dean of St Asaph. Apparently a certain Mr Pilling as a youngster, had aspired to be a Cathedral Organist but instead, had been sucked into the family business. When he retired he was worth several million pounds and with this money, he and his wife, having no children, had set up a Trust Fund to support Cathedral Music. The Dean of St Asaph gave me the relevant address whereupon I wrote a begging letter enclosing with it a letter from Dean Geraint from which, to my horror, I had discovered that the Dean and Chapter of Brecon Cathedral actually were considering cutting back on musical expenditure as money was in short supply. To my astonishment and relief, I received a kind reply from the Pilling Trust, offering £10,000 annually, for five years, making a total grant of £50,000. Overjoyed, I quickly worked out a scheme of payments which I submitted to the Dean and Chapter. I raised my own salary from £7,488 to £10,000; Hazel's salary as Assistant Organist I raised from £300 to £2,000; I doubled the choristers pay, and increased the amount of money which was allocated to help pay for their instrumental tuition; finally, I made sure that there was enough money set aside to pay for the Lay Clerk's annual dinner because in the past they had paid for most of this themselves. Much to my amazement the Dean and Chapter expressed a wish to divert £1,000 of this £10,000 to supporting Royal School of Church Music activities in Swansea. I told the Dean in no uncertain terms, that if this was done and the Trustees found out, we might end up losing all the money. Amazement turned to anger when the Canons sent back a message to say that if I wanted £10,000 a year then I would have to pay their extra Statutory National Insurance payments myself as they could not afford to pay them. Apart from doubting the legality of such action, I was also annoyed that they seemed to have overlooked how this extra money in fact, was helping to make the financial savings on the music that they had been looking for. The kindly Cathedral Treasurer came to my rescue. She worked out that if I was actually paid £7,700 while Hazel was paid £4,300 per annum, then no extra National Insurance payments were necessary; all that was necessary if this was done was for me to pay Hazel £2,300 less Housekeeping Money every year! So my scheme went through although I was unhappy about the National Insurance arrangement as it seemed dishonest, also there was the nagging feeling that the business could have been sorted out far more easily and amicably if the Dean and Chapter had let me in on their deliberations about the 'windfall' which I, and not they, had acquired for their Cathedral.

Other problems were arising at the Cathedral. Dean Geraint was still anxious to persuade people to sit in at the youngsters' choir practices so to comply with an EEC ruling concerning the supervision of young people, but, as I expected, only one mother was prepared to help and she on a very irregular basis. Then there was an incident on the previous All Saints Day. When I arrived for Choral Eucharist I found for the first time, a nave altar. Wynn was next to arrive and when he saw this he went immediately to see Geraint in the Dean's vestry. Pointing out to him that when he had worked in Llandrindod Wells and had worshipped at Geraint's former church in the town, he had become used to a nave altar and a westward facing celebrant, he went on to remind Dean Geraint that here at Brecon Cathedral he was in charge of the servers, therefore he would have expected to have been told of any change to the normal arrangements, so as to be able to inform and instruct the servers of any new movements. Amazingly, considering the fact that Geraint had been Dean now for more than a year, he denied any knowledge of Wynn being in charge of the Servers. Then there was Palm Sunday and afterwards Easter Day, when like Christmas Day, no procession was allowed yet the processional hymns were still sung but with the choir rooted in the choir stalls. That particular Easter Day saw the inauguration of Dean Geraint's new Children's Area in the Cordwainers' Chapel, at the 11.00 am Choral Eucharist. This led to some letters in the Brecon and Radnor Express, addressed to the Editor:

> 'Sir, As I am not a regular attendant of Cathedral services I have hesitated in writing this letter.
>
> However, I cannot be the only person to have had the Easter morning service ruined for me by the apparent children's crèche in a side chapel, provided with a box of toys similar to a doctor's surgery. At one point, a wheeled toy could be heard on the stone floor of the Cathedral.
>
> The quiet moments of the service were lost and I found it impossible to concentrate on the sermon – I have no idea what the Bishop said.
>
> There was no benefit for the children, who did not attend the service, so one must assume this arrangement to be for the convenience of the parents.
>
> A wooden partition is no barrier to sound.
>
> I wonder if any of the Cathedral regulars, will have the courage to complain.'

Another member of the congregation wrote piously in the course of a letter:

> 'Please do not let us exclude anyone to 'Our Lord's Supper.'
>
> If we wish to have a time of quiet prayer and contemplation we may go into the Cathedral when it is quiet'.

One of the Cathedral regulars was

> 'sure our Lord was delighted that the children and their young parents were there', and expressed the hope that 'more young families will come to join us in worship', concluding with the hope that, 'When they do, we want them to feel welcome and at home.'

However, it was bass Lay Clerk Trevor Benwell who made the most sensible observation:

> 'There are other rooms in the Cathedral complex where children could be happily accommodated and even brought back at the end of the service for a blessing and the closing hymn, uniting the family in Cathedral worship.'

Indeed, tenor Lay Clerk, Bernard Adams, in his usual forthright manner, reinforced this observation:

> 'As a member of the Cathedral Choir, I was not aware beforehand of the arrangements that had been made for the crèche that was set up in St Keyne's Chapel on Easter Day. It seems to me that consultation on the scheme cannot have been carried out on a very wide basis, or I would at least have heard of the proposal ....

....It was interesting to note that on Low Sunday no use was made of the crèche facility. If in fact there is demand for it on a regular basis use could surely be made of the extensive premises in the Close .... In this way no one need be debarred from church, no one need suffer irritation and the children – too young to understand the service – would be properly cared for.'

Cathedral Singer Audrey Doughty, ever sensible and humorous, who had attended the service, commented:

'I live in Llandrindod where, at Holy Trinity Church, the children arrive after the sermon and potter around making the sort of noises one expects from toddlers etc.. However, we do not give them toys which encourage commotion. What on earth were they playing with at Easter?

It sounded like saucepan lids and metal lorries. I couldn't hear part of the sermon – and I am not deaf. I can honestly say that in all my years as a church goer, I have never heard such a racket during a service ....

....I am a frequent visitor to the Cathedral where I expect an opportunity for a peaceful religious experience combined, incidentally, with a dignified service (not the alternative 'Rocky Horror' one which appears once a month). Come on Brecon. Get your act together. You have a magnificent Cathedral which has a special status – it's called heritage and tradition. Treat it with the respect it deserves.'

The Brecon and Radnor Express milked this story for all it was worth but on the other hand, was useless at doing something like supporting the Cathedral's Easter music programme. Somehow the Easter Bank Holiday was mixed up with the May Bank Holiday while Brecon Cathedral Singers were mixed up with Crickhowell Choral Society. So the following article had appeared in the week leading up to the Easter holiday, on the 'What's On' page:

'At long last Easter, the first Bank Holiday of the year, is here. And if you haven't got a lot planned then just check the many and varied events on this page. You are bound to find something for all the family.

And let us not lose sight of the true meaning of Easter, and the many services which will be held in churches throughout the region to celebrate the first major Christian festival of the year. The Crickhowell Choral Society will present an Italian Festival performing Vivaldi, Venice (sic!) and Vespers at St Edmund's Church in Crickhowell on Easter Saturday and Easter Sunday at 7.30 pm and at 3.00 pm on Easter Monday.'

Not being very amused by this, I wrote to the Editor:

'Dear Mr Sivier
What do I have to do to get the Brecon and Radnor Express on the side of the Brecon Cathedral Music Programme? A month ago I sent a detailed letter

explaining the background of the orchestral and choral concerts on Good Friday, Holy Saturday and Easter Day but none of this information has been used. Last week I submitted a detailed advertisement which will cost in excess of £75 + VAT. I open today's Brecon and Radnor Express to discover in the page about Easter attractions, the opening paragraph which should have mentioned our Easter concerts instead has them credited to Crickhowell Choral Society yet these concerts actually take place a week later, on the weekend following Easter. To organise entertainment of the quality being put on in the Cathedral over the Easter weekend costs a lot of money, time and energy. It would be lovely to have some help and support from the Brecon and Radnor Express.'

Actually, the concert on Easter Sunday Evening contained a rarity – a Concerto for violin, piano and string orchestra composed by the famous Felix Mendelssohn when he was only twelve years old. Tracking down the orchestral parts had been a nightmare but eventually I met with success when I telephoned Breitkopf and Härtel at Hamburg. The lady who answered my telephone call, not surprisingly, spoke little English, but she put me onto another lady who spoke fluent English. She asked me my name and when I replied: 'David Gedge', she exclaimed excitedly: 'Harriet's Dad.' Apparently she and Harriet met every year at the Frankfurt Music Fair.

By now Geraint Hughes had been Dean of Brecon Cathedral for almost two years; approaching sixty-six years, he had been heard to say recently that 'as he was doing such a good job he would stay until he was seventy.' Why then, just one week later, on May 1st, did he give three months notice of his retirement to the Bishop? There was time, however, for just one more misfortune. Ever since we had come to Brecon back in 1966, whenever the Diocesan Mothers Union Services had been held in the Cathedral, either Hazel or I had played the organ; indeed it was the only diocesan service for which we had ever been paid a fee! This year, 2000, however, the service was special. It was to take the form of a Millenium Service which was to be attended by Mothers' Union members from throughout Wales, while the Guest Preacher was to be Lady Eames, the wife of the Anglican Archbishop of Armagh, who was the World-Wide President of the M.U.. Shortly before the day of the service, I received a letter from the Provincial President of the Mothers' Union, who happened to be the wife of one of the Brecon Cathedral Canons:

'Dear David

The Dean has asked me to write to you to let you know formerly (sic!) that we shall be using the Swansea and Brecon Mothers' Union Organist, the Revd. Hugh Lervy, to play the organ at the Provincial Mothers Union Millenium Service at the Cathedral on 21st June next.

My regards and good wishes to Hazel.

Yours sincerely

This came as a shock, especially as young Hugh Lervy had been a good friend to us during his time as a Minor Canon here not long before. He was in no way responsible for this situation. I sent the following reply:

> 'Thank you for your letter.
>
> I had no idea that there was a Swansea & Brecon Diocesan Mothers' Union Organist, especially as in past years, whenever the service has been in the Cathedral Hazel has played the organ – and that goes back to the days of Bishop J J A Thomas.
>
> I would be grateful if you would include on the service sheet, the information that the Organist for the service is The Revd. Hugh Lervy.
>
> With good wishes
Yours sincerely
David

At the same time, I wrote the following letter to Dean Geraint, who in no way had been responsible for this situation:

> 'Dear Geraint
>
> I enclose a copy of Ann's letter.
>
> I hope that you, as Dean, will ensure that the customary fee for such a service is paid to Hazel as this is part of her income, as is the case when someone else requests to play the organ for a funeral at St Mary's Church or here in the Cathedral – this, by the way, is an Incorporated Society of Musicians ruling. Incidentally, Hazel has played the organ at all major Mothers' Union services in the Cathedral going back to the days of Bishop J J A Thomas, and has always received a fee.
>
> Out of interest, you may be fascinated to know that when I was appointed Organist back in 1966, I was paid £450 pa by the Cathedral, £100 paid by St Mary's and Dean Gwynno James promised me £50 pa in fees, and worked hard to ensure that I got this although sadly he died within nine months of my arrival here. Now that I am paid £10,000 pa this £50 fees represents some £500 pa which I certainly do not get in extra fees although I have not complained about this.
>
> If I sound militant it is because I am not happy that Hazel should be treated in so cavalier a fashion. She is, after all, a soloist in her own right, who has broadcast recitals and services on TV and the radio, and has made recordings both as a soloist and accompanist. This could all have been done in so better a way. Incidentally, since when has there been a Swansea and Brecon Diocesan Mothers' Union Organist!?
>
> With good wishes
Yours sincerely
David'

Sadly, Dean Geraint made no attempt to obtain a fee for Hazel, nor did he reply to my letter. So we sat back and waited with interest to discover who was to be the seventh Dean that we would have to work for.

LXIV

This inter-regnum witnessed certain events which, I suppose, ideally should not have happened; these, however, stemmed mostly from problems that had arisen during the past year or so, which had left so many people uneasy about life in the Cathedral. It had just seemed inconceivable that Dean Geraint should not only have tried to revive the parish of St John the Evangelist, but had also set about trying to compile an Electoral Roll for this parish. All this despite the stone set in a pillar at the back of St Mary's Church, Brecon, which had carved thereon in bold lettering:

'St Mary's becomes the Parish Church, 1923.'

So Hazel's and my names were on the Electoral Roll of St Mary's and there they stayed, despite the fact that Archdeacon Elwyn John had made it impossible for us to attend the 'Easter Vestry', as the Annual General Meeting used to be called, by always arranging it for 3.00 pm on a Sunday, when we were involved in Choral Evensong at the Cathedral. Even so, there was no way that Hazel and I were going to transfer our names to an Electoral Roll of St John the Evangelist, as we doubted its legality. So many people were bothered about the Cathedral's future that an informal meeting was arranged to enable everyone to air their views and, I suspect, to gain comfort by strength of numbers. Hazel and I also tried to have a chat with the Bishop, but when we took Kelvin with us he refused to discuss anything, joking that three was a meeting!

The new Dean was John David Edward Davies who, like John Harris before him, had been Vicar of Maindee in Newport. Interestingly earlier in his life he had been Organist and Choirmaster of Bassaleg Church, where apparently we had met when I had taken a rehearsal for 'Celebration 80', at which time he had been practising as a Solicitor. He, his wife Jo, and children Kate aged 12, and Christopher aged 10, moved into The Deanery early in September and therefore were witnesses to a most unfortunate event which must have made them wonder why on earth they had come to Brecon. It began when the choir returned from its holiday, part of which had been spent blissfully in Cork, yet again singing services at Cork, Cöbh, Cloyne and Lismore Cathedrals, while enjoying the facilities at Brookfield Holiday Village and the wonderful Enterprise Lounge. As the choir processed into Brecon Cathedral for the 11.00 am Choral Eucharist it was confronted for the first time ever at this service, by a Nave Altar. The Lay Clerks were so taken aback by this that without any prompting at all, not a single one of them could bring himself to receive the Holy Sacrament when that time in the service arrived. After the service there was understandably much discussion about what had happened and this continued over lunch at The Bull's Head with the result that as the choir lined up for the Vestry Prayer before processing into Evensong, I started to make an apology on its behalf, to the Minor Canon only to have my words drowned out by his announcing the Prayer. To many this was the 'last straw', especially when it was discovered that it was the Minor Canon himself who had instigated the use of the Nave Altar in this way, without consulting anyone. The repercussions that followed were many. From Bass Lay Clerk Wynn Davies I had the following note:

'Dear David
I was not at all happy with the events of this morning and have written to the new Dean. I enclose a copy of my letter for your information ....'

This read:

'Dear Mr Dean
I withdrew the servers from this morning's Eucharist for the first time in the fifteen years that I have been organising the serving in this Cathedral. I did so because I had not been consulted beforehand about the use of a nave altar. I therefore had no time to work out what the servers were supposed to do, where they were supposed to go, how and when. It seemed best to leave them in the choir, where at least they would be on sure ground and not lost and confused.
I am very angry about this. This is a Cathedral. We expect things to be done properly. There is no place for ad hoc, unplanned, unrehearsed chaos here.
I note that the next Choral Eucharist will be the day after your installation. I would like that service to be a happy, well organised, joyful occasion, unlike this morning's unhappy, potentially chaotic affair.
I would be most pleased to meet with you at your earliest convenience in order to plan how the serving at the 11.00 o'clock Eucharist is to proceed in the future ...'

At the same time Bass Lay Clerk Colin Chapman also wrote to the new Dean:

'Dear Mr Dean
I joined Brecon Cathedral Choir in January 1989. At that particular time I was employed by British Coal and subsequently moved to Derby where I was also a member of the Cathedral Choir. Following the demise of the Coal Industry in the mid 90s, I moved back to my home town of Neath. Upon my return home, I resumed links with the Cathedral Choir – I was made so welcome – it was as if I had never been away!
I have always been impressed by Brecon Cathedral and what it stands for, its liturgy and the high standard of choral services. I was particularly impressed by the way in which the services were conducted. In particular the High Altar, Sanctuary, Altar Servers, Crucifers, Gospel Processions and the like, which added to the atmosphere of what I would describe (with no disrespect) as a typically 'Welsh Cathedral', ie a special character of its own.
During the course of a normal week, my daughter Nia (who also sings in the choir) and I travel over 135 miles for Evensong on Fridays and for the Sunday

Services. My love of Brecon Cathedral and its tradition has not waned at all over the years.

However, I was rather saddened to find that on Sunday 10th September the High Altar was not in use, and was replaced by a sub-standard 'Nave Altar'. I understand that the High Altar was not used at the 8.00 am Eucharist either. The use of the 'Nave Altar' dispensed with the need for Altar Servers and indeed the Gospel Procession. The whole service took a turn for the worse, even the sermon was preached from the 'portable' lectern. The combination of all these events put those present in a position of embarrassment and disapproval (and indeed prompted many to decline the offer of the Eucharist).....'

On the following Sunday, the Cathedral Bulletin opened with this statement:

'Last Sunday, there was a degree of confusion followed by some wholly inappropriate hostility at the Cathedral. The former can lead to the latter, but in a Christian community we should try to overcome this. It will do nobody who claims to be a Christian any harm to read and re-read Luke 18 (9-14), to-day's Prayer Book Gospel.'

This prompted Tenor Lay Clerk Bernard Adams to write in his own inimitable way, in the course of a letter to the Dean:

'I was present at both choral services on 10 September, and was not aware of any confusion. No-one was rude or hostiley disposed toward me, nor in my presence towards anyone else – with one most regrettable exception. In the morning services the lay clerks to a man refrained from communicating, in the main because of their dislike as individuals of the manner in which this was done, standing at the portable nave altar. This was, I must emphasise, not a premeditated action, the outcome of discussion or plotting; I for one only learned the minute before going into church that the said altar was in use, and frankly we are too busy before a service with final musical preparations to have much chance of discussing anything of weight. I understand that a number of the congregation also declined to receive.

Any individual entitled to receive the sacrament has, I believe, the right to choose not to receive it. If one adopts the latter course it should certainly not be with the intention of causing offence to the celebrant, who should in any case regard himself as a mere persona and without standing in the matter. In the afternoon, however, as the choir was about to enter the church for evensong, Mr Gedge began publicly to utter what was clearly intended to be a word of conciliation to the Minor Canon. As I saw nothing for which to apologise this seemed unnecessary, but Mr Jarvis, instead of letting Mr Gedge have his say and accepting his conciliatory remarks in the spirit in which they were offered, shouted him down with brutally forceful repetitions of 'Let us pray'; surely a sad, indeed uncouth misuse of the phrase. That was the only instance of rudeness or hostility of which I was aware in the Cathedral that day, and if, as

I suspect, Mr Jarvis was the author of the words on the Bulletin, he should be reminded of Proverbs 15:1'*

Given out with the Bulletin was a letter from the new Dean which began:

'Dear friends

I am taking the most unusual step of writing to you prior to my installation as Dean in order to put beyond any doubt certain matters in relation to the use of a nave altar at the Cathedral and also the associated matter of the position of the high altar.

I have decided to do this since I am given to understand that both these matters have been, and in some cases remain, the source of controversy. I have long believed it to be one of the important tasks of the clergy to teach, especially about change or experiment ....'

Later, turning his attention to the High Altar he wrote:

'Some time ago, the Chapter agreed to seek a faculty for the permanent repositioning of the high altar some 9'6" away from the reredos. I have been told that little teaching about the basis for this decision had been given and I am therefore not surprised that several people were taken aback by the proposal.

I take the view that there should have been more teaching. Further the distance which it was proposed that the altar should be moved could have resulted in the destruction of the unity of the high altar with its reredos and surroundings. I believe that a much more modest change is appropriate. I therefore propose to simply move the high altar to the edge of the first altar step and into a position in which the president of the Eucharist will be able to celebrate facing east or west....'

Finally, he wrote:

'It is my intention to put in place a Liaison Group through which communication with the Chapter can take place. A lack of communication can lead to misconception and misunderstanding ....'

In his letter, Bernard Adams had this to say about what the Dean had written:

'I see that it has become painfully clear to you that your predecessor's insatiable desire for change, coupled with a singular determination to ignore the thoughts of others, has led to a considerable rift in the laity ...'

After pointing out that 'the regular congregation of Brecon Cathedral clearly had not wished for 'a nave altar', he also explained that the only teaching advanced on the subject by Dean Geraint had been that nowadays in most other churches 'the celebrant at the Eucharist faces west', although, he added, 'not all see this as a reason why he or she should do so here.' Turning to the

'Alternative Order for the Eucharist' Bernard Adams suggested that it was 'by no means universally admired by the laity', indeed:

> 'Under Dean Hughes the name 'Alternative' Order became a joke, as little else was ever to be encountered.'

According to Bernard Adams:

> 'Many would welcome the reintroduction of the 1662 Book of Common Prayer, which is, after all, an acknowledged monument of the English language. It is reappearing in ever more churches and cathedrals as the value of what has been lost is appreciated and the futility of the exercise recognised.'

Earlier in the year, before the new Dean had accepted the job, at least three members of the Chapter of Brecon Cathedral had told him about the problems of working with me, the Organist, indeed one had said: 'I was the most difficult person he had ever had to work with'. So the new Dean had come to Brecon Cathedral toying with the idea of making changes to the musical set-up. Fascinating to learn, therefore, that after he had met with Bass Lay Clerk Wynn Davies to discuss the servers, the two had become good friends; indeed eventually the Dean's own two children, Kate and Christopher, became Servers. As for Bass Lay Clerk Colin Chapman, the new Dean eventually made use of his professional IT skills, giving him the task of setting up a Cathedral web site. Soon the Verger's job became vacant and the Dean appointed Bass Lay Clerk David Walker. Before long it became obvious that the Dean and the Lay Clerks were on the same wave-length; so, after his first Christmas at Brecon Cathedral, Dean John Davies was able to write:

> 'First impressions are often said to be impressions which last. With this thought in mind, it seems to me appropriate to reflect upon some of my own first impressions of Advent and Christmas in Brecon. I am bound to say that those impressions have been positive. The quality of worship at the Cathedral has been high, and this has been due, in no small part to the efforts of all those who, under the guidance of David Gedge, have produced wonderful music to enhance that worship. We should all be immensely grateful for the commitment to church music from which we benefit'.

Meanwhile, Alto Lay Clerk Dudley Palmer had purchased a thurible for the Cathedral in preparation for Friday, January 5th 2001, the Eve of the Epiphany, when the first Solemn Evensong in living memory, was sung in Brecon Cathedral. Young Daniel, one of the trebles, acted as Thurifer. However, transported into another world by the ceremonial, he soon succeeded in knocking over the thurible and then spent the First Lesson wetting his fingers and trying to retrieve the white-hot charcoal in time for the censing of the High Altar during the Magnificat. On the next morning, the Feast of the Epiphany, the Lay Clerks sang Jean Langlaise' 'Missa in Simplicitate' at Solemn Eucharist when the smell of the incense took me back to my days at my father's Holy Trinity, Lambeth, and my days at Fr.Timms's St Mary the Virgin, Primrose Hill; I was in my seventh heaven! By now the Dean was making his presence felt, and for the right reasons. No more was the 11.00 am Sunday service governed by the clock as it had been during Dean Geraint's reign when it had always had to finish by 12.00 noon; now the service was allowed to run its natural course. Nor did the Dean court popularity by insisting that attending Cathedral services was not just a Sunday occupation; he expressed his displeasure at the lack of worshippers at mid-week Festivals like The Epiphany, Ascension Day or Corpus Christi, not forgetting All Saints Day, All Souls Day and major Saints Days. He was, however, delighted with his first taste of Holy Week and Easter with its ten sung services and four concerts, so much so that as the augmented choir was rehearsing for Evensong in the Choir room, he slipped the following letter on to the piano:

> 'My dear David and Hazel
>
> This is but a brief, and probably quite inadequate note, to thank you both for all your efforts this Holy Week.
>
> The way in which others have responded to your personal enthusiasm has meant that, for many, Holy Week has been a wonderful experience of faith, enriched by liturgy and music.
>
> Personally, I have found the whole experience of my first Easter in Brecon utterly captivating.
>
> Please accept my warmest thanks, and pass these on to the Cathedral Choir, Singers and other involved.
>
> As Ever
> John '

Here, at last, was someone who understood what we had been trying to do over the years. All the more illuminating, therefore, was the note that he published in 'The Beacon', the Cathedral's magazine:

> 'My first Holy Week and Easter at the Cathedral was an experience, which I will value for the rest of my ministry. Whilst it was tremendously demanding for many of us in terms of preparation and planning, it was also tremendously rewarding, and a number of you have expressed your own sense of having shared in an enriching journey of faith.
>
> Prior to taking up my appointment as Dean I had been told, quite falsely, several tales about what to expect at Easter. All these tales proved to be idle, and misleading – one or two even proved to be malicious gossip. What, I believe, we actually experienced was Anglicanism at its best – worship composed of a rich mixture of teaching, ceremonial, music, prayer and scripture. No one element obscured or detracted from another; rather all combined to allow the week to be a powerful walk with Jesus along the way of the cross.'

By now the Dean had fallen in love with the Cathedral Organ, particularly its Fanfare Trumpet stop. Sadly, however, he was having hearing problems with one ear, so, wanting to hear better his favourite stop, he found the money to have it extended to provide a stop one octave higher. This stop was duly named affectionately 'Dean's Clarion'! At Choral Evensong one Friday the Dean played the final organ voluntary; at another Choral Evensong he played both the opening and closing voluntaries. Meanwhile, more internal jobs came the way of the Cathedral choir when Alto Lay Clerk Paul Jackson was appointed Diocesan Web Master while Tenor Lay Clerk Arwyn Davies became Editor of The Beacon. Christmas 2002, found the Cathedral Choir singing Hungarian Folk Carols the melodies of which had been discovered by Tenor Lay Clerk Bernard Adams, to which I added harmonies – in his spare time Bernard translated Hungarian books into English, many of which were published. During this time Assistant Organist Hazel took over running the Cathedral Welcomers while Sub Organist Kelvin Redford continued to put together and photocopy the monthly Cathedral Service Sheets. So much for the rebellious Cathedral musicians, indeed when the Dean celebrated his fiftieth birthday and was taken away for a surprise holiday by his wife, Jo, it was the Organist and Assistant Organist, Hazel and me, who moved into The Deanery to look after their two children, Kate and Christopher.

The staff now had weekly meetings attended by The Dean, his secretary, David his Verger, Roger Taylor the new Minor Canon who used to be a professional French Horn player, Fr Michael, the recently appointed Residentiary Canon and Director of Ministry, a lovable New Zealander, and me, the Organist. For the first time we all knew what was happening every week. Better still, Roger and Fr. Michael frequently dined with the Lay Clerks in the Bull's Head after Choral Evensong on Fridays and this did wonders for choir morale. The Cathedral musicians had never had it so good, especially me as the Dean ensured that I was no longer the lowest paid Cathedral Organist in England and Wales, furthermore, he ensured that I had enough money to subsidise concerts and recitals without having to dip too deeply into my own pocket.

By now the Cathedral grounds had taken a turn for the better, largely because the Dean's wife, Jo, chose to relax from her onerous nursing duties at The Heath Hospital, Cardiff, by driving a motor mower over the lawns. On her first Christmas here, I presented her with a sweat shirt bearing the logo 'Official Lawnmower Operator'. As for the Cathedral Café, 'Pilgrims' , that picked up two awards including one from Giles Coren of The Times Newspaper, who included it among the ten best restaurants in England and Wales. Now as my time as Organist and Choirmaster of Brecon Cathedral was drawing to a close, the Dean instigated a million pound appeal to have the Cathedral's music properly endowed; the distinguished list of patrons was headed by none other than Prince Charles himself. Feeling that Brecon Cathedral had its Organist and Assistant Organist on the cheap, (back in 1966, when Dean Gwynno James had appointed me he had said: 'Two for the price of one') Dean John Davies now wanted the next Organist to be paid the same wage as a Vicar and given a pension along with somewhere to live while the Assistant Organist also was to be paid a reasonable wage and given accommodation. Finally, he wanted all the trebles to be properly paid and given free instrumental or singing lessons. In addition, mindful of what the Cathedral Choir had given to its youngsters from the council housing estate in the way of security, love and care, along with a glimpse of Christian life, he was anxious that this particular ethos should continue.

In my thirty-seven years at Brecon Cathedral, I had really travelled a full circle. When I had arrived in Holy Week 1966, Dean Gwynno James had been planning then to put the trebles on contracts, making £500 available for this purpose. Sadly, ten months later he had died, shortly before the Chapter Meeting when this was to be ratified, leaving the scheme to be abandoned by the very Canons whose support he had been relying on. Now it really did look as if at last what had been planned then was about to come to pass, thereby ensuring the future of what had been built up with the Cathedral Choir, the Cathedral Singers and in the diocese. As for the Cathedral itself, the building which had captivated and mesmerised me back in August 1962, when Hazel and I had called in on our way to Selby, had never looked better. Comfortable, attractive chairs had replaced the uncomfortable Victorian oak pews; the red carpet had quietly been removed from the Sanctuary by the Minor Canon, leaving the High Altar surrounded only by lovely stone which did not fight the liturgical colours of its seasonal frontals; the heating system was now being used properly so that the Cathedral was always comfortably warm and without those biting downdraughts that had made life so miserable in the winter. Most important there was now meaningful worship going on, with that rare commodity: a happy Cathedral Close, so unlike Trollope's 'Barchester', with a caring Dean at its head. When Harriet, my daughter, came home to tell Hazel and me that she had breast cancer, within minutes the Dean was at Hazel's side to share our shock, dismay and anxiety. Over the year when Harriet was receiving treatment and Hazel wanted to be free to be with her when necessary, the Dean made money available to enable young Bass Lay Clerk Timothy Morgan, who had just won an Organ Scholarship to Selwyn College, Cambridge, and was enjoying a 'gap year', to do her work for her at both the Cathedral and St Mary's Church. Indeed, when the Cathedral Choir toured Idaho, Wyoming and Utah in April 2002, Tim it was who played most of the organ accompaniments so that Hazel could stay at home. It was indeed a Golden Age.

LXV

As my time at Brecon Cathedral now slowly began to draw to a close, so the choir tours appeared to materialise more quickly than ever, so too did the Coffee Mornings which moved from being occasional affairs in Bishop Bevan Hall to being monthly. These raised valuable cash, usually between £150 and £200 a time, which was used to subsidise the cost of these trips for the youngsters in the Cathedral Choir. A visit to Brittany found the choir one Autumn Sunday morning during the school Half-Term holiday, singing Matins in the English Church of St Bartholomew, Dinard. Later that day the choir sang at an epoch-making service lasting more than two hours, at which the church and its parish were accepted into the Diocese of Europe by the Bishop of Gibraltar. During their stay in Brittany the choir resided nearby in L'Abbaye at Saint-Jacut de la Mer on the Côte D'Emeraude, an idyllic seaside village. That Sunday night the lay Clerks, exhausted by both the journey from Brecon on the Saturday, and by their labours on the Sunday, wanted to relax in a hostelry. Unfortunately, they discovered that lock-up time at L'Abbaye was at the early hour of 9.30 pm, therefore after delicate negotiations a key was obtained for the main gate. Unfortunately, one of the lay clerks, Peter Rose, always a model of discretion, decided to have an early night but did not realise that he needed the key. Not wanting to spoil the festivities he slipped out of the bar and made his way back to L'Abbaye only to find the main gate locked. What Peter did not know was that L'Abbaye was run by a group of nuns who had retired to their bedrooms for their devotions and nightly sleep. When he rang the bell at the gate, Peter roused the 'Mother Superior' from her bed as she had to come to the gate to let him in; not surprisingly she was somewhat disgruntled at this intrusion into her slumbers. Meanwhile the remainder of the lay clerks were having a riotous time in the village bar, especially as it housed a table-football game! When eventually they came to leave the hostelry they found to their horror that not only had all the street lights been extinguished but, worse still, all the house lights in the village had been rendered invisible by individual shutters. Never having been there before and with it being a particularly dark night, they couldn't see anything at all and proceeded to stumble around, first one way then another, like the blind leading the blind, eventually breaking up into two groups both searching for L'Abbaye. That still could have been alright had not one group become so hopelessly lost that it never found L'Abbaye until almost 3.00 am, by which time the other lay clerks were on the point of telephoning the police and the 'Mother Superior' had been roused from her slumbers again. Next morning an irate 'Mother Superior' read the riot act and Brecon Cathedral Choir was threatened with eviction.

Over the next few days the choir anxiously set out to win 'Brownie Points'! On Tuesday night the lay clerks sang plainsong Compline in the chapel in

L'Abbaye; so beautiful was this that the atmosphere which previously had been highly charged, now began to thaw out. Later on in the week the full choir sang some unaccompanied motets in the dining hall after dinner and immediately were back in favour. With the last night being the Eve of All Saints Day, the choir decamped to the local parish church, which had a ravishing acoustic, and there sang a Palestrina Latin Mass so meaningfully that all was finally forgiven.

Meanwhile the choir had created a favourable impression in Dinard itself when it had given a charity concert in support of 'Medicins sans frontiers' in the Roman Catholic Church. This was attended by none other than Sir John Holmes, 'Son Excellence L'Ambassadeur de Grande Bretagne en France'. It was rumoured that the Ambassador had flown from Paris to somewhere near to Dinard where he had been met by his chauffeur driving the ambassadorial Rolls Royce (which had actually been driven down from Paris), in order to make a fitting entrance to Dinard. By some strange coincidence, the ambassador's wife's mother lived in Gwenddwr, a village near to Builth Wells, where lived one of the Cathedral Singers sopranos, while a son (by another marriage) attended Christ College, Brecon's public school.

It was not all work. One day the choir was driven to the amazing Mont Saint-Michel where the choristers climbed to the top of the mountain to see the amazing church and the views around. On the way back to Saint-Jacut de la Mer the choir stopped off at the gorgeous, cavernous mediaeval cathedral of Dol-de-Bretagne, there to sing an unaccompanied Evensong (Gibbons 'Short Service' and Byrd 'Ave Verum') in a most wonderful acoustic, which was blissful.

Nine months later the Cathedral Choir was back in its beloved Cork for the fourth time. That the choristers did not arrive there until after 11.00 pm, did not deter dear Finbarre and Dolly O'Shea from serving more than thirty suppers at the Enterprise Lounge. So began yet another memorable visit to the Emerald Isle during which the choristers discovered Killarney with its wonderful Pugin Roman Catholic Cathedral, so obviously modelled on Salisbury Cathedral. Many choristers kissed the Blarney Stone at Blarney Castle nearby and lived to tell the tale. Also discovered was majestic Kilkenny Cathedral, the second largest in Ireland; here Tim Morgan coaxed the ailing, ancient 1853 Bevington organ into accompanying Evensong – Brewer in D, a wonderful sound and a glorious service.

As usual other services were sung at William Burges's fantastic St Finbarre's Cathedral in Cork, and at lovely Lismore Cathedral where time stands still and where dear Dean Beare was as hospitable as ever as was Cathedral Organist Colin Nicholls, and Angela his wife, at Cork. Again a famous trip.

Finally, the school Half-Term holiday in October 2005, found the Cathedral Choir with some of the Cathedral Singers flying out from Cardiff Airport to Prague in Czechoslovakia. Arrangements for this trip had been problematical, leaving me apprehensive about its outcome, but I need not have worried; it was wonderful both musically and socially. On Sunday morning 'Holy Mass' was celebrated in English at the early Baroque church of Our Lady of Victory, once a Carmelite monastic church. So we were able to recognise enough of the readings and liturgy to realise that these were more or less identical to what was being used in Brecon Cathedral that day. That evening another Mass was sung at the former Jesuit church of St Salvator which faced the famous Charles Bridge and stood on the banks of the even more famous River Vltava. This time the service was conducted in Czechoslovakian by a cleric who had been a candidate for the country's Presidency. With so famous a political clergyman at the helm the church was packed full of people young and old. At the conclusion of the service, the choir and Singers sang the three extracts from Mendelssohn's 'Christus' which end with 'There shall a star from Jacob come forth'; when they had finished the entire congregation stood, faced the choir which was standing high up on a gallery at the west end of the great church, and applauded enthusiastically. It was an emotional moment. Yet for all that, perhaps the highlight of the week was the visit to Karlovy Spa where the choir and Singers gave a joint concert with the famous Karlovy Children's Choir in the Baroque Church of St Mary Magdalen. During the Communist era, this church had been allowed to fall into a ruinous state, indeed part of the nave roof was only prevented from descending upon the congregation below by a mountain of scaffolding. Such also was the ruinous state of the organ that initially we weren't allowed to use it, but Tim worked his magic and produced some lovely accompanimental sounds from it. The local children's choir were wonderful, having had many years of experience at competitions throughout the world; however, the Brecon choristers were not overawed, they sang their music with great sincerity before joining with the children's choir to sing Mozart's 'Ave Verum'. It was a very moving experience. Afterwards everyone repaired to a nearby hosteltry to eat supper together and socialise but not before many of the choir and Singers had contributed generously to the restoration fund for this lovely church. During supper, a poster announcing the concert, was signed by many of the Karlovy Children's Choir; this, now framed, hangs in the Brecon Cathedral Choir Room. Towards the end of our stay in Prague, the Cathedral Choir and Singers gave a lunchtime concert in St Nicholas Church in the Old Town Square, a magnificent Baroque church famous for its dome which is covered with frescoes of the lives of St Nicholas and St Benedict. The church possesses a magnificent pipe organ but Tim had to make do with playing an electronic keyboard because, so I was told by the concert organiser, the choir was not sufficiently famous! The next day was our last and as it was a free day, many of the choristers made the most of Prague's underground trains and fabulous trams, neither of which were familiar to the Brecon youngsters. I went around shouting to passers-by 'Smile' because they all looked so glum, nor did their eyes meet our eyes. Later it was explained to me that smiles were few and far between because there was so much poverty, nor was there much eye contact because during the Communist era (and that was not long ago), if you did catch someone's eye it could be a member of the Secret Police and this could lead to you being arrested and taken away for questioning. Indeed, freedom, which we took for granted, was something new for Czechoslovakians. As for wealth, when Don, my Selby friend, and I put all our loose change together at the hotel and gave it to the only waitress who had smiled, her joyous reaction made us think that we had presented her with a vast fortune.

On returning to Brecon we found the Cathedral in turmoil; electricians were installing a £100,000+ new lighting scheme. To our amazement the main light fittings resembled those that we had just seen in the remarkable castle at Cesky Krumlov, except that the Bohemian ones had been coloured. When, four months later, the electricians had finished, the Cathedral had been dragged into the twenty-first century with regard to its lighting and the way that Health and Safety regulations governed all electrical fittings. However, for the first time, W. D. Caröe's magnificent Reredos of 1935, was properly illuminated and its beauty revealed for all to see. So too was Gilbert Scott's magnificent chancel vault of 1862, suitably lit and, for the first time, displayed to good effect. That was not all. In so many ways the Cathedral was becoming more 'user-friendly'. Attractive signs explained its most interesting features while a wooden model of the Cathedral was covered with signs in braille. Brief, attractively produced guide leaflets were now available for visitors in a variety of languages, furthermore a ramp was installed to make it easier for those in wheel chairs to enter the Cathedral. And there was more. Daily celebrations of the Holy Eucharist were now at times which were more acceptable to most worshippers, also the heating system was properly used so that they would be warm in the Cathedral. It was all so different from forty years ago when I had first come to work here. On the other hand the Choir Rooms now were locked by order of the Ecclesiastical Insurance Company – a sign of the times, furthermore, the more valuable items in the Cathedral were wired to a burglar alarm, in addition security cameras were now installed at various places in the Cathedral. Yet despite all this the ancient Priory Church still had that wonderful aura of holiness which so forcefully captivated me when I had called in on my way to Selby Abbey back in 1962. Indeed if I had my life over again, I would change it hardly at all and would answer that summons in more or less the same way. However, there is one last job scheduled to be done that I would like to see finished before I leave. Firstly, the transept walls which last were covered with a plaster that did not marry to the plaster that was already there and therefore are now bubbling and flaking; these need correct treatment. Then there are the sanctuary walls which not all that long ago were smothered incorrectly with an oil-based magnolia-coloured paint; these too are to be stripped bare and also given the correct treatment. After that the Cathedral building will be well-nigh perfect apart from the re-polishing of the tiles on the Sanctuary floor; then it will be time to go........

LXVI

That's how it should have been had not the Almighty intervened. On Saturday, July 8th, 2006, the Cathedral Singers and Gwent Chamber Orchestra were due to perform Joseph Haydn's oratorio 'Creation'. Unfortunately, somehow, a wedding had been booked into the Cathedral on that day at 2pm, the very time when the full rehearsal should have begun there. Through the kindness of Head Teacher, Audrey Bayliss, I was allowed to borrow the hall in nearby Priory Church in Wales Primary School for this rehearsal and so arranged to set out the chairs and music stands that Saturday morning. Accordingly on that morning I arrived at the school at 10am accompanied by my Yorkshire friend from Selby, Don Riches, who had come down to sing tenor in the chorus, and by Cathedral Head Chorister, Bethan Moses. Unfortunately, not being very conversant with matters of security I immediately succeeded in locking the front door key inside the school with the three of us still outside in the playground. It took an hour to sort that out before we could get into the hall to prepare for the rehearsal! Some time before there had been the additional problem of securing a bass soloist because while I had dearly wanted my son, Nick, to sing this, he protested that part 3 was pitched too high for his voice. So he asked me to find someone else to sing the final part and, as usual, we enlisted the help of his old teacher Mark Wildman. To our delight Mark suggested himself, despite the fact that he had an Associated Board of the Royal Schools of Music seminar to conduct that day somewhere in Kensington. However, he had worked out that by taking a taxi to Paddington Station, he could board the 5.45pm train to Newport and arrive in Brecon in time for Part 3 at around 8.45pm. So, early that Saturday morning I had booked and paid for a taxi to meet Mark at Newport Station and bring him to Brecon. For the remainder of the day Hazel and I had prayed fervently, firstly that Mark would arrive in time at Paddington Station and secondly, that the train would arrive on time at Newport because trains on that line could be notoriously late at weekends on account of track maintenance work. One further complication arose unexpectedly that day. Soprano soloist, Nikki Kennedy, was driving to Brecon accompanied by her new-born babe, when unfortunately her car broke down on the A40 road, near to Abergavenny, not long before the rehearsal was due to start.

Nevertheless at around 2pm, with almost one hundred and twenty performers stuffed into the school hall, the rehearsal began, while over in the Cathedral, where we should have been, Hazel played the Organ for the intrusive wedding. By 3pm, the wedding had ended leaving bass lay clerk Richard Williams along with young Bethan Moses and her team of chorister helpers free to erect the staging so that by 4pm the rehearsal could be transferred to the Cathedral by which time our soprano soloist had joined us and all was going well. During tea Hazel received a mobile phone message to

say that Mark was on the train; so far so good! At 7.30pm but not too promptly
so as to allow Mark more time to reach Brecon for Part 3, the performance
started. All bowled along happily to the end of part 2 when there was an
interval during which wine and soft drinks were sold while I walked home
across the churchyard to discover the whereabouts of Mark. I need not have
worried for there he was, in the bathroom, changing into his suit, making a few
preliminary singing noises! As the soloists lined up to return for part 3, Mark
looked at his tatty copy of 'Creation' and asked if he could borrow another copy
as his was missing the final two pages which were rather important. However,
he need not have worried because just before the final chorus began, I felt a
strange tingle travel upwards from my left foot, up my leg and left side into my
head. Suddenly I could no longer turn the pages of my score, nor could I give
leads with my left hand. As I uttered the words: "I cannot go on", so I toppled
over on my left side, landing on top of a bemused orchestra leader, John
Roberts. I had suffered a stroke with the result that Haydn's 'Creation' had
come to a premature end; Mark hadn't needed those final two pages!

Pandemonium reigned as various people rushed to my aid, the remaining
details naturally are a little hazy in my mind! Amazingly quickly an
ambulance arrived and among the paramedics was the father of chorister,
Kate Robinson, so that I felt among friends. Soon I was being transported in
the ambulance down Priory Hill, past the Bulls Head where I should have
been enjoying a party, down the A40 road to Nevill Hall Hospital on the
outskirts of Abergavenny, accompanied by Hazel and Nick while Harriet
followed in her car. There we found ourselves mixed up with policemen and
the remnants of a brawl that must have occurred earlier in Abergavenny
which added to the excitement of the night! Eventually I was found a bed in
the hospital and was settled in for the night with a paralysed left hand and
left arm. Back at the Cathedral, Nikki the soprano had assumed control and
had asked the bemused audience to go home whereupon certain of the
musicians and Singers, along with the Dean and his wife Jo, had decamped to
Garth Cottage, there to drink coffee and my favourite Redbreast Irish Whisky
while they awaited the return of Hazel, Harriet and Nick with news of me.

Strangely, while surfing the internet, Harriet had come upon the following
statement which had been sent from the USA shortly after the concert:

> Blogs are a somewhat clumsy place to talk about things that really matter, but
> I want to go on record as wishing a speedy recovery to one of my favorite
> colleagues, David Gedge, who collapsed tonight during a performance of The
> Creation in Brecon. I know an awful lot of conductors, famous and not, bad
> and good, but David is someone whose human qualities represent the best of
> what a conductor can be.
>
> David has been the conductor of the Gwent Chamber Orchestra and organist
> at the Brecon Cathedral for many years, and my wife has been a regular
> collaborator with him since her first year at music college. David's
> inspirational leadership and warm humanity has touched the lives of countless

choristers during his tenure. He does more than conduct music- time and again he has been a needed mentor or friend to someone for whom the Brecon Cathedral Choir was an all-important refuge. Music can and does change lives, and David's work has changed and bettered the lives of many, many people. He has built his choir not from the children of the great and the good, but with young people from disadvantaged backgrounds, broken homes and profoundly challenging circumstances. Lest I make him out to be a boring, pious do-gooder, I also want to point out that he's a great guy to go for a beer with- funny, laid-back and wise.

His son was singing in tonight's concert, and his wife (who has been the assistant organist at the Cathedral all these years) was also there. I can't begin to imagine how they are feeling tonight. Our thoughts are with them and David, as we hope for a full and speedy recovery.

The next day the damage done to me was assessed by Professor Saunders of Nevill Hall Hospital, two of whose daughters had at one time played in the Gwent Chamber Orchestra. As we knew him well, he was very helpful to my family and kept them informed of developments. Four days later I was transferred to Bronllys Hospital, close to Brecon, where some time before Hazel's mum and dad had been cared for whenever Hazel needed a rest. There for nearly five weeks I received the most marvellous care and attention as the resident team of nurses and physiotherapists set about me, my left hand and arm. They had me walking around with the aid of a stick, riding a fixed bicycle, doing all sorts of exercises under the watchful eye of a minute Sri Lankan lady who answered to the name of Kumari, who would appear when I was least expecting her and bark at me if I was dragging my left foot! It was like being in a hotel so good was the care and attention, so how the N.H.S can contemplate closing such an hospital as this, as it is doing as I write, I know not. So many people were so kind to me that I filled six scrap books with their lovely cards, caring letters and Aunty Aud's poem, I did the pasting while Bethan, the Head Choirgirl who used to visit me almost daily to play rummy and won the series of games 62-58, did the sellotaping. Aunty Aud's poem reads:

From two till six last Saturday we practiced hard and tried
To ignore the blinkin' wedding bells that we could hear outside.

Pre-concert runs are something else. Patience has to be the rule
We really are quite used to it BUT NOT IN PRIORY SCHOOL

Some were squashed in midget chairs-knees jammed beneath the jaw
For those stuck on a vaulting horse, feet did not touch the floor.

We really did our very best to tackle 'The Creation'
But little children's furniture plays hell with circulation.

The evening came-we all turned up to stand and sit and stand
(The Singers did their utmost to be heard above the band!!!)

We had a break, a little wine and some went for a wee
And then we climbed back up again to wrestle with part III.

'Watch' Watch' shouts David frequently. We obey these rules with care
But when we looked-just for a check, the blighter wasn't there.

We thought he'd just gone down the pub-that made us pretty sad.
We'd worked quite hard. We didn't think we'd been quite THAT bad.

Alas, we had misjudged him. It really was no joke.
*Cos just **three pages from the end**, he'd gone and had a stroke.*

Now, David-that was most unkind. Our glory was diminished
*If you're going to do that sort of thing. **Please wait until we've finished.***

But we forgive you everything. We really won't complain
If you criticise or shout at us. JUST COME BACK WELL AGAIN.

After those five weeks such was my progress that I was sent home to continue with my miraculous recovery, aided by two physiotherapists who visited me three times every week. One in particular, Richard by name, seemed to specialise in hands and inflicted the most marvellous 'torture' on my left hand and arm that within a short time I was playing five-finger exercises on the piano, although not very successfully at first. Once back at home I took it upon myself to attend all the choral services at the Cathedral as a member of the congregation. The choir had been faultless throughout my illness. My friend John York Skinner directed the choristers at all these services while another friend, Cathedral Choir tenor Lay Clerk ex teacher and organist, David White took all the practices. The choristers, boys, girls and gentlemen were marvellous and just continued as normal without me. Bethan drove the choristers along and with Amy Morris led the treble line with their lovely soprano noises while Hazel, Hugh Thomas, Tim Morgan and Robert Green presided at the organ. Especially wonderful was the way in which Bethan organised the choristers and some of the Lay Clerks for the Litter Picking during the Jazz Festival, a thankless task.

Much to my joy while I had been out of action, the ancient Choir Room had been decorated, the first time since 1981; the walls were whitewashed and a new blue carpet was laid. Much to my sorrow, however, afterwards the many photographs which had to be taken down for the painting, were not returned to the walls, nor it seems was there any intention of their being returned as all the nails upon which they had been hung, were removed by order of the Dean who quoted advice from Cadw (the Welsh equivalent of the 'National Trust') and the Cathedral architect. So tragically, more than one hundred years of choir and Cathedral history was removed from view, something which had always interested visitors to the Choir Room, especially relatives of former choristers. Even the news that an exhibition of choir photographs was to be hung and lit properly downstairs did little to soften the blow as there would not be room enough for all the photographs. However, this tragedy should not be allowed to cloud the fact that a fine job of redecoration has been accomplished by Lay Clerk Richard Williams, Head Chorister Bethan Moses, along with choristers Matthew Morris, Kate Robinson, Charlotte Hacche and Natalie Brown, all of whom had been released from school for 'Work Experience'; this room is both large and high and the work had taken many hours.

This was not the only slight aggravation. The Dean, quoting from Health and Safety Regulations this time, would not allow me to draw up the monthly Service Music List. This had always been one of my monthly recreational jobs and I had always taken great care over this, always giving a key scheme to the music of the Canticles, Anthem, Hymns and Psalm Chants also Responses at every service, so that the musical flow would be smooth. The first music list not done by me caused me more agitation than would have been the case had I put it together myself. So two Advent anthems adorned services in September, while at another, canticles in Emajor jarringly partnered an anthem in Aflat. I was horrified.

However, order was restored by October when that month's Service Sheet was compiled by the Dean, the Minor Canon and me and sanity prevailed in the choice of music and tonalities. Meanwhile the Cathedral Singers had been preparing Gabriel Faure's lovely 'Requiem', working not with me but with another of my friends John Cynan Jones, former conductor of the famous Treorchy Male Choir, the Treorchy and District Choral Society and Organist of St George's church, Cwmparc in the Rhondda. Come October and I resumed working with the Gwent Chamber Orchestra and the Cathedral Singers. On Tuesday, October 31st, instead of taking the Cathedral Singers rehearsal, I was off to London, to Lambeth Palace, with Hazel and some friends as Hazel and I were each to be presented with the Cross of St Augustine by the Archbishop of Canterbury. For me this journey was special as I was returning to the Lambeth of my youth, indeed we even enjoyed lunch in the café that now adorned the precincts of Southwark Cathedral, where I had found so much happiness in my youth. It was the nearest I could think of to coming home.

On medical advice I had now brought forward the date of my retirement, from August 2007, to Easter Day which in any case did seem rather appropriate since my first service in the Cathedral had been on Good Friday 1966. In the process of looking after me following my stroke, a rail had been installed on the wall of the staircase of Garth Cottage by Health Authority workers, to enable me to walk up and down stairs. This necessitated removing an antique corner cupboard and a large number of prints and pictures. This started Hazel and me moving pictures, books, videos and CD's down to our future home in Kidwelly where work was being done to make the bathroom easier for me. The end was in sight as we emptied Garth Cottage but for now, hopefully, I would soon be working again with my beloved choir in lovely Brecon Cathedral, preparing for the J.S.Bach Advent Cantatas, which had been the spur to my rapid recovery. Imagine my dismay therefore when I started to prepare the December Service Sheet to discover that the Advent Sunday Cantata had been replaced by the

Advent Sunday Carol Service which for as long as I can remember had taken place in the morning, while the Advent II Cantata had been cased out by the Installation of a new Residentiary Canon. This left room for one J.S.Bach Cantata only at Evensong on the afternoon of Advent III because the fourth Sunday in Advent was Christmas Eve and when that clash occurred, Christmas Music from Handel's 'Messiah' was always sung, ending rather appropriately with the chorus 'For unto us a child is born'. So ended a tradition that had lasted more than twenty-five years, much to the sorrow of the Choristers and Lay Clerks who had grown to love singing in German J.S.Bach Cantatas 36, 61, 62, 140 and part one of the 'Christmas Oratorio' (in English) with orchestral accompaniment at Choral Evensongs during Advent, an experience which had been of particular educational and musical value for the youngsters.

I resumed taking choir practices on Tuesday, November 21st and directed the music at Evensong on Friday, December 1st, so by then almost all was back to normal whatever that may be at Brecon Cathedral.

Of particular interest now was the appointment of my successor as Organist of Brecon Cathedral. Remembering how at Selby Abbey, back in 1966, I had resigned in November thereby allowing the Vicar to appoint a new Organist in time for the successful candidate to give three months notice and so take over on Easter day in order that there would be no interregnum to disrupt the choir, I sent in my letter of resignation to the Dean at the end of August but to my horror, he did not advertise the job in The Church Times until the end of November, with interviews planned for January and the starting date for the new Organist suggested as September, thereby causing an interregnum of four months which would not be good for the choir.

The great surprise to Hazel and me was the annual salary on offer to the new Organist, £21,030, equivalent to the salary of a Residentiary Canon, very considerably more than was paid to me, furthermore also on offer was the chance for the successful candidate to pay into a pension scheme, something which had never come my way!

However, the Dean was only being realistic, even if it was at our expense; he wanted the best and was prepared to pay for it. Forty-one years ago I had only survived financially because a part-time teaching job had been available to swell my meagre Cathedral income, but now nothing like that was available. Yet one had to admire the single-mindedness of the Dean. In his short time here he had supervised the installation of comfortable chairs, magnificent lighting and at least the building was warm, even the Liturgy had improved out of all recognition. Furthermore in his prayers he had the ability to incorporate words from anthems and the lessons to add extra relevance and bind into one single, suitable theme, all the many loose elements. He had accomplished so much.

Meanwhile, daughter Harriet had been negotiating to purchase a gorgeous house in Abergavenny, "Brecon is my home" she had said and she wanted to stay in touch with the friends of her youth. Abergavenny had seemed ideal as it had a railway station and was thirty minutes driving time nearer to London. Typical of her thoughtfulness was the idea that Hazel and I would be able to keep in close touch with Nick and Kate and our grandchildren, also with all our friends in Brecon so that moving away would not be so much of a wrench. She even planned to employ our Kidwelly builder-friend who at that time was working to prepare our house in Kidwelly, to work on her property in Abergavenny.

So for the second time, all was set for retirement, this time on Easter Day. On the day before, Holy Saturday, there was my final concert in the Cathedral with the Cathedral Choir, the Cathedral Singers and Gwent Chamber Orchestra. The review by Rian Evans, published in the Musical Opinion, says all that needs saying about the evening:

> 'Easter music at Brecon Cathedral has always been special: the music making utterly professional yet demonstrating the spirit and dedication of musicians rooted in their community. This Easter was particularly special for marking the last concerts given under its Director of Music, David Gedge, before his retirement. The concert on 7ᵗʰ April epitomised the nature of Brecon: the Brecon Cathedral Choir and the Cathedral Singers joining forces with the Gwent Chamber Orchestra for Faure's Requiem, while distinguished soloists paid their tribute to David Gedge in Beethoven's Triple Concerto. Brothers Paul and Huw Watkins, respectively cellist and pianist, are among Britain's most brilliant musicians and have been associated with Brecon since they were boys: they were joined by violinist Miranda Dale, another frequent visitor to Brecon over the years. The collective artistry of these three players in the Beethoven was exceptional and in the circumstances deeply touching.
>
> Huw Watkins was the most perceptive pianist in Britten's Canticle Abraham and Issac, with Rogers Covey-Crump and William Purefoy equally eloquent. The latter pair brought to the sometimes overburdening role of the Voice of God, where tenor and counter-tenor sing together, a refined beautifully harmonious blend.
>
> David Gedge has always been ambitious in his programming and Faure's Requiem may have been slightly more tame a choice than David would have liked, but the miracle was that he was there to conduct it at all. Last summer he collapsed with a stroke on the podium while directing a performance; this Faure was testimony to David's remarkable determination and tenacity in which he enjoyed the luxury of a Cathedral so jam-packed as surely to regret his impending retirement.
>
> With the Gedge's veritable teamwork, David's wife Hazel as assistant organist and his son Nicholas singing the baritone solo in the Libera Me, it was a moving night, but without undue sentiment. David Gedge ensured the characteristic French aura of the work while fastidiously observing its musical discipline and dynamics shone through. Soprano Ruth Lowther sang the Pie Jesu with exactly the right pure sound.
>
> Hazel and David Gedge have devoted themselves to Brecon and the warmth of the audience's reception surely spelled out just how much they will be missed.'